The Chowhound's™ Guide to
the San Francisco Bay Area

The Chowhound's™ Guide to
the San Francisco Bay Area

Chowhound.com

Introduction by Jim Leff

penguin books

PENGUIN BOOKS
Published by the Penguin Group
Penguin Group (USA) Inc., 375 Hudson Street, New York, New York 10014, U.S.A.
Penguin Group (Canada), 10 Alcorn Avenue, Toronto, Ontario, Canada M4V 3B2
    (a division of Pearson Penguin Canada Inc.)
Penguin Books Ltd, 80 Strand, London WC2R 0RL, England
Penguin Ireland, 25 St Stephen's Green, Dublin 2, Ireland
    (a division of Penguin Books Ltd)
Penguin Group (Australia), 250 Camberwell Road, Camberwell, Victoria 3124, Australia
    (a division of Pearson Australia Group Pty Ltd)
Penguin Books India Pvt Ltd, 11 Community Centre, Panchsheel Park, New Delhi—110
    017, India
Penguin Group (NZ), cnr Airborne and Rosedale Roads, Albany, Auckland 1310,
    New Zealand (a division of Pearson New Zealand Ltd)
Penguin Books (South Africa) (Pty) Ltd, 24 Sturdee Avenue, Rosebank, Johannesburg
    2196, South Africa

Penguin Books Ltd, Registered Offices:
80 Strand, London WC2R 0RL, England

First published in Penguin Books 2005

10 9 8 7 6 5 4 3 2 1

Some of the contents of this book first appeared in *ChowNews,* an e-mail newsletter.

CIP data available
ISBN 0 14 30.440 5

Printed in the United States of America
Set in New Century Schoolbook with Trade Gothic
Designed by Sabrina Bowers

Contents

A Dining Guide Like No Other

You'll notice that many popular and excellent places like Chez Panisse, La Folie, Merenda, and El Farolito aren't mentioned in these pages. It's not that we don't like them. We do! But our Greek restaurant roundup doesn't survey every *saganaki*; our pizza roundup is missing a slice or two. *The Chowhound's Guide* doesn't aim for comprehensiveness (though it does offer exhaustive surveys of area dim sum, BBQ, breakfast, bakeries, ice cream, farmers' markets, Thai temple dining, Wine Country picnics and provisions, etc.). Over the years, Chowhound.com has covered nearly the entire universe of edibility, but this guide focuses on recent "chowconnaissance," to ensure the freshest possible info and to fit it into a portable size.

The goal is not to catalog every obvious choice. We've concentrated on places that are white hot among those who eat to a different drummer; the front-line food lovers determinedly smoking out the sensations of tomorrow. *The Chowhound's Guide* is an eye-opening plunge into the world of adventure dining, spotlighting places that have recently excited the expert and iconoclastic diners known as chowhounds. Most eateries described herein will be completely unknown to you—virgin finds never before mentioned in guidebooks or newspaper food sections. Here, for your chowing pleasure, are well over a thousand cutting-edge dens of deliciousness—intriguing alternatives to the oft-hyped usual suspects. It's the ultimate hip map to edible treasure, by and for those who live to seek it out.

Everyone knows the Mission abounds in burritos; that's old news. Chowhound attention is drawn more to the unbelievably wondrous taco trucks of Sonoma County, which may one day be equally famous. Other guides list sake places in Japantown, but we lead you to a barbecue joint run by a guy whose passions bridge both smoky meat and subtle rice wine, and who loves to share his deep knowledge of both. We've discovered a laundromat stocking thirty flavors of Mitchell's ice cream, and an itinerant challah bread baker who delivers perfect crusty, shiny loaves to your door. Oh, and rarity of rarities, a place making real old-fashioned frozen custard.

You may have heard of China Village, the landmark Sichuan. This place, hidden in Albany, was first ferreted out by our battalions of chowhounds. In these pages, we analyze its menu (including untranslated secret dishes) as a biblical scholar examines scripture, plumbing for esoterica beyond the reach of the laity. We've sent in Mandarin speakers to unlock mysteries. Ardent chowhounds of every creed pool knowledge and expertise, jubilantly switching teams—Koreans delving into quesadillas, Jews scouting chopped pork barbecue . . .

No other guide rounds up all the surprisingly varied chow choices in SBC Park, or all the best farmers' market vendors, or where to buy armadillo, crispy fresh-fried churros, or bourbon banana cream soft cake. We'll clue you in on expensive splashy meals where deliciousness exceeds splash, as well as the best spot on Pescadero Beach for gathering mussels.

Chowhounds are always refining their strategies, searching for greatness with blithe disregard for conventional wisdom. Any food guide will tell you where to buy great cheese. Only *The Chowhound's Guide* will hip you to where to score a seasonal aged Brescianella. And introduce you to the South Bay guerilla blini ladies, and steer you from the long queue at Ton Kiang to nearby Mayflower (whose dim sum is better), and tell you where to buy wormwood to make your own absinthe. Do you know where to grab scrumptious crab salad sandwiches on Dutch crunch rolls right near SFO to bring on your flight? No?!? Then dive into this book and don't expect to come out for a good long while. And expect to get very, very hungry!

○◯○ Tips for Using *The Chowhound's Guide*

The central presumption of this guide is that, as a chowhound, you're willing to go out of your way for greatness. If you must have the most extremely delicious pizza or souffle, you only want to hear about the standouts, and will gladly trek across town for them. Those who feel a need to eat near where they happen to currently be lack, in our opinion, the necessary enthusiasm. If you can approach this guide with a free-ranging, ready-to-chow mindset, let us make you so cuckoo-for-Cocoa-Puffs ravenous that you jump out the door in a delirious frenzy. But if you're determined to settle for options close by, our neighborhood index will direct you to nearby killer chow (and tempt you into ranging just a bit wider.)

There are two very different ways to use this guide. We expect that you'll flip between the two.

1. Right Brain: If you don't know what or where you feel like eating, boy, is this the guide for you. The following is pure, distilled gastronomic foreplay, designed to get you "in the mood." Just browse; we'll soon have you on your way to satisfying cravings you didn't realize you had.

2. Left Brain: If you hanker for a given cuisine, search the cuisine index. If you want to stay local, check the nabe index. If you'd like to see our thoughts on a specific restaurant, rifle through the restaurant index.

Our respondents take pride in their opinions because their names are attached to them. It pays to note whose taste matches your own and weight tips accordingly, but don't feel obliged to pay close attention to the players (whose Chowhound.com nicknames appear within asterisks). Our editors have selected only the most promising tips from reliable reporters, always watching for corroboration, so if we note that a restaurant is recommended by *Jack Sprat*, that doesn't mean we haven't weighed other opinions as well.

Alternative eating doesn't mean "cheap eats." Different pleasures come at different prices. Both snobs and reverse snobs miss out on too much enjoyment, so chowhounds embrace the full spectrum. Their mantra is "deliciousness is deliciousness"; a wonderful brownie baked with ample love, skill, and pride is as worthy of respect as the richest Persicus Caviar. You'll get the best possible use from this guide if you, too, embrace deliciousness in all its many manifestations.

Finally, there's no thrill like making your own finds. Put this guide to ample use, but don't be a slave to it. Sever the cord sometimes and adventurously chow where no hound has ever chowed before. Report back on Chowhound.com, and maybe we'll include you and your tip in our next edition!

○◯○ How Do You Build a *Chowhound's Guide?*

Easy! First, build a Web site and attract five hundred thousand people per month. Prevent its savvy intensity from diluting as the community grows huge. Manage to keep conversation focused, rather than lapsing into brawls, ads, and chatty digressions—as large online discussions do. Train teams to watch vigilantly for sham testimonials, deflect the nutty .01 percent who try to derail things, and keep it all rolling on a shoestring budget with a skeleton staff out of pure chowhound fervor. The result: a deliriously informative unorganized mayhem of thousands of daily reports, penetrable only by the most ardent chowhounds. Like a good used bookstore, everyone leaves with an armful of bounty, but few ever find exactly what they were looking for.

So, recruit fleets of chow-savvy editors to read through each posting, scouring for the primo tips. Organize the information, weigh opinions, gauge consensus, and look up addresses and phone numbers, producing an e-mailed summary called *ChowNews* (in editions for New York Tristate, San Francisco Bay Area, and Greater Los Angeles) each week (information at www.chowhound.com/chownews/sf.html).

But *ChowNews* isn't indexed or portable. So cull the best recent *ChowNews* info, reedit, reconsolidate, index, and cross-reference, and have throngs of chowhounds vet all for currency and quality—working quickly so the tips don't go stale.

If this guidebook seems unlike any other, now you understand why. Only obsessed raving zealots could produce a food guide this good. Swarms of them at every stage, contributing, supervising, and editing with ferocious intensity. It's a rare occurrence, and we invite you to savor the unique results.

○○○ Don't Trust This Book

All prices and hours mentioned in this guide are iffy. For that matter, so are the tips themselves. Why? Because things change fast in the food world. So call ahead to make sure that dynamite lasagna deal is still on, and that the place hasn't turned into a tanning parlor. And don't shoot the messenger if a new chef has come aboard and is blithely melting Velveeta all over everything. Restaurants go downhill and out of business with dismaying frequency. The complacent are left in the cold when their favorites tank, which is why chowhounds continuously scan the horizon for new deliciousness. They're trying to stay ahead of entropy.

If everything's so flaky and changeable, why bother with

this guide? Simple: Even though chow information, like crois-sants, starts to stale from the moment it's produced, you will still eat a quadrillion times better if you crib from *The Chowhound's Guide* than if you don't. The goal—of this guide, of dining out, of life itself—is to increase your odds of eating deliciously, and we are your best possible ally, because we are battalions of obsessive-compulsive true believers who are at least as picky as you are. And this is literally as fresh as a guidebook can possi-bly be. Since the users of Chowhound.com sign their names to their opinions, pride compels them to offer only timely ones. And this guide's editors have selected recently confirmed information. Plus, the folks at Penguin, themselves chowhounds, have expe-dited production.

But still, caveat eater. Call ahead to confirm prices and other details and always remember that last week's superb artichoke pizza might be next week's inedible nightmare.

○◯○ Chowhound Profiles

Profiles of some randomly selected Chowhound.com regulars are scattered throughout the guide. We've asked them a number of questions, and predictably, everyone offered different perspec-tives on everything . . . with one unexpected exception. When asked about their favorite guilty pleasures, fully half our re-spondents (in both New York and San Francisco) cited Popeyes fried chicken. We swear we weren't paid for the mass-market product placement.

○◯○ The Real Purpose

Finally, let me confess something. In the end, it doesn't matter if you're out there reading this . . . *any* of you. I've recruited the most obsessive and fussy eaters to build the largest food com-munity in the world, tended to its growth, appointed staff to en-capsulate its output into *ChowNews,* and convinced Penguin to release this volume all from one motivation: For many years I have lusted to hold exactly this book in my hands. Yes, this has all been a grotesquely elaborate vanity project for me, me, me. I've tricked hundreds of thousands of experts into coughing up their best tips, created machinery to process and cull those tips, and duped a major publisher into spitting out the savviest, deep-est, chowiest guide to Bay Area dining ever produced. It all stems from my dream of harnessing the know-how of chowhounds everywhere to ensure that I'll make out sublimely wherever I go or whatever I crave. You can all go do as you like. I've got my book and I'm ready to go eat.

Ciao,
—**Jim Leff**, Alpha Hound

About Chowhounds

Chowhounds existed long before a Web site gathered them into an international network. Chowhounding predates even prostitution. Among Neanderthals were those who roamed a valley or two out of their way to where the mastodons ran particularly tasty—and who always insisted on the tender cheek meat.

Chowhounds ignore conventional wisdom and hype. They refuse to eat where they're told, preferring to scout for hidden gems. This culinary treasure hunting is fueled by the conviction that the landscape is rife with unheralded greatness awaiting joyful discovery. And so chowhounds plumb outlying neighborhoods; they screech their cars to a halt upon spotting promising-looking Peruvian chicken parlors; they horde take-out menus with a covetousness that would alarm even fervent butterfly collectors. All this to avoid the unthinkable horror of ingesting a bite lacking the potential to change their lives. A chowhound cannot bear the thought that something shatteringly wonderful might have been discovered if they'd only trekked another two blocks.

Chowhounds are open to the full spectrum of deliciousness. They sit up straight in four-star palaces and swirl their Merlot with eyebrow-cocked insouciance, yet they also know to ask curbside tamale vendors for atole, the traditional accompanying beverage. They appreciate subtle cooking where poetic statements are made with ethereal gestures as much as lusty cooking requiring hearty digging in. They adjust; they acclimatize; they're culinary chameleons gleaning the essential experience from each milieu.

If one knows one's options, one can always score. Being a chowhound is all about acquiring the ability to sate every craving not just adequately but extraordinarily. Since even billionaires find themselves in formal dining settings for less than 10 percent of their ingesting lives, all chowhounds build portfolios of superior breakfast muffins, falafel sandwiches, and ice cream sundaes as well as options for swanky business lunches and

Saturday-night dates. You may grab a quick sandwich at work. A chowhound goes twenty blocks out of the way for a better one. You may pick up a bag of cookies from a convenience store. A chowhound orders cookies from a certain bakery in Wisconsin.

Chowhounds eat on the cutting (and spooning and forking) edge; they're aware of a new immigrant group's influx before city agencies catch on, they navigate the roads of obscure corners of the city with more aplomb than cabbies, and most of all, they know all the best places to eat. They won't settle for anything less than cooking that makes them shut their eyes and moan with pleasure. Chowhounds are always on the lookout for greatness, and their discoveries will be tomorrow's vaunted places. They are the buzzers rather than the buzzies.

One joy of this peculiar hobby is that the objects of a chowhound's affections are more viscerally satisfying than those of, say, antiques collectors. After all, you can't literally consume your new Hepplewhite mahogany Pembroke table. You can only look at it, point at it, show it off—locked in the cold dualism of finder and found. Compare and contrast, if you will, with a slice of fresh, eggy, golden brown coconut custard pie. Food is not just acquired, it's encompassed at the cellular level. And while Mr. Hepplewhite is as dead as his era, the cultural aspects of cuisine are vividly alive, immersive, *ingestible*.

There is much to be experienced on the chowhounding trail; adventures to undertake and otherness to embrace and internalize. In the end, it's more than just about food. In an age when humongous engines of marketing ensnare multitudes to blandly familiar brands, chowhounds are the conscientious objectors. Having resisted the hypnotic trance of directed consumption, they use their free will to make smart choices. By refusing to settle for easy mediocrity, they ensure that a great many of their occasions are special ones—and support the artisans, holdouts, and geniuses who aim for more than extraction of maximal profit from minimal effort. The more people awakened to the heady pleasures of treasure hunting, the more treasures there'll be for us all to enjoy.

Acknowledgments

The Chowhound's Guide to the San Francisco Bay Area was edited by Limster, with Jake Klisivitch, Jim Leff, Fred Manny, Caitlin McGrath, Karen Ostler, Cheryl Pochapin, Chris Van Der Rhodes, and Melanie Wong, with an assist from Julie Woo.

The material in this guide was adapted and edited from *ChowNews,* a weekly e-mail publication chock full of primo chow tips culled from the Chowhound.com message boards (read a sample issue at www.chowhound.com/chownews/sf.html). The editorial staff of San Francisco Bay Area *ChowNews* is

Editors: Caitlin McGrath, Cheryl Pochapin
Associate Editors: Ruth Lafler, Melanie Wong, Diana Wynne
Assistant Editors: Gordon Wing, Kenneth Hoffman,
    Nancy Berry, Judith Lessow-Hurley, Jennifer Fish Wilson,
    Rochelle Foles
Executive Editor: Jim Leff
Managing Editor: Pat Hammond
Copy Editor: Caitlin McGrath
Linker: Karen Ostler

The Wait Staff for the Chowhound.com Web site is

Alpha Hound: Jim Leff
Web-Tamer: Bob Okumura
Pack Management: Pat Hammond
Technical Attaché: Pierre Jelenc
Bone Counter: Leslie Huang
Legal Beagles: Andrew "Wonki" Kim and Molly McEnery
    (Wilson Sonsini Goodrich & Rosati)
LSD (not the drug): Jeremy Osner and Pierre Jelenc
Logo Artist: Cecil Lehar
Korean Military Advisor: Michael Yu

Brad Heintz is the evil genius behind CHEW (the Chowhound Editing Wizard), which makes these guides possible. Limster created Nabe Converter, our program for indexing, and Pierre Jelenc and Paul Trapani provided technical help. Office space provided by Lawsuites.net. This guide would have left several dead and countless wounded without BBEdit, Bare Bones Software's legendary text-editing software.

The editors would like to thank our agent, Daniel Greenberg of Levine Greenberg Literary Agency (and Melissa Rowland and Elizabeth Wooldridge of LGLA, as well), and, at Penguin, our editors Jennifer Ehmann and David Cashion and managing editor Matt Giarratano, copy editor Carol Cassady, production editors Noirin Lucas and Jennifer Tait, and designer Sabrina Bowers.

Deep debt of gratitude to Bob Okumura (Chowhound co-founder), Pat Hammond, Andy Penn, and Wayne Frost; Diane Cabell, Dave Feldman, Seth Godin, Jay and Michelle Itkowitz, Brian Platton and George Sape of Epstein Becker & Green, David Shenk, the aggrieved spouses and varyingly significant others, the lard fried potato chips at La Palma Mexicatessen. And, most of all, the awesome hounds of Chowhound.com.

A Most Dignified Lunch at
ALFRED'S

Alfred's Steakhouse (Financial District)
659 Merchant St.
San Francisco, CA
415-781-7058
Steak house

The decor is elegant in an old-fashioned men's club way, the clientele is well dressed and sedate, the service professional and solicitous, and the meat's perfectly cooked. Seventy-five-year-old **Alfred's** is the ideal place for a quiet, carnivorous meal. And lunch is a bargain!

Half rack of lamb, New York steak, salad, crisp fries, and garlic mashed potatoes are all recommended, as is the world's most elegant chicken-fried steak: high-quality beef, panko-breaded and fried to a tender medium rare(!), with a milk gravy more akin to fine bechamel. Entrees come with the soup of the day or a generous salad, and the $19.28 Merchant Street Special adds dessert and a glass of house wine (respectable cabernet from Geyser Peak).

○ **Alfred's Steakhouse:** *see also* **p. 56.**

Killer Smoked **BACON**

A.G. Ferrari
www.agferrari.com
Italian store

Bryan's Quality Meats
 (Pacific Heights)
3473 California St.
San Francisco, CA
415-752-3430
Store

Dittmer's Gourmet Meats
 (Peninsula)
400 San Antonio Rd.
Mountain View, CA
650-941-3800
German/American store

Hobbs' Applewood Smoked Meats
 (Marin County)
1201 Andersen Dr., H
San Rafael, CA
415-453-0577
Mail order source

Lucca Ravioli Co. (Mission)
1100 Valencia St.
San Francisco, CA
415-647-5581
Italian store

Molinari Delicatessen
 (North Beach)
373 Columbus Ave.
San Francisco, CA
415-421-2337
Italian store

Neuske's Smoked Meats
www.nueskes.com
800-392-2266
Mail order source

Niman Ranch
www.nimanranch.com
Farm or Farm stand

San Francisco Ferry Plaza
 Farmers' Market
 (Embarcadero)
Foot of Market St. on the
 Embarcadero; Ferry Building
 Marketplace
San Francisco, CA
415-353-5650
Farmers' market

Mmm . . . bacon! Hounds sing the praises of applewood-smoked bacon available from **Niman Ranch** or via mail order from **Hobbs'**, or **Nueske's**. **Bryan's** is a retail outlet for Hobbs' bacon.

Niman's bacon is available with or without nitrates. They've also started making guanciale (cured fatty meat from the pig's jowl, cured with more salt and black pepper and less sugar than pancetta, and without the nutmeg or other sweet spices). Ask for it at markets that carry Niman products, or you can special order and pick it up at their Ferry Plaza market stand on Saturdays.

Molinari makes pancetta two ways: regular and affumicata (smoked). It's available at Molinari's shop in North Beach and at **Lucca's** and **A. G. Ferrari**. (*Victoria Libin* reports better prices at the latter).

The selection at **Dittmer's Gourmet Meats** is huge, ranging from good old regular bacon to Canadian, English rasher, Gypsy, pancetta, pepper, garlic and herb, and back bacon.

○ **San Francisco Ferry Plaza Farmers' Market:** *see also* **pp. 26, 52, 79, 104.**

Monster **BAKERY** Crawl

Acme Bread Co. (East Bay)
1601 San Pablo Ave.
Berkeley, CA
510-524-1327
Bakery

Acme Bread Co. (Embarcadero)
One Ferry Bldg., Embarcadero
San Francisco, CA
415-288-2978
Bakery

Alex Bakery (Richmond)
431 Clement St.
San Francisco, CA
415-387-0151
Chinese (Hong Kong) bakery

Anna Bakery (Chinatown)
715 Clay St.
San Francisco, CA
415-989-8898
Chinese (Cantonese) bakery

Anna's Danish Cookie Co.
  (Peninsula)
1007 Howard Ave.
San Mateo, CA
Danish bakery

Arizmendi (East Bay)
3265 Lakeshore Ave.
Oakland, CA
510-268-8849
Bakery

Arizmendi (Sunset)
1331 9th Ave.
San Francisco, CA
415-566-3117
Bread/Pizza bakery and sitdown
  café

Arizmendi Bakery and Pizzeria
  (East Bay)
4301 San Pablo at 43rd St.
Emeryville, CA
510-547-0550
Bread/Pizza bakery and sitdown
  café

Bette's-To-Go (East Bay)
1807 4th St.
Berkeley, CA
510-548-9494
Diner or coffeeshop

Boniere Bakery (East Bay)
1417 Park St.
Alameda, CA
510-522-0110
Bakery

Bouchon Bakery (Napa County)
6528 Washington St.
Yountville, CA
707-944-2253
Bakery

Bovine Bakery (Marin County)
11315 Hwy. 1
Point Reyes Station, CA
415-663-9420
Bakery

Bread Basket Bakery (Peninsula)
7099 Mission St.
Daly City, CA
650-992-1932
Filipino bakery

Cheese Board (East Bay)
1504 Shattuck Ave.
Berkeley, CA
510-549-3183
Pizza bakery/Cheese shop/Pizzeria

Emporio Rulli (Marin County)
464 Magnolia Ave.
Larkspur, CA
415-924-7478
Italian café

Emporio Rulli II Caffe
(Union Square)
255 Stockton St.
San Francisco, CA
415-433-1122
Italian café

Golden Gate Bakery (Chinatown)
1029 Grant Ave.
San Francisco, CA
415-781-2627
Chinese (Cantonese)/Chinese
(Hong Kong) bakery

Hopkins Street Bakery (East Bay)
1584 Hopkins St.
Berkeley, CA
510-526-8188
Bakery

Il Fornaio (Embarcadero)
1265 Battery St., in Levi's Plaza
San Francisco, CA
415-986-0100
Italian

La Farine Bakery (East Bay)
6323 College Ave.
Oakland, CA
510-654-0338
French bakery

Nabolom Bakery (East Bay)
2708 Russell St.
Berkeley, CA
510-845-2253
Bakery

Noe Valley Bakery & Bread Co.
(Noe Valley)
4073 24th St.
San Francisco, CA
415-550-1405
Bakery

Pilgrim Kitchen (Peninsula)
311 El Camino Real
Belmont, CA
650-592-0638
Bakery

Preston Vineyards & Winery
    (Sonoma County)
9282 W. Dry Creek Rd.
Healdsburg, CA
707-433-3372
Winery

Schat's Bakery (Sonoma County)
534 N. Cloverdale Blvd.
Cloverdale, CA
707-894-0211
Café

Sheng Kee Bakery
www.shengkee.com
Chinese (Hong Kong) bakery

Stella Pastry Cafe (North Beach)
446 Columbus Ave.
San Francisco, CA
415-986-2914
Italian café

Tartine (Mission)
600 Guerrero St.
San Francisco, CA
415-487-2600
French café

West Portal Bakery
    (Westportal/Ingleside)
170 W. Portal Ave.
San Francisco, CA
415-681-4546
Bakery

Start out your bakery tour in the South Bay with Filipino breads at **Bread Basket**, especially their wonderful *siopao* (the Filipino version of steamed pork buns), cloudlike rolls filled with pork, chicken, or *bola bola* (meat balls). *Ube ensaymada* is a wonderful, yeasty sweet roll streaked purple with purple yam and frosted with not-too-sweet buttery topping. Linger on in the South Bay for cookies from **Anna's**—especially the chocolate-covered coconut ones—and hit **Pilgrim Kitchen** for pies like the pies of old from Marie Calendar. Their fruit pies, Boston cream pies, cream pies, old-fashioned Danish, coffee cake rings, donuts, etc., are all calories well spent, says *Stanley Stephan*.

In San Francisco, visit **Emporio Rulli**—especially during holiday season for their Sacchetto di Marroni, a Milanese autumn specialty of candied chestnuts, rum-infused savoiardi (lady fingers), and mascarpone chocolate cream encased in a marzipan "burlap sack," serving 6–8, $32; 8–10, $42. Described by a smitten *Melanie Wong* as a rich edible tromp l'oeil. **Tartine** is terrific for croissants, pain au chocolate, eclairs, and French-style breads (especially the country loaf bread—best afternoons, when it comes out of the oven), and they also make great bread pudding, chocolate mousse, and pumpkin pie. **Noe Valley Bakery** makes breads with fruit and/or chocolate (chocolate chip, chocolate-cherry, apricot ginger, fig, the latter especially good with cheese). Legendary **Acme Bread Co.** bakes vaunted levain, rustic rolls, olive bread, rustic sweet baguette, ham and cheese croissants, and cinnamon rolls. **Stella's** is one of the best bets in town for sacra-pantina, a sponge cake that makes for a perfect light dessert. **West Portal Bakery** is important for sour date rolls and chewy seeded baguette. Perennial Chinatown favorite **Golden Gate Bakery** is a must for coconut macaroons, coconut tarts, egg custard tarts (best warm, so reheat in toaster oven at home), vanilla sponge cake, and the "pineapple bun" (sorry, no actual pineapple, just a hundred or so folds of flaky dough). **Anna Bakery** and **Alex Bakery** make similar egg tarts—both almost as good as the ones at Golden Gate. **Sheng Kee Bakery** makes great red bean buns and sponge cakes. And **Il Fornaio** has great cookies, especially chocolate chip.

Crossing into the East Bay, **Boniere**, run by a former owner of Flying Saucer on Guerrero in San Francisco, offers an ever changing selection, but among the perennials are frangipane tarts that will blow your mind, says *Fish butcher*, who also recommends passionfruit-mango mousse cake, very good croissants, sandwiches, tarts, foccacia. Other favorites include tomato-pesto-feta foccacia, cream biscuits, ham and cheese biscuits, coconut kisses. **Arizmendi**, home of thin-crusted pizza, also does killer scones (especially cornmeal-cherry) and luscious shortbread cookies. Same with Berkeley's **Cheese Board**, to whom they're related. **La Farine** is always a favorite; *dml* recommends—with a straight face!—the Swisstwinkies; morning buns and croissants are excellent. **Nabolom** is recommended for fruit Danish with buttery pastry filled with chunks of whole fruit. (Skip other items, just go for the Danish!) **Bette's-To-Go** does fruit tarts right; good pâte brisée, custard, and check out the cookies, especially pistachio lemon. **Hopkins Street Bakery** sells almond cupcakes called *friandises,* rich, thick, moist chocolate walnut cookies, and fine cakes.

Now chomp on up to Wine Country, where *Melanie Wong* recommends old-fashioned **Schat's Bakery's** Cloverdale location for great pastries and breads in a rustic style reflecting the proprieters' Dutch roots. Cinnamon rolls are huge, but have real integrity of texture and flavor, and whole wheat rolls freeze well. Pizza bread isn't a favorite, though (sweet/jammy sauce and cheddar cheesey). Others like **Schat's** Calistoga and Bishop locations, and several single out their wonderful macaroons. **Bovine Bakery** offers high-quality brickmaiden breads, pumpkin muffins, and pumpkin pie squares. **Preston Vineyards** makes bread and olive oil. Preston's bread is very rustic, and only one kind's made each day, for $4 a loaf. Arrive early (around 11 A.M.) and it'll be fresh from the oven. Olive oil is a light, flavorful French-style, the picnic grounds are lovely and open to the public, but only Preston wines may be consumed on premises (note that the picnic grounds and boccie courts can be reserved in advance for large groups, in return for minimum wine purchase). We hear breads at Thomas Keller's **Bouchon Bakery** are pretty good, including a campagne similar to Acme's levain (4 lb loaf for $12, or $4 for a ¼ loaf), rustique rolls similar to ciabatta, and baguettes. *lm* is less impressed with the pastries, saying most are pretty but don't have great flavor. Exceptions: fantastic lemon–pine nut tarts, nice financiers, and bouchons (little chocolate items, moist and not too sweet, for a perfect chocolate fix).

- **Acme Bread Co.:** *see also* p. 97.
- **Arizmendi:** *see also* pp. 102, 238.
- **Arizmendi Bakery and Pizzeria:** *see also* p. 238.
- **Cheese Board:** *see also* pp. 51, 54, 198, 238.
- **Golden Gate Bakery:** *see also* pp. 100, 288.
- **Hopkins Street Bakery Inc.:** *see also* p. 48.
- **La Farine Bakery:** *see also* p. 81.
- **Stella Pastry Cafe:** *see also* p. 45.
- **Tartine:** *see also* pp. 8, 133.

BANANA Fans Rejoice!

FatApple's Restaurant and Bakery (East Bay)
1346 Martin Luther King Jr. Way
Berkeley, CA
510-526-2260
Diner or Coffee shop

FatApple's Restaurant and Bakery (East Bay)
7525 Fairmount Ave.
El Cerrito, CA
510-528-3433
Diner or Coffee shop

Hot N Hunky (Castro)
4039 18th St.
San Francisco, CA
415-621-6365
American

Liberty Cafe (Bernal Heights)
410 Cortland Ave.
San Francisco, CA
415-695-8777
American

Lido Market (East Bay)
35219 Newark Blvd. B
Newark, CA
510-745-0696
Store

Mel's Drive-In (Richmond)
3355 Geary Blvd.
San Francisco, CA
415-387-2244
Diner or Coffee shop

New Yorker's Buffalo Wings
   (Marina)
2499 Lombard St.
San Francisco, CA
415-931-8181
American

Peninsula Creamery (Peninsula)
900 High St.
Palo Alto, CA
650-323-3175
Diner or Coffee shop

The Smokehouse (East Bay)
3115 Telegraph Ave.
Berkeley, CA
510-845-3640
American

Tartine (Mission)
600 Guerrero St.
San Francisco, CA
415-487-2600
French café

Walker's Restaurant & Pie Shop
   (East Bay)
1491 Solano Ave.
Albany, CA
510-525-4647
Diner or Coffee shop

Han Lukito has found (no drooling, please) bourbon banana cream soft cake at **Lido Market** in Newark. It's a soft-textured cake with banana-flavored cream filling and banana-flavored white chocolate on the ends. **Liberty Cafe** is a longtime chowhound favorite for banana cream pie. But there are alternatives: Don't bother sitting down for a meal at **Walker's Pie Shop**—the food's nothing special—just grab one of its pies to go; **FatApple's** is so tasty it will slay even non–banana cream pie fans, promises *Alexandra*; **Tartine** has been known to tart up its banana cream pie by coating the crust with chocolate (not consistently, though); **Peninsula Creamery** has awesome pies and other baked goods. Rumor has it that banana milkshakes at the Castro **Hot N Hunky** are great. *Targ Sarvarge* likes the **Smokehouse's** banana shakes for their flavor of banana candy (think Runts), and says that **New Yorker's Buffalo Wings** makes a good one, too, with plenty of real banana flavor (albeit very frothy). Another recommended banana shake: **Mel's** Geary location. *But*, whatever you do, don't actually *eat* anything at Mel's or New Yorker's. Hounds have roundly panned the food at both spots. You've been warned!

○ **Liberty Cafe:** *see also* pp. 20, 97.
○ **Tartine:** *see also* pp. 5, 133.

BANH MI Outside the Tenderloin

Thanh Thanh (Richmond)
2205 Clement St.
San Francisco, CA
415-387-1759
Vietnamese

Vietnam Restaurant (Chinatown)
620 Broadway
San Francisco, CA
415-788-7034
Vietnamese

Tweety Deli (Potrero Hill)
1200 Vermont St.
San Francisco, CA
415-642-1189
Vietnamese

Hounds know San Francisco's best *banh mi* (Vietnamese sandwiches, chock full of meaty goodness) are in the Tenderloin, but sometimes the craving hits when you're elsewhere. Try these satellite picks: **Thanh Thanh** offers a superlative vegetarian version, with big chunks of fried tofu. Roast chicken and pork banh mi at **Vietnam** are $3, larger than average, and generously filled with carrots and daikon, a few long slices of cucumber, cilantro, jalapeño rings, and scallions. **Tweety Deli** is a rare source for banh mi in Portrero Hill. You may have to ask for jalapeños at some of these places, so inquire when ordering.

Eating at the **BAR**

Blue Plate (Mission)
3218 Mission St.
San Francisco, CA
415-282-6777
American

Chenery Park Restaurant
   (Noe Valley)
683 Chenery St.
San Francisco, CA
415-337-8537
New American

Chez Nous (Pacific Heights)
1911 Fillmore St.
San Francisco, CA
415-441-8044
French

Eos Restaurant & Wine Bar (Haight)
901 Cole St.
San Francisco, CA
415-566-3063
Pan-Asian fusion/New American

Hayes Street Grill (Civic Center)
320 Hayes St.
San Francisco, CA
415-863-5545
New American/Seafood

Jardiniere (Civic Center)
300 Grove St.
San Francisco, CA
415-861-5555
French/New American

Last Supper Club (Mission)
1199 Valencia St.
San Francisco, CA
415-695-1199
Italian/New American

Luna Park (Mission)
694 Valencia St.
San Francisco, CA
415-553-8584
New American

Piperade (Embarcadero)
1015 Battery St.
San Francisco, CA
415-391-2555
Basque/French

Solstice (Pacific Heights)
2801 California St.
San Francisco, CA
415-359-1222
New American

Timo's (Mission)
842 Valencia St.
San Francisco, CA
415-647-0558
Spanish

Town Hall (SOMA)
342 Howard St.
San Francisco, CA
415-908-3900
New American

Zuni Cafe (Civic Center)
1658 Market St.
San Francisco, CA
415-552-2522
New American/American

When you're in the mood for an upscale bite but don't want to wait or book a table, eat at the bar! These San Francisco restaurants offer full food service and a congenial staff at the bar.

Jardiniere, Last Supper Club, and Luna Park are all great places for a bar dinner, but bar seats are scarce at peak hours. Blue Plate and Chez Nous are fun bar-dining choices, since bar seats come with a view of the kitchen. Chez Nous only serves beer and wine, and the bar at the back of the room is tiny. The wine bar at Eos has a huge by-the-glass selection, and you can order off the full restaurant menu. Chenery Park, with around eight bar seats, is a mellow, non-sceney place for a bar meal. Piperade is great for small, Basque-inflected bites at the bar. Solstice is a loungey spot serving appetizer-sized portions of chicken potpie, fruit and cheese plate, etc., at the bar for $5 to $7. One makes for a snack; several, a meal. At busy Hayes Street Grill, it's fun to watch the hustle and bustle of the restaurant from behind a martini and fries at the bar, says *jen maiser*, who actually prefers the bar here. The bar at Timo's is perfect for ordering tapas. At Zuni Cafe, fresh oysters and exemplary caesar salad are favorites for late-night bar dining. Town Hall has very good food but a short wine list.

○ Chenery Park Restaurant: *see also* p. 118.
○ Jardiniere: *see also* p. 159.
○ Piperade: *see also* p. 18.
○ Zuni Cafe: *see also* p. 323.

Monster BARBECUE Survey: East Bay

Barney's Hickory Pit (East Bay)
3446 Clayton Rd.
Concord, CA
925-680-9761
Barbecue

Bobby's Cajun BBQ (East Bay)
4261 Hilltop Dr.
Richmond, CA
510-262-0694
Barbecue

Carmen & Family Bar-B-Q
  (East Bay)
41986 Fremont Blvd.
Fremont, CA
510-657-5464
Barbecue

Carmen & Family Bar-B-Q
  (East Bay)
692 W. A St.
Hayward, CA
510-887-1979
Barbecue

Chef Edward's Barbeque
  (East Bay)
1998 San Pablo Ave.
Oakland, CA
510-834-9516
Barbecue

Doug's Barbecue (East Bay)
3600 San Pablo Ave.
Emeryville, CA
510-655-9048
Barbecue

Everett & Jones Barbeque
  (East Bay)
1955 San Pablo Ave.
Berkeley, CA
510-548-8261
Barbecue

Everett & Jones Barbeque
  (East Bay)
296 A St.
Hayward, CA
510-581-3222
Barbecue

Everett & Jones Barbeque
  (East Bay)
126 Broadway
Oakland, CA
510-663-2350
Barbecue

Everett & Jones Barbeque
  (East Bay)
3411 Telegraph Ave.
Oakland, CA
510-601-9377
Barbecue

KC Barb-Q (East Bay)
2613 San Pablo Ave.
Berkeley, CA
510-548-1140
Southern/Barbecue

Why *ericf* loves **KC's**: (1) meat is almost never overcooked, (2) nice spice rub, and (3) links are coarsely ground with mild spicing. Why *ericf* thinks others might object to KC's: (1) BBQ sauce is sweet, (2) meats are not obviously smoky, and (3) only potato salad and baked beans for side dishes. Also, KC's accepts phone orders for take-out and your order is always ready when promised.

Carmen's has its partisans, especially for their complex sauce. Both meat and sauce are theorized to be better at the Hayward location than the Fremont one. Sampling a few locations of **Everett & Jones** demonstrates the wide variability of BBQ: the Jack London Square location has juicy meat and a spicy Lousiana-style sauce, while the Berkeley location can be more dry. Two noteworthy sides: candied yams (with hints of molasses and spice) and collard greens (real Southern style with meat) from the Jack

London Square location (which is a real sit-down restaurant). Pork ribs from E & J's Hayward location are most succulent and toothsome, and have great sauce.

Bobby's Cajun BBQ features excellent juicy meat, both ribs and brisket, mildly smoked with a tangy/spicy sauce. They make their own *boudin* and Cajun sausages. At **Chef Edward's**, the piggly wiggly sandwich is a fave. Brisket's tender and juicy and has good smoke flavor, but ribs are bland and the sauce is too ketchupy. The side of candied yams are a sweet complement to the meat; mac and cheese is dry. Local favorite **Barney's Hickory Pit** has been serving up BBQ chicken, ribs, and pork for years and years, and it's still going strong. Here, you'll find a distinctive sauce specific to the Hickory Pit restaurants; mild and brown, it's more like a smoky, nonsweet gravy than the usual, reports *Ken Hoffmann*. With or without sauce, meats are well made— slow-cooked, smoky, and flavorful.

Doug's, another luminary, disappoints with jerkylike thin-sliced brisket devoid of smoke flavor. The smokier ribs are slightly better, but it's the stellar beans (flavored with all the bits and scraps of various smoked meat and fat from the chopping blocks) and rich, flaky sweet potato pies that get us going. They also make interesting things like barbecued goat and deep-fried turkey. The chowhoundish option is to get meat elsewhere and then hit Doug's for your beans, sides, and pie—and more meat, if they've made up anything interesting.

Monster **BARBECUE** Survey: San Francisco

Big Nate's Bar-B-Que (SOMA)
1665 Folsom St.
San Francisco CA
415-861-4242
Barbecue

Brother-in-Law's Bar-B-Que
  (Pacific Heights)
705 Divisadero St.
San Francisco, CA
415-931-7427
Barbecue

Cliff's Bar-B-Q & Sea Food
   (Potrero Hill)
2177 Bay Shore Blvd.
San Francisco, CA
415-330-0736
Barbecue

Memphis Minnie's BBQ
   (Haight)
576 Haight St.
San Francisco, CA
415-864-7675
Barbecue

Johnson's Barbeque
   (Westportal/Ingleside)
2646 San Bruno Ave.
San Francisco, CA
415-467-7655
Barbecue

Johnson's Barbeque is obscure but good, in the Flint's style, with a dark Louisiana-style sauce on smoky ribs and brisket. Their collard greens also shine. At **Memphis Minnie's**, the brisket has the essential rosy smoke ring BBQ expert *Rochelle McCune* says to look for; choose spicy mustard or Texas-style red sauces. **Big Nate's** brisket is wonderful. Cut up into chunks and bathed in a fiery dark-red sauce (it looks like pot roast), it has an intense flavor and tender but unmushy texture. Despite its reputation as one of the top BBQ joints in San Francisco, **Brother-in-Law's** ribs are poor quality, and lack any smoke flavor. **Cliff's** is a top pick of several chowhounds.

○ **Memphis Minnie's BBQ:** *see also* p. 224.

Monster **BARBECUE** Survey: Far North and Far South

Central Texan BBQ
   (Monterey County)
10500 Merritt St.
Castroville, CA
831-633-2285
Barbecue

D's Bar-B-Q (Solano County)
2909 Sonoma Blvd.
Vallejo, CA
707-557-6765
Barbecue

Gracie's Family Bar-b-cue
  (Solano County)
2525 Springs Rd.,
  William Kims Tae Kwon Do
  Center parking lot
Vallejo, CA
Barbecue street cart/Truck

JC's Bar-B-Q (South Bay)
1080 Saratoga Ave.
San Jose, CA
408-246-2146
Barbecue

Mr. Ribs (Marin County)
100 Red Hill Ave., in front of
  United Market
San Anselmo, CA
Barbecue

New Sweet Home Church of God
  (Peninsula)
2170 Capitol Ave., a block
  behind Ikea's parking lot
East Palo Alto, CA
650-325-1467
Barbecue

Pack Jack Bar-B-Que Inn
  (Sonoma County)
3963 Gravenstein Hwy. S.
Sebastopol, CA
707-823-9929
Barbecue

Uncle Frank's House-Barbecue
  (Peninsula)
2417 Pulgas Ave.
East Palo Alto, CA
650-321-6369
Southern/Barbecue

Searching outside the 'cue epicenters of San Francisco and the East Bay . . .

'Cue-loving hounds in Marin County have found happiness at **Mr. Ribs,** a portable operation that sets up seasonally (through Halloween) on Fridays, Saturdays, and Sundays, dispensing tender and smoky ribs, chicken, tri-tip, and pulled pork. Meat's not smoked at the selling location, but hounds smell and taste true wood smoke at work. **D's Bar-B-Q** produces uniformly high-quality meats: sliced beef brisket has good smoky tones says *Melanie Wong*, but could be more tender; pork ribs have a nice crust and deep smoke ring; and hot links are excellent (coarse ground, pretty lean with a dryish texture and the afterburn of lots of black pepper). Sauce is well-balanced, and medium's plenty spicy. Skip inedible sides.

Doing business from a trailer, **Gracie's** specializes in baby back ribs they call "smoked to the bone." They're meaty, juicy, moist, and not fatty. Gracie's lean, savory sauce is superfluous, as a subtle rub, the smoke treatment and the natural sweetness of the smooth and succulent pork provide all the flavor for these toothsome beauties. Baby backs are served after 3 p.m. and often sell out before closing time. Chicken and regular pork spareribs are good, too. There are a couple of picnic tables and umbrellas for eating "in." **Pack Jack's** makes funky, fatty lamb ribs.

On the Southern route, there are a couple of neat spots in the Pennisula, one serious deal in the South Bay, and then a place as far south as Monterey County.

In the parking lot of **New Sweet Home Church**, there's a big smoker rig and a small greenhouse/kitchen on blocks. Inside, you'll find ribs, chicken, and hot links. Ribs are "nice and meaty, tender yet the right resistance to the bite and well-rendered of excess fat," and sauce has "moderate heat and a nice spicy complexity . . . barely sweet and very different from the thick and jammy style of Flint's or E & J. We liked how it complemented the smoky meat instead of overwhelming it," says *Melanie Wong*. Sides are forgettable. Friday and Saturday only, sunrise(!) to 7 p.m.

Of **Uncle Frank's Cafe**, *Ken Hoffman* says to "make sure you come here not just to eat, but to talk to Frank. He's a stickler for quality and his mission is to transport true Southern smoking ideals to the mouths of mid-Peninsulans. On this score, he has performed his task to the highest levels." Meats are smoky and tender, sauce is thick and sweet, but there's Crystal hot sauce and vinegar on the tables for perking up. Delicious fried catfish is done in a light, greaseless batter.

JC's offers a $10 combo plate with two pieces of moist and flavorful chicken and three tender ribs, beans, and salad that's lots of good food for the money. Some people like the tangy sauce from **Central Texas BBQ** in Castroville, but the meat can be slightly chewy (note: our taster had traveled far with this 'cue, so it may have deteriorated in transit).

BARS AND BREWPUBS

Eldo's Grill & Microbrewery
(Sunset)
1326 9th Ave.
San Francisco, CA
415-564-0425
American

Half Moon Bay Brewing Company
(Peninsula)
390 Capistrano Ave.
Princeton-by-the-Sea, CA
650-728-2739
New American pub

Oaks Kitchen (East Bay)
4099 San Pablo Ave.
Emeryville, CA
510-652-1133
German pub

Prince of Wales Pub (Peninsula)
106 E. 25th Ave.
San Mateo, CA
650-574-9723
British pub

Rogue Brewpub (North Beach)
673 Union St.
San Francisco, CA
415-362-7880
American pub

Rosamunde Sausage Grill
(Haight)
545 Haight St.
San Francisco, CA
415-437-6851
American/German

Toronado (Haight)
547 Haight St.
San Francisco, CA
415-863-2276
Pub

One of *Jim Leff*'s preferred ways of combining great food and drink is to grab a sausage to go (and some of Miss Vickie's potato chips) from Chowhound favorite **Rosamunde,** and bring it next door to enjoy at **Toronado,** one of the country's foremost beer bars (with much greatness on tap, hand pumps, and in bottles). The following are a few of the many great area places to eat fine food and drink appealing ales under one roof.

Rogue Brewpub's buckwheat beer is particularly good, and there's word of an occasional soba ale (yet more buckwheat!) and hazelnut ale. The menu is typical pub grub, but there's a wonderful Kobe beef burger, at $9 big enough for two to share. Mediocre fries, though.

Half Moon Bay Brewing Company is known for excellent beer, and their chef is whipping up some relatively ambitious dishes. Between that, cozy atmosphere, and full bar (with creative cocktails and full range of tequilas), this is a destination even for non–beer drinkers. Pub grub remains on the menu, but also a half dozen daily fish specials, creative appetizers, and Mayan-influenced preparations (the latter Wednesdays only). Dungeness crab cakes are full of fresh crab with no filler, and are spiced to a subtle bite. Beer-batter dipped artichokes (well-prepared with no greasiness) come with a blue cheese dip. Choose an outdoor table overlooking the harbor or a comfy seat by the fire in the bar area. Live music every night but Monday.

Busy **Prince of Wales Pub** is known for its "wallys," or deep-fried dill pickle spears ($3 for 6). A crackly crisp batter coating gives way to rubbery skin and juicy interior. The combination of mouth-watering sourness and salty oiliness makes them an ideal bar food, according to *Melanie Wong*. Mix-and-match with eight beers on tap. **Oaks Kitchen** is a well-executed hofbrau with a good bar for catching a game. *Shep* advises you get a meaty sandwich and a beer, but never dessert, and adds that it's a lot of fun watching the poker players in the big card room. If wings are your ideal bar snack, head to **Eldo's** for a very respectable spicy version, accompanied by good beer.

For more bars and brewpubs, check the Cuisine Index.

○ **Rosamunde Sausage Grill:** *see also* **pp. 134, 236.**

Cozy Family-Style **BASQUE**

Piperade (Embarcadero)
1015 Battery St.
San Francisco, CA
415-391-2555
Basque/French

Meals are meant to be shared, family style, at cozy, Basque-influenced **Piperade**, just as they have been in California's simple Basque restaurants for decades. Flavors are fresh and bold throughout the menu of small and large plates and desserts.

Small plate highlights: warm sheep's milk cheese and ham terrine ("many layers of melted cheese and crispy ham, so it was like crispy-soft-crispy-soft-crispy-soft-crispy-soft" reports *felice*) and warm piquillo peppers with goat cheese, raisins, and moscatel vinaigrette. Large plate highlights: steamed pacific snapper with fried garlic vinaigrette and marinated lamb chops with thyme and aged sherry vinegar (juicy—especially the bone-in pieces—with onions cooked in sherry vinegar). Dessert highlights: turron mousse cake with roasted almonds, Gateau Basque with mango coulis (like pure mango extract), and walnut and sheep's milk cheese gratin (salty and sweet and then a bit tangy right at the end). Service is generally excellent and friendly.

○ **Piperade:** *see also* p. 10.

Drinks at **BEAUCOUP**

Beaucoup (Union Square)
1001 California St.
San Francisco, CA
415-409-8500
French/New American

Beaucoup boasts an interior that architecture magazines are made of, according to *Jupiter*, who recommends the back room with fireplace, comfy chairs, and good drinks—especially mojito with cassis; *dp* would return for very fine risotto, well-executed molten chocolate cake, and rave-worthy skate wing and tempura sardines. Unflappable service is a big plus.

Mysterious **BERBERE** Spice Mix

Brundo Meats & Deli (East Bay)
6419 Telegraph Ave., adjoins
   Cafe Colucci
Oakland, CA
510-601-7933
Ethiopian or Eritrean store

Yum (Castro)
1750 Market St.
San Francisco, CA
415-626-9866
Store

Berbere is an intriguing and unusual Ethiopian spice mix made from hot red chilies, toasted ginger, cardamom, garlic, fenugreek, and cinnamon, often used as a rub on chicken, duck, or fish. Find this mix at **Yum** or very possibly at **Brundo**, an Ethiopian/Eritrean market next to Cafe Colucci. Check out www.recipesource.com for berbere recipe ideas.

Chowhounding in **BERNAL HEIGHTS**

Angkor Borei Restaurant (Mission)
3471 Mission St.
San Francisco, CA
415-550-8417
Cambodian

Liberty Cafe (Bernal Heights)
410 Cortland Ave.
San Francisco, CA
415-695-8777
American

Good Life Grocery (Bernal Heights)
448 Cortland Ave.
San Francisco, CA
415-648-3221
Store

Maggie Mudd (Bernal Heights)
903 Cortland Ave.
San Francisco, CA
415-641-5291
Ice cream or Gelato

Good Life Grocery (Potrero Hill)
1524 20th St.
San Francisco, CA
415-282-9204
Store

Mitchell's Ice Cream (Mission)
688 San Jose Ave.
San Francisco, CA
415-648-2300
Ice cream or Gelato

Chowhound Nametag: Nancy Berry

○◯○

Location: San Francisco

Occupation: Social psychologist, Internet search specialist, software tester, and book editor

Nabe Most Full of Explorable Unknown Chow: The Redwood City section of Middlefield Rd., full of all sorts of little regional Mexican places—some identified on Chowhound.com, but loads of others that haven't been! Also, there's an area of Mountain View near California that has lots of interesting-looking restaurants.

Favorite Comfort Chow: Lam Hoa Thuan on Irving near 25th Ave. in San Francisco for soup 4, or orange preserved duck wonton noodle soup with thick noodles

Guilty Pleasure: Popeyes fried chicken

Favorite Mail Order Chow:
- Nueske's bacon (*nueskes.com*)
- FireGirl's Hot Sauce (*firegirl.com*)
- Dave's Albacore (*davesalbacore.com*)
- Tony Packo's pickles, peppers, and hot dog sauces (*tonypacko.com*)
- Morton & Bassett Spices (*worldpantry.com/morton*)
- Dat'l Do It hot sauces, relishes, mustard, etc. (*datldoit.com*)
- Da Vero Extra Virgin Olive Oil (*davero.com*)
- Monastery Fruitcake (*trappistabbey.org/fruitcake.html*)
- Usinger's Sausage (*usinger.com*)
- King Arthur Flour (*kingarthurflour.com*)
- Southern foods (*peasandcornco.com*)
- Fabulous cherries and dried fruit (*cjolsoncherries.com*)
- See's Candy (*sees.com*)

Chowhounding Rules of Thumb:
1. Talk to people.
2. Look for lines at lunchtime.
3. Ask the folks in line what they're going to order.
4. Point to stuff that looks good on other folks' plates (especially if there's a language problem).
5. If you're a tourist, ask people where they go for certain specific dishes.
6. Never ask what's the best restaurant in town—you'll be sent to all the tourist traps.

Moki's Sushi & Pacific Grill
   (Bernal Heights)
830 Cortland Ave.
San Francisco, CA
415-970-9336
Japanese

Progressive Grounds
   (Bernal Heights)
400 Cortland Ave.
San Francisco, CA
415-282-6233
Café

Palatino Restaurant
   (Bernal Heights)
803 Cortland Ave.
San Francisco, CA
415-641-8899
Italian

Way out on Cortland in Bernal Heights lies a cute little shopping and eating district. Best bet for food and service is **Liberty Cafe**, always good for chicken potpie and much more. **Good Life Grocery** is a small, high-quality local market carrying grass-fed beef. Both locations in San Francisco are well loved. **Maggie Mudd's** ice cream is excellent, *svL* reports. **Progressive Grounds** serves Mitchell's ice cream, and if they don't have the flavor you crave, the original **Mitchell's** location is only a few blocks away (though usually crowded). **Palatino** and **Moki's** are both good eateries for the neighborhood, though not destination spots. **Angkor Borei**, just off Cortland on Mission, is a favorite for Cambodian.

- ○ **Angkor Borei Restaurant:** *see also* p. 38.
- ○ **Liberty Cafe:** *see also* pp. 8, 97.
- ○ **Mitchell's Ice Cream:** *see also* pp. 26, 139, 285.

BIRTHDAY CAKE

Dianda's Italian American Bakery
(Mission)
2883 Mission St.
San Francisco, CA
415-647-5469
Italian bakery

Patisserie Delanghe
(Pacific Heights)
1890 Fillmore St.
San Francisco, CA
415-923-0711
French café

Jolt N' Bolt Bakery (Potrero Hill)
2325 3rd St. #100
San Francisco, CA
415-863-8761
Bakery

Schubert's Bakery (Richmond)
521 Clement St.
San Francisco, CA
415-752-1580
German/Austrian bakery

Sheng Kee Bakery
www.shengkee.com
Chinese bakery

Happy birthday, hound! Here are some worthy cakes to celebrate. *Nancy Berry* loves **Schubert's** wonderful genoise layer cake filled with strawberry mousse and beautifully decorated with chocolate leaves. If you want something lighter, head to one of the many locations of **Sheng Kee**, where delicious sponge cakes are frosted with whipped cream, and light mousse cakes come in flavors like mango or green tea with red bean. They're inexpensive, and there is always a wide selection. Some deem the St. Honore cake at **Dianda's** tops. It's delicious and always makes a big hit at parties, reports *RCWFoodie*. Some celebrants insist on a princess cake (a many layered confection covered in marzipan) from **Patisserie Delanghe. Jolt N' Bolt** is a bit hard to find, on the first floor of an industrial-looking building with no sign on the outside, but it's worth the search, says *felice*, who loves its light strawberry cake. Order two days ahead.

French **BISTROS**

Baker Street Bistro (Marina)
2953 Baker St.
San Francisco, CA
415-931-1475
French bistro

Bistro Clovis (Civic Center)
1596 Market St.
San Francisco, CA
415-864-0231
French bistro

Bistro Elan (Peninsula)
448 S. California Ave.
Palo Alto, CA
650-327-0284
New American/French
  bistro/Swedish

Chapeau! (Richmond)
1408 Clement St.
San Francisco, CA
415-750-9787
French brasserie

Chez Maman (Potrero Hill)
1453 18th St.
San Francisco, CA
415-824-7166
French

Clementine Restaurant
  (Richmond)
126 Clement St.
San Francisco, CA
415-387-0408
French bistro

Florio Bar & Cafe
  (Pacific Heights)
1915 Fillmore St.
San Francisco, CA
415-775-4300
French bistro

Hyde Street Bistro (Russian Hill)
1521 Hyde St.
San Francisco, CA
415-292-4415
French bistro

Metro Cafe (Haight)
311 Divisadero St.
San Francisco, CA
415-552-0903
French bistro

Ti Couz Creperie (Mission)
3108 16th St.
San Francisco, CA
415-252-7373
French

We've got reports on bistros all over the Bay, starting with **Hyde Street Bistro.** *Melanie Wong* says, "next time I'm missing France, this is where I'll find the cure." *Frisee aux lardons* was "everything I could hope for, simple and perfectly executed. It was true to its roots, and the best part is hot, freshly fried croutons that released a gusher of garlicky butter with each bite." Very good moules and frites. Small, well-chosen wine list includes not just one, but two bottlings of Cahors, the "black wine" of southwest France, by the glass. There's a draped alcove tucked in the front corner, designed just for cozy romantic dining. Service is friendly and helpful. They also offer three-course prix fixe for $27.50.

Bistro Elan starts all meals with house baked breads and butter from Normandy (the apricot-studded loaf is particularly good). Fusion dishes are definitely not the strong point here. Stick with delightful seared foie gras, a dilled prawns appetizer special that's very Swedish, and duck confit and crème fraiche risotto. For dessert, date cake is "unbelievably good. An individually molded cake, very moist and almost puddinglike, encasing fresh dates, rests in a pool of deep dark caramel studded with juicy surprises—which turned out to be caramelized apples" (*Melanie Wong*). Can be very noisy when crowded, especially on weekends.

Of **Florio** *ed k* says: "this restaurant definitely falls into the bistro category, with its compact interior (not cramped, just not huge), lively atmosphere and menu of bistro favorites like steak frites and roast chicken. As a roast chicken fanatic, this was the best roast chicken I've ever had." Only drawback, the battered fries look great, but are no better than mainstream fast food spuds. Excellent service.

Here are some particularly good value bistros: **Metro Cafe** offers $15 entrees, relaxed bistro atmosphere, easy seating (indoors or garden), and French staff. This is the kind of place where they remember the locals, reports *krafter*. **Baker Street Bistro**, a good quality and value place with a standard bistro menu, does a prix fixe dinner for about $20. **Bistro Clovis** charges around $10 for entrees and has "nice ambience, good service, tasty food (and lots of it, more than even I could truly eat), and reasonable prices," says *Judith Hurley*. Symphony lovers should note that it's near all the essential concert venues around the Civic Center. Desserts are a specialty, reportedly worth traveling for. Nice big room, but not too noisy. **Ti Couz** is an authentic Breton creperie with a nice list of hard ciders, but the menu goes beyond buckwheat galettes and dessert crepes. Large salads are a good deal and sized to share (try an authentic salade verte or a hearty seafood salad) and cheese plates offer a nice selection of fromage. **Chez Maman** also has crepes, as well as heartier entrees like steak frites and couscous with house-made *merguez*, along with bistro classics like endive salad.

Chapeau! and Clementine, two much-recommended pricier bistros, have well-priced early bird deals with plenty of choices.

- Baker Street Bistro: *see also* p. 217.
- Chapeau!: *see also* pp. 75, 217.
- Chez Maman: *see also* p. 236.
- Clementine Restaurant: *see also* p. 75.
- Metro Cafe: *see also* pp. 217, 219.
- Ti Couz Creperie: *see also* p. 227.

Stalking BLACK WALNUTS

Heart of the City Farmers' Market
    (Civic Center)
1182 Market St. #415
San Francisco, CA
415-558-9455
Farmers' market

Joe's Ice Cream (Richmond)
5351 Geary Blvd.
San Francisco, CA
415-751-1950
Ice cream or Gelato

Mitchell's Ice Cream (Mission)
688 San Jose Ave.
San Francisco, CA
415-648-2300
Ice cream or Gelato

San Francisco Ferry Plaza
    Farmers Market (Embarcadero)
Foot of Market St. on the
    Embarcadero; Ferry Building
    Marketplace
San Francisco, CA
415-353-5650
Farmers' market

Black walnuts are rare and wonderful, with a delicate flavor many find addictive. In the fall, watch for them at the walnut/almond stand (look for the gal with the teddy bears) at **Ferry Plaza Farmers Market**. They also sell them at the Civic Center Market at the nut stand nearest the Asian Art Museum end of the plaza.

Napa's a hotbed of black walnut trees. Look around there in the fall and you might beat the squirrels to some. If you find black walnuts fresh, it's best to freeze them, as they don't stay fresh for long. A trick: put unshelled nuts briefly in the freezer to make them easier to shell. Speaking of freezing, check out the black walnut flavor at **Joe's Ice Cream** or at **Mitchell's**.

○ **Heart of the City Farmers' Market:** *see also* p. 103.
○ **Joe's Ice Cream:** *see also* pp. 139, 285.
○ **Mitchell's Ice Cream:** *see also* pp. 20, 139, 285.
○ **San Francisco Ferry Plaza Farmers Market:** *see also* pp. 2, 52, 79, 104.

BLUE BOTTLE COFFEE

Blue Bottle Coffee Co. (East Bay)
5002 B Telegraph Ave.
Oakland, CA
510-653-3394
Store

James Freeman, owner of **Blue Bottle Coffee Company**, roasts, brews, and serves exceptional coffee. His beans come from a specialty broker, and though his primary focus is on quality, Freeman purchases beans that are organic, traditionally cultivated, or fair trade whenever he can find a suitable supply. Freeman is particularly fanatical about freshness. The roasting, grinding, and brewing steps are performed as close as logistically possible to actual consumption. Beans are never roasted more than twenty-four hours before being sold or brewed. Find this elixir at the Berkeley farmers' market on Tuesday and Saturday or have it delivered if you live in San Francisco, Berkeley, Oakland, Alameda, Mill Valley, Larkspur, Corte Madera, or San Rafael. All blends (delivered to all regions) are $15 a pound, including delivery or postage. SFers can also score some of this coffee from Blue Bottle's stand inside the Ferry Building Market, where even regular drip coffee is brewed to order, one cup at a time.

BOULEVARD

Boulevard (Embarcadero)
1 Mission St.
San Francisco, CA
415-543-6084
New American/French/Italian

Hounds agree that the food at **Boulevard** is terrific—some of the best in the city. The tough part is choosing what to order from their mouthwatering menu. Soups like lobster bisque (topped with shrimp and thin fries) and creamy white asparagus (with rock shrimp and bacon) draw raves. Seasonal, innovative entrees include duck breast over wild rice with chanterelles and blueberries; stuffed pork loin wrapped in bacon; and "Kobe Kobe Kobe" (braised shortribs, a big raviolo, and seared steak tartar). Terrific wine list with affordable choices.

Less adventurous eaters leave happy, too. Indian-spiced tuna tartare with cucumbers, and walu (Hawaiian butterfish) served with an array of colorful vegetables is "inventive and interesting; one of the most beautiful dishes I've ever eaten, like mardi gras on a plate," raves *nja*. Culinary conservatives will also find bliss in heirloom tomatoes with buffalo mozzarella made in-house each morning, Kobe steak, and a grilled pork sampler. Boulevard's service is lauded, along with its buzzy-but-informal attitude.

○ **Boulevard:** *see also* **p. 271.**

The **BRAZILIAN RODIZIO** Craze Hits San Francisco

Espetus Churrascaria (Civic Center)
1686 Market St.
San Francisco, CA
415-552-8792
Brazilian

Espetus Churrascaria is San Francisco's first *rodizio*—a Brazilian churrascaria (grill restaurant) offering an endless parade of skewered, grilled meat carved tableside. A generous salad bar features interesting choices like spicy chopped avocado and tomato salad and brined melon; also, hot fish, chicken, and bean dishes. There are currently five grilled meat choices at lunch and a dozen at dinner, including homemade beef sausage, chicken, pork, and various cuts of beef. The owners are said to have imported an experienced churrasco chef from Brazil to oversee the kitchen. The all-you-can-eat feast is priced at $8.95 (salad bar only) and $14.95 (salad bar plus hot dishes) at lunch; $24.95 for complete lunch or dinner with salad bar and grilled meats.

Artisan **BREAD BAKING** Tools

San Francisco Baking Institute (Peninsula)
480 Grandview Dr.
South San Francisco, CA
650-589-5784

SFBI is a great source for baking tools, and it offers short courses on artisan baking, too. If you want to start doing some home baking, check out *Artisan Baking Across America: The Breads, the Bakers, the Best Recipes* by Maggie Glezer.

Bay Area Monster **BREAKFAST** Survey

Bechelli's Restaurant (Marina)
2346 Chestnut St.
San Francisco, CA
415-346-1801
Diner or Coffee shop

Cafe Barbara Restaurant
 (East Bay)
1005 Brown Ave.
Lafayette, CA
925-284-9390
Diner or Coffee shop

Chow Market (East Bay)
Lafayette Circle, La Fiesta Sq.
Lafayette, CA
925-962-2469
American

Half Day Cafe (Marin County)
848 College Ave.
Kentfield, CA
415-459-0291
Diner or Coffee shop

Hide-Away Cafe (East Bay)
1920 Dennison St.
Oakland, CA
510-533-1211
Diner or Coffee shop

Judy's Cafe (Marina)
2269 Chestnut St. #248
San Francisco, CA
415-922-4588
Diner or Coffee shop

Millie's Kitchen (East Bay)
1018 Oak Hill Rd. #A
Lafayette, CA
925-283-2397
Diner or Coffee shop

Mountain Home Inn
   (Marin County)
810 Panoramic Hwy.
Mill Valley, CA
415-381-9000
New American

Q Restaurant (Richmond)
225 Clement St.
San Francisco, CA
415-752-2298
American

Soscol Cafe (Napa County)
632 Soscol Ave.
Napa, CA
707-252-0651
Diner or Coffee shop

Town's End Restaurant & Bakery
   (SOMA)
2 Townsend St.
San Francisco, CA
415-512-0749
American

Willie's Cafe (Marin County)
799 College Ave.
Kentfield, CA
415-455-9455
Diner or Coffee shop

Woodward's Garden (Mission)
1700 Mission St.
San Francisco, CA
415-621-7122
New American

Some breakfasts of particular interest: **Mountain Home Inn**, near
Mt. Tam, a small restaurant with an outdoor deck and gorgeous
views, is a great undiscovered bargain considering what you
would pay at any breakfast place in San Francisco with a view
says *Bay Gelldawg*. Breakfast plates are $10 (blueberry pancakes

served with honey butter, real maple syrup, crispy designer bacon; ham and onion hash with cheese grits, two eggs, English muffin, and berry puree—just two favorites). They serve freshly squeezed blood orange juice, and coffee's repeatedly refilled. Reservations are recommended, especially for deck seating.

Half Day Cafe's a chic breakfast/lunch/brunch destination in Marin serving enormous freshly baked scones (flavors change daily) and happening blueberry (or lemon blueberry) pancakes. Nearby **Willie's** serves the best buttermilk pancakes on the planet according to *StraightTalk*. **Soscol Cafe** up in Napa is the spot for a hearty workingman's breakfast: good quality, big portions, and huevos rancheros with black beans come highly recommended.

Oakland's **Hide-Away Cafe** has its fans, including *Eric Eto*, who really likes its potatoes and notes that the place is never crowded and is "a chill and unpretentious place." Inside can be very dreary, so hit the patio if weather cooperates.

Back in San Francisco . . . In peach season, hit **Town's End** where they put the fruit to excellent use in Swedish oatmeal pancakes with peaches and almonds. Fresh peaches and slivered almonds are added right into the batter for sweet, crunchy goodness in every bite. Icing on the (pan)cake is fresh raspberry fruit butter in lieu of syrup (dinner-wise, Town's End sometimes offers a killer three-course meal for only $12, Wednesdays through Sundays). **Woodward's Garden**, long hidden below a freeway since removed, has started serving breakfast. Try savory breakfast soup and/or Valrhona hot chocolate. *Celeste* says prices seem low for the quality. **Q** has cheap and interesting food—what *Stanley Stephan* describes as diner comfort food for the new millennium. With its thrift store decor and a magnetic board for playtime, it's a great place to bring kids. They serve a bacon, blue cheese, and red onion marmalade omelet Stanley calls worth a heart attack. Baked beans, good enough to please a transplanted New Englander, are smoky-sweet and loaded with bacon. It's very veggie friendly, especially for breakfast, and gets bonus points for a waitstaff that's quick with coffee refills (also, their fried chicken compares favorably to Powell's and is served with nice, spicy gravy and mashed potatoes). Note, though, that not everyone seems to love Q equally.

Bechelli's is another great breakfast spot, serving good omelets, chunky home fries, and blueberry pancakes in generous portions. **Judy's** serves delicious pumpkin bread with breakfasts.

Three good tips in Lafayette: **Chow Market** (new twists on old favorites such as herbed hash, poached eggs, and French toast made with baguettes), **Millie's Kitchen** (crowded, best coffeecake in town), and **Cafe Barbara** (nice patio, delicious waffles, fruit salad, and omelets).

Also see "*Diner* Survey."

○ **Chow Market:** *see also* **p. 226.**
○ **Town's End Restaurant & Bakery:** *see also* **p. 217.**

Cajun Sunday **BRUNCH**

Pam's Cajun Sunday Brunch at Piccadilly Gourmet Catering (Peninsula)
1072-K Shell Blvd., at Charter Sq. Shopping Center
Foster City, CA
650-573-0444
Cajun/Creole

Run by a catering company, **Pam's Cajun Sunday Brunch** buffet is offered each week. Best dishes: catfish two ways (grilled and cornmeal-fried), succulent crayfish, mashed potatoes with gravy, macaroni and cheese, fried chicken, shrimp fritters, three kinds of hot links, warm sweet potato pie with ice cream, and bread pudding with whiskey sauce. Best of all, though, is gumbo, featuring succulent crawfish tails and big shrimp, chicken, and sausage. It's thickened with file, has the nutty taste of a well-turned roux, and is made with wonderful broth, reports *Melanie Wong*. Brunch is served every Sunday, 10:30 a.m. to 4:30 p.m.; $23 plus tip. Punch, juice, mimosas, coffee, and tea are included. Seniors get a 10 percent discount. Call ahead to check all info!

BRUNCH in the East Bay

Bette's Oceanview Diner
  (East Bay)
1807 4th St.
Berkeley, CA
510-644-3230
Diner or Coffee shop

Cafe Fanny (East Bay)
1603 San Pablo Ave.
Berkeley, CA
510-526-7664
New American/French/Italian

Chester's Bayview Cafe (East Bay)
1508 Walnut St., B
Berkeley, CA
510-849-9995
American

Claremont Resort & Spa
  (East Bay)
41 Tunnel Rd.
Berkeley, CA
510-843-3000
New American

Homemade Cafe (East Bay)
2454 Sacramento St.
Berkeley, CA
510-845-1940
Diner or Coffee shop

Inn Kensington (East Bay)
293 Arlington Ave.
Kensington, CA
510-527-5919
American

La Note (East Bay)
2377 Shattuck Ave.
Berkeley, CA
510-843-1535
French/American

Makri's Coffee Shop (East Bay)
2105 University Ave., east of
  Shattuck
Berkeley, CA
510-843-7653
Diner or Coffee shop

Mama's Royal Cafe (East Bay)
4012 Broadway
Oakland, CA
510-547-7600
Diner or Coffee shop

Rick & Ann's Restaurant
  (East Bay)
2922 Domingo Ave.
Berkeley, CA
510-649-8538
American

Royal Cafe (East Bay)
811 San Pablo Ave.
Albany, CA
510-525-6066
Diner or Coffee shop

South Shore Cafe (East Bay)
531 S. Shore Ctr., W.
Alameda, CA
510-523-3663
Diner or Coffee shop

Venus (East Bay)
2327 Shattuck Ave.
Berkeley, CA
510-540-5950
New American

A nice round-up of the 510 brunch scene is offered by *garcon*.

Bette's is the best all-around with varied menu including fantastic pancakes and fruit pancake-souffles. Everything they do reflects the perfectionist approach of the owners. The only downside is the wait, although you can use it to enjoy the Fourth Street shops. **Royal Cafe** is a good no-fuss alternative with less wait. They do some fine specials, especially the scramble with sun-dried tomatoes, Asiago, and mushrooms, and worthy pancakes. Super service.

Makri's is a super-cheap greasy spoon not far from UC Berkeley—a great breakfast dive run by a friendly Korean couple. Breakfast sandwiches and shredded potato hash browns are great. But *garcon* thinks the best breakfast, dollar for dollar, in the East Bay is the egg, onion, mushroom, and tomato breakfast sandwich with a big side of golden crisp hash browns for under $5.

Mama's Royal Cafe has a hip Temescal vibe, sort of like the Mission used to be five to ten years ago—a bit Betty Page/Johnny Cash. Solid brunch items include eggs Benedict and breakfast burritos. **Homemade Cafe**, filled with lots of regulars, has a nice cozy vibe. Food's good, though not quite up to Bette's or Mama's. **Chester's** has an upstairs deck with bay views and serves great waffles and very good frittatas. The sight of the Golden Gate glowing under the late morning rays between sips of orange juice is one of those quintessentially Bay Area moments. **Inn Kensington** is another solid brunch place with lots of regulars. Their speciality is big (though maybe a tad too sweet) biscuits. **Venus** has really good ultra-rich walnut pancakes and homemade sausages. Small spot, expect a wait on weekends. **La Note's** French vibe might seem a bit touristy, but eating their French breakfast under the olive branches on the lavender-lined patio can more than make up for it.

Fans of **Rick & Ann's**, across from the Claremont Resort's tennis courts, willingly wait in line for brunch. As *garcon* puts it so aptly, "lines don't lie, though they sure can be annoying."

Cafe Fanny is tasty, but be aware that portions are small yet prices aren't. This is more of a light breakfast spot than full-out brunch place, but after eating you can enjoy shopping for wine at Kermit Lynch and for breads at Acme. Be aware that specials run out early.

The **Claremont Resort** Pavillion Room does a big upscale brunch buffet with the best setting and view of all, but the food's inconsistent. **South Shore Cafe** serves breakfast all day, but don't expect fancy brunchy atmosphere. *Ruth Lafler* rates it "zero (or perhaps minus five) for atmosphere, unless you like your coffee shops as dark as your bars." Ask for loco moco (it's not on the menu): mounds of fluffy white rice, topped with big flat hamburger patties, topped with fried eggs, all soaked in oniony brown gravy.

○ **Bette's Oceanview Diner:** *see also* p. 37.
○ **La Note:** *see also* pp. 227, 236.

Best **BURMESE** Bets

Burma Super Star Restaurant
  (Richmond)
309 Clement St.
San Francisco, CA
415-387-2147
Burmese

Mandalay Restaurant
  (Richmond)
4348 California St.
San Francisco, CA
415-386-3895
Burmese

Innya Lake Restaurant
  (Peninsula)
586 San Mateo Ave.
San Bruno, CA
650-873-1388
Chinese/Burmese

The kitchen at Burma Super Star uses a light hand, preserving the freshness of its ingredients. This is an easy and approachable place to try Burmese cuisine, says *Melanie Wong*. *Patrick* agrees: "every dish we have tried has tasted impeccably fresh and well flavored, and all meat has been tender and beautifully cooked." Its food travels and keeps well, and makes really good leftovers. Burmese specialties are noted with stars on the menu. Only on Chowhound.com would you get a wine recommendation to go with Burmese food. Melanie suggests: Bonny Doon's Cardinal Zinfandel. As for best dishes, *Patrick* recommends: *shan kaukswer* (number 1 dish! rice noodles with spicy tomato sauce and piles of cilantro and toasted chili flakes), Burmese samosas (veg and chicken), Burmese style chicken salad (bits of fried chicken in saucy cabbage salad), chickpea curry (chana dhal with tasty, tea-flavored sauce—good cold, too), and dried fried string beans (excellent version of this menu standard).

Innya Lake's Burmese specials are also asterisked on the menu—plus, check the house specials section. Or look for the Burmese script (written over the leader dots between the English name and Chinese characters) next to each item. Overall food quality's high, but service is a bit quirky. Recommended dishes: samosa, green onion beef, palada (thousand layer bread), fermented tea salad (particularly intense), ginger salad (bright, refreshing flavors), pork and potato curry, curried fish balls, tampoi rice (sweet savory rice cooked in spices), coconut curry chicken noodle soup (both crispy fried noodles and regular soup noodles), satay combo (sweet pork especially good), Burmese eggplant, coconut rice. And, for dessert: paluda ice cream, "resembles ice cream soda, served in a soda glass with tapioca, coconut jelly, other tasty but unidentifiable fruit and jelly bits, coconut juice, paluda syrup, topped with vanilla ice cream and peanuts. Weird but good" (*Ruth Lafler*). Lots of free parking.

Mandalay's an old-time Burmese where *Melanie Wong* feels the kitchen is calling it in and no longer paying attention to details. Service can also be uneven.

Meaty Dining at **CAFE ROUGE**

Cafe Rouge Meat Market (East Bay)
1782 4th St.
Berkeley, CA
510-525-1440
Store

Cafe Rouge doubles as a high-end meat market, so meaty entrees are the way to go. Hounds universally acclaim what *Hapa-Girl* droolingly describes as an insanely good burger—not on the dinner menu but always available—and excellent frites and hanger steak. Best starters are oysters, charcuterie, salads, and housemade beef jerky (good to snack on with their excellent cocktails). If you haven't got time to sit down, just grab a Niman Ranch dog to go from the meat counter. The butcher shop has great meat quality, but the butchers don't do a great job with special requests, so reconcile to having it *their* way.

A Good Unfancy Slice of **CAKE**

Bette's Oceanview Diner
(East Bay)
1807 4th St.
Berkeley, CA
510-644-3230
Diner or Coffee shop

Crixa Cakes (East Bay)
2748 Adeline St.
Berkeley, CA
510-548-0421
Bakery

Comforts (Marin County)
335 San Anselmo Ave.
San Anselmo, CA
415-454-9840
Pan-Asian Fusion

If you don't feel like fancy European patisserie—just a slice of homey layer cake or a tasty cupcake—here's where to go: In Berkeley, **Crixa Cakes** serves up slices of moist ginger cake, Boston cream pie, and other traditional favorites. **Bette's Oceanview Diner,** also in Berkeley, stocks large, appealing cupcakes in its pastry case. And in San Anselmo, **Comforts** goes traditional with chocolate layer cake, coconut cupcakes, and blueberry corn cakes served on Sundays only.

○ **Bette's Oceanview Diner:** *see also* **p. 33.**
○ **Crixa Cakes:** *see also* **p. 223.**

Friendly, Delicious **CAMBODIAN**

Angkor Borei Restaurant (Mission)
3471 Mission St.
San Francisco, CA
415-550-8417
Cambodian

Outer Mission's Angkor Borei serves up Cambodian specialties in a nice neighborhood setting. The friendly owner will recommend authentic dishes and share her knowledge. It's hard to go wrong with most dishes, which ranged from fair (at very worst) to really, really good. An appetizer of fresh spinach leaves is a do-it-yourself affair: make bite-sized treats by wrapping fresh leaves around bits of coconut, jalapeño, limes, dried shrimp, ginger, peanuts, and red onion. It's a very refreshing way to start a meal. Salads of ground pork, chicken, squid, and beef were a bit heavy on the lime, but still good. Crispy Cambodian crepe was very crispy and featured a surprising bite of coconut. Crispy rice chips are served with a dipping sauce of shrimp, pork, coconut, and tamarind. Might be best ordered early in the meal (before spicy salads dull your tastebuds). Recommended entrees: Pan-fried fish fillet with garlic sauce, stewed ground pork (*prahok*)—a pork dip served with fresh veggies—and mock duck claypot. Rich, tangy Ahmonk (curry fish mousse) is a definite must order; *Suzy, Joanne, and Spencer* say that "each spoonful is a bite of soft mousse and more solid pieces of fish with the flavor and smell of a lemongrass curry." One dud: prawns baked in foil have come out overcooked.

○ **Angkor Borei Restaurant:** *see also* p. 20.

Chowhound Nametag: Han Lukito

○◯○

Location: Hayward, California

Occupation: Distributor of machine parts

Cholesterol Level: Excellent (I take Lipitor)

Farthest Out of the Way Traveled Just for Chow: Two hours one way for oysters at Hog Island Oyster. Result: very disappointed, almost give up on chowhound worthiness, but came back to my senses shortly after.

Nabe Most Full of Explorable Unknown Chow: San Jose, South Bay area for Asian/Indian cuisine

Top Chinatown Pick: Hon's Won Ton for the curry beef and wonton in San Francisco Chinatown; Goldmedal in Oakland Chinatown for the wonton soup

Underrated by Chowhounds: Ton Kiang Noodle House receives low marks but undeservedly so especially for the #1 and #8 combo noodle soup but must be ordered with flat egg noodle and separate soup

Favorite Comfort Chow: Fu Lam Moon for dim sum; Raffles in Milpitas for hokkien mee and hainam chicken rice; Lechon Manilla in Fremont for Filipino food like chicken adobo, kare-kare; Taiwan Restaurant in Union City for South Taiwanese noodle soup; Cheese Board in Berkeley for pizza; Shanghai Restaurant in Fremont for sliced five-spiced beef, omelet, halibut, shrimp, twice-cooked pork, spicy side pork, etc.; Fresh Choice in Hayward.

Guilty Pleasure: Chive fries and hot fudge sundae at Belle in Hayward

Touring Local **CANDY FACTORIES**

Jelly Belly Candy Company
(Solano County)
One Jelly Belly La.
Fairfield, CA
1-800-953-5592
Chocolate/Candy shop

Scharffen Berger Chocolate Maker
(East Bay)
914 Heinz Ave.
Berkeley, CA
510-981-4050
Chocolate/Candy shop

Here are a couple of very different opportunities to see candy makers in action, making small-batch artisan chocolate or super-automated gourmet jelly beans. Go on a weekday when the factories hum to see the actual process.

Scharffen Berger makes high-end chocolate and takes it seriously, and its tours are geared toward those who want to hear chcocolate history and learn how it gets from bean to bar (while tasting it at every stage). You won't find high-tech assembly lines, just vintage equipment straight out of Willy Wonka, per *JimA*'s description. This tour's not for everyone, but curious (and patient) chocophiles will come away happy.

A **Jelly Belly factory** tour is for everyone with a sweet tooth. You get to see the whole process, from tons of plain sugar to boxed beans (and these *are* high-tech assembly lines), with descriptions and free tastes. There's even a cafe that serves jelly bean-shaped burgers and pizza.

Both, of course, have factory stores on location. Get tour schedules and details from their Web sites: www.scharffenberger .com and www.jellybelly.com.

○ **Scharffen Berger Chocolate Maker:** *see also* p. 73.

CANTONESE Banquet

Great Eastern Restaurant (Chinatown)
649 Jackson St.
San Francisco, CA
415-986-2500
Chinese (Cantonese)/Chinese (Dim Sum)/Chinese (Hong Kong)

Not only is Great Eastern a Cantonese banquet legend, it's also one of the easiest Chinese restaurants for non-Chinese to navigate, says *Melanie Wong*. Best choices:

- sticky rice–stuffed chicken (order forty-eight hours in advance) stands up to R & G Lounge's version, although *Melanie* feels that R & G's stuffing is a bit more complex
- cold plate of appetizer meats (soy sauce chicken, stuffed skin of pork shank with cured pork, anise beef shank, jellyfish)
- sauteed sea conch and scallops with yellow chives (a "playfully textured dish, with firm conch, soft scallops playing against refreshing crunch of bean sprouts and soft savory sweet onioniness of chives," says *Bryan Loofbourrow*)
- lobster with green onion and ginger (sparklingly good)
- perfectly steamed sea bass
- roast squab: "flat-out superb, with wonderfully textured skin, just the right amount of spice, and flavorful meat that showed off the intensity of squab without crossing over into heavy liverish territory"
- steamed oysters with black bean sauce—very fresh, juicy, and cooked to perfection

Melanie Wong shares some info to keep in mind about service here (and in many other Chinese restaurants): "Sunday is the busiest night and places will be filled with Chinese families. I avoid Chinese restaurants on Sundays until after 7:30 or 8:00, when you'll find many of them cleared out after the earlier chaos, din, and pandemonium. The staff is breathing much easier at this time. Also, I don't expect anything in the way of wine service from Chinese restaurants. If they know how to open a bottle, it's a pleasant surprise. I bring my own corkscrew and wine glasses."

○ **Great Eastern Restaurant:** *see also* **p. 85.**

CANTONESE Favorites

China First Restaurant
  (Richmond)
336 Clement St.
San Francisco, CA
415-387-8370
Chinese (Cantonese)/Chinese
  (Hong Kong)

Daimo Chinese Restaurant
  (East Bay)
3288 Pierce St., at Pacific East
  Mall
Richmond, CA
510-527-3888
Chinese (Cantonese)/Chinese
  (Hong Kong)

Gold Medal Restaurant (East Bay)
381 8th St.
Oakland, CA
510-268-8484
Chinese (Cantonese)/Chinese
  (Hong Kong)

Joy Luck Place (Peninsula)
98 E. 4th Ave.
San Mateo, CA
650-343-6988
Chinese (Cantonese)/Chinese
  (Dim Sum)/Chinese
  (Hong Kong)

Joy Luck Place (South Bay)
10911 N. Wolfe Rd.
Cupertino, CA
408-255-6988
Chinese (Dim Sum)/Chinese
  (Cantonese)/Chinese
  (Hong Kong)

Legendary Palace (East Bay)
708 Franklin St.
Oakland, CA
510-663-9288
Chinese (Cantonese)/Chinese
  (Hong Kong)/Chinese
  (Dim Sum)

Louie's California Chinese Cuisine
  (Chinatown)
646 Washington St.
San Francisco, CA
415-291-8038
Chinese (Hong Kong)/Chinese
  (Dim Sum)/Chinese
  (Cantonese)

Silver House (Peninsula)
2224 S. El Camino Real
San Mateo, CA
650-571-1298
Chinese (Cantonese)/Chinese
  (Hong Kong)

Silver Lake Seafood Restaurant
   (Peninsula)
2291 S. El Camino Real
San Mateo, CA
650-578-1678
Chinese (Cantonese)/Chinese
   (Hong Kong)

South Sea Seafood Village
   (Sunset)
1420 Irving St.
San Francisco, CA
415-665-8210
Chinese (Hong Kong)/Chinese
   (Cantonese)/Chinese
   (Dim Sum)

Gold Medal in Oakland is among this guide's most well-rounded restaurants, appearing in best-of round-ups for jook, kidneys, tripe, and chow fun. There are other good things here, such as soy sauce chicken and salt steamed (aka salt poached) chicken. *Margret* says not to miss the gnow (or ngow) lay sow (fried bread). Look for them stacked in the corner of the steam table (in the window); they're football shaped with a slit on top, crunchy and donutlike (kind of a cross between yau tiu and a donut) and a little sweet. Avoid roast duck.

South Sea Seafood Village in San Francisco is a good choice for a wedding or other big banquet. Fancy Hong Kong–style decor, bilingual staff, and an accommodating attitude set it apart. You can customize your menu (picking from banquet menus and regular menu items), and it will even provide separate menus for vegetarian and fish-allergic guests. Excellent service goes beyond the call of duty (*tyler*).

Good special-request dishes at **Louie's** in San Francisco's Chinatown: dried scallop fried rice (like fried rice from another dimension), e-fu noodles, chicken stuffed with glutinous rice (order in advance), fried bean curd skin roll, gai lan with garlic, thousand layer cake.

Silver House in San Mateo is *KK*'s Cantonese favorite. Stick with white board specials or any steamed fish. Other favorites: steamed razor clams, salt-baked fishlings (aka white rice fish), and minced beef with spinach.

Daimo in Richmond garners praise for salt and pepper crab and wontons. A report on their BBQ sampler plate of roast duck, roast suckling pig, and *gui fei ji* (poached empress chicken) raises our hopes that the BBQ station's improving. Skin-on duck and pig is perfectly crispy and meat's flavorful without being too oily. *Yvonne* finds its BBQ good but not as first class as some of the little hole-in-the-wall places in Oakland and San Francisco. This jibes with *Yimster*s take: "BBQ, like dim sum, can sometimes be hit-or-miss at bigger places. The master of the kitchen may be off that day. That's why a hole-in-the-wall is less hit-and-miss because the owner/chef will be there every day they're open."

China First in San Francisco still serves old-fashioned *gon low won ton* (meat and sauce served over boiled won tons in place of rice or noodles). *Sarah* found beef stew gon low won ton nice and tender, with the right amount of meat, gristle, and tendon (very, very good!), and salted spicy fried chicken wings fried to perfection. The wings, plus two large plates of gon low won ton and a gratis homey beef-veggie soup starter ran around $12.

Joy Luck Place in Cupertino is a big fave for dim sum and much more. Its San Mateo branch is much smaller (so reservations are strongly suggested), but it is open late and is especially good for roasted squab, steamed tofu with seafood in bamboo steamer, and mango pudding (including fresh diced mango).

At **Silver Lake** in San Mateo, *Yimster* enjoys Chinese comfort food "what mom used to make at home." Staff speaks good English. Recommended specials can be found listed on the wall (Chinese only), but here are some tips: tofu goose (better than average in both flavor and texture), bitter melon stir-fried with frog, Chinese drunken chicken with wood ears, and taro root stewed with roast duck

At **Legendary Palace** in Oakland, these dishes (mostly from the menu) are recommended: sauteed scallops and calamari with sugar peas; jumbo prawns with honeyglazed walnuts; lettuce cups with diced squab; lobster with supreme sauce; steamed live fish; braised crab meat noodles. Longevity buns and winter melon soup (served in whole melon) must be special ordered in advance.

Also see "*Cantonese* Banquet." Also see the Cuisine Index for more Cantonese tips.

○ **Gold Medal Restaurant:** *see also* pp. 73, 162, 167, 294.
○ **Joy Luck Place:** *see also* p. 82.
○ **Legendary Palace:** *see also* pp. 68, 90.

North Beach **CAPPUCCINO** Crawl

Caffe Italia (North Beach)
565 Green St
San Francisco, CA
415-576-1033
Italian café

Caffe Puccini (North Beach)
411 Columbus Ave.
San Francisco, CA
415-989-7033
Italian café

Caffe Sempione (North Beach)
641 Vallejo St.
San Francisco, CA
415-362-6317
Italian café

Caffe Trieste (North Beach)
609 Vallejo St.
San Francisco, CA
415-982-2605
Italian café

Stella Pastry Cafe
  (North Beach)
446 Columbus Ave.
San Francisco, CA
415-986-2914
Italian café

Steps of Rome Trattoria
  (North Beach)
348 Columbus Ave.
San Francisco, CA
415-397-0435
Italian

Cappuccino expert *Stanley Stephan* shares top picks for frothy joe in North Beach. For scientific precision, all were tried early in the morning. Results may vary at other times!

1. **Stella Pastry Cafe** (made from Lavazza beans) a thick creamy layer sits atop the perfect espresso
2. **Caffe Puccini** (from Cafe Puccini roast beans): the best foam, almost dessertlike, not too dense, not too foamy; savor spoonfuls of this sweet froth—and good house-made Italian tortes, including ricotta
3. **Caffe Italia** (from Caffe Italia roast beans): the most impressive cloudlike foam, good strong espresso—my whole cappuccino crawl was worth it for discovering this brew

Honorable mentions: **Caffe Trieste's** cappuccino has thick foamy cream with a swirl of crema. Strong, full bodied, bordering on a good bitter brew. **Steps of Rome** adds imported powdered chocolate between espresso and foam, and the result has less bite than Puccini's. And in the early morning, there was none of the rumored attitude; staff was gracious and friendly. **Caffe Sempione** gets points for being the artiest café in North Beach, with works by local painters on the walls, books by local authors for sale, free poetry magazines, and a piano for anyone who plays. Open at 6 a.m. Unfortunately, their cappuccino is more of a pleasant lattelike drink.

○ **Stella Pastry Cafe:** *see also* p. 5.

Bay Area **CARIBBEAN**

Adobe House (Napa County)
376 Soscol Ave.
Napa, CA
707-255-4310
Caribbean/Filipino

Mango Cafe (Peninsula)
435 Hamilton Ave.
Palo Alto, CA
650-324-9443
Jamaican/Caribbean

We've had just a couple of recommendations for good and inexpensive island cuisine (which is hard to find hereabouts). The food at **Mango Cafe** seems to have been toned down in recent years, but there are still good choices, especially goat roti, beef patties, mango chutney, and hearts of palm salad. Jerk chicken legs are tender and well cooked, but wings should be avoided. There's a large collection of bottled hot sauces, too, and twenty or so smoothies served in large globes. **Adobe House**, with a Filipino owner and Puerto Rican chef, currently serves Cuban, Puerto Rican, Dominican, Mexican, and Filipino dishes, plus burgers, salads, and sandwiches. They plan to turn more Caribbean, but, meanwhile, the Filipino dishes—lechon and pork adobo— are recommended.

CATCH: Good Food in a Glitzy Scene

Catch (Castro)
2362 Market St.
San Francisco, CA
415-431-5000
New American

"Delicious, surprised, happy, filled," is how *Spencer* felt after dining at **Catch**. "The food was very good, but the design, the live music, and the vibe were distracting. The hired pianist dressed like Elton John at a funeral and there was a distracting glare from a backlit bar that stretched up to a twenty-foot ceiling. But I enjoyed the food." Pepper-seared ahi tuna and crostini trio, pepper broiled opah on sea of garbanzo beans is "steaky, full of flavor and texture, pepper marinade is primo for the fish and whatever they do to the garbanzo beans is well worth it." Wines served by the glass and (how often do you see this in San Francisco these days?) also by the half or whole pitcher.

East Bay Retail **CAVIAR**

Berkeley Bowl (East Bay)
2020 Oregon St.
Berkeley, CA
510-843-6929
Store

Beverages & More
www.bevmo.com
877-772-3866
Wine store

Pasta Shop (East Bay)
1786 4th St.
Berkeley, CA
510-528-1786
Store

Pasta Shop (East Bay)
5655 College Ave., at Rockridge
    Market Hall
Oakland, CA
510-655-7748
Store

Ver Brugge Meat Fish Poultry (East Bay)
6321 College Ave.
Oakland, CA
510-658-6854
Store

When springing for expensive, high-quality caviar, you want to make sure your source has taken good care of it. In North Oakland and Berkeley, the **Pasta Shop, Berkeley Bowl,** and **Ver Brugge** all sell well-cared-for caviar. **Beverages & More** in Walnut Creek not only keeps caviar properly chilled, but will pack it in ice for your trip home.

- ○ **Berkeley Bowl:** *see also* **p. 206.**
- ○ **Pasta Shop:** *see also* **p. 156.**
- ○ **Ver Brugge Meat Fish Poultry:** *see also* **pp. 79, 230.**

CHALLAH Options

Bay Breads (Pacific Heights)
2325 Pine St.
San Francisco, CA
415-440-0356
French bakery

Grand Bakery (East Bay)
3264 Grand Ave.
Oakland, CA
510-465-1110
Bakery

Hopkins Street Bakery (East Bay)
1584 Hopkins St.
Berkeley, CA
510-526-8188
Bakery

Irving's Premium Challahs
www.greisman.org
415-753-5474
Mail order source

Moscow & Tbilisi Bakery
   (Richmond)
5540 Geary Blvd.
San Francisco, CA
415-668-6959
Russian bakery

Semifreddi's Bakery (East Bay)
3084 Claremont Ave.
Berkeley, CA
510-596-9942
Bakery

Semifreddi's Bakery (East Bay)
4242 Hollis St.
Emeryville, CA
510-596-9930
Bakery

Does true challah, the Jewish bread with crisp outer crust and moist, eggy, slightly sweet interior, exist in the Bay Area? For *notmichaelbauer* **Irving's Premium Challah** is easily the best he's had in decades of Bay Area challah eating. It's got the requisite eggy flavor and nice crust, and is available in various sizes—the small is big enough to feed a family of three. Orders via phone only, but Irving delivers! Oakland's **Grand Bakery** is another fave, with **Semifreddi's** (nice flavor, lousy crust, per *Howard Freedman*) running second.

Bay Breads makes a nice, less-sweet challah on Fridays using oil, not butter. *Howard Freedman* notes that "real challah uses vegetable oil because the Friday night meal is traditionally a meat meal, and Jews are required to refrain from consuming meat and dairy in the same meal." So this is the authentic item, though many bakeries (e.g. Arizmendi, Cheese Board and Noe Valley Bakery) have followed Julia Child's lead since she published a famous challah recipe calling for butter. **Hopkins Street Bakery** makes challah recommended by *Nathan Landau*, and **Moscow & Tbilisi's** version is crusty but less sweet than many traditionalists prefer.

○ **Bay Breads:** *see also* **pp. 76, 214.**
○ **Hopkins Street Bakery:** *see also* **p. 4.**
○ **Moscow & Tbilisi Bakery:** *see also* **p. 98.**

The **CHANA** Syndrome

Chutney (Tenderloin)
511 Jones St.
San Francisco, CA
415-931-5541
North Indian/Pakistani

Darbar (Russian Hill)
1412 Polk St.
San Francisco, CA
415-359-1236
Pakistani/North Indian

Naan N' Curry (Tenderloin)
478 O'Farrell St.
San Francisco, CA
415-775-1349
Pakistani/North Indian

Shalimar Restaurant (Tenderloin)
532 Jones St.
San Francisco, CA
415-928-0333
Pakistani

Pakwan Restaurant (Tenderloin)
501 O'Farrell St.
San Francisco, CA
415-776-0160
Pakistani

Vik's Chaat (East Bay)
726 Allston Way
Berkeley, CA
510-644-4412
Indian

Saravana Bhavan (Sunnyvale)
1305 South Mary Ave.
Sunnyvale, CA 94087
408-616-7755
South Indian

Chowhound *squid-kun* has sacrificed for all hounddom by rigorously sampling chana, channa, chole, and chollay—all terms for chickpea—dishes at pretty much all the Tandorooloin restaurants. His general take: "Despite similarities in the menus, especially among the Punjabi places, each is staking out a distinct style."

Shalimar: Kabli channa ($4.95), tender chickpeas flavored with cumin, tamarind, and medium chile heat. The gravy's smooth, thick and medium golden-brown, and there isn't much of it. A small amount of spice-red oil pooled on top (*squid-kun* doesn't mind, though others might).

Pakwan: Chana masala ($4.50) is lighter in color and has more gravy, more chile heat, and some whole spices—nigella and flecks of red chile—but less tamarind tang and an overall thinner flavor.

Chutney: Chana masala ($3.99) has the firmest peas in the 'hood, a quality some may prefer. Chile heat is comparable to Pakwan's—a surprise, since other dishes here are mild—and flavors are nicely balanced. Also in the sauce: chopped cilantro and a couple of green cardamom pods.

Naan N' Curry: Chana masala ($3.99) has medium-high heat, lots of smooth golden gravy, little whole spice presence. Slices of tomato contribute some sourness. A small amount of chopped cilantro tops the dish.

Darbar: This relative newcomer serves a familiar Punjabi menu—the owner is from Lahore. Lahori choley ($4.95) is unusually red with lots of liquid and maybe not as much garbanzo as the other places. Strong cumin flavor, chopped cilantro, sliced onion, tomato, and green bell pepper. Hot, as ordered, but a one-dimensional heat. The decor is a cut above the other places, and there is full table service.

A couple of other tips: in Berkeley, *Kathleen Mikulis* likes chole at **Vik's** (comes with orders of samosa, aloo tikki chole or bhature). And *Preeth Chengappa* likes chole and chana masala best at **Sarvana Bhavan**, served with flaky layered paratha, made with a spice paste including coconut and fennel.

○ **Chutney:** *see also* p. 146.
○ **Darbar:** *see also* p. 146.
○ **Pakwan Restaurant:** *see also* p. 196.
○ **Shalimar Restaurant:** *see also* p. 146.
○ **Vik's Chaat:** *see also* p. 57.

C'est **CHEESE**

Andante Dairy (Embarcadero)
Ferry Plaza Farmers
    Market (Sat.)
San Francisco, CA
707-526-0517
Farmers' market vendor

Artisan (Pacific Heights)
2413 California St.
San Francisco, CA
415-929-8610
Cheese shop

Cheese Board (East Bay)
1504 Shattuck Ave.
Berkeley, CA
510-549-3183
Pizza bakery/Cheese shop/Pizzeria

Coopers (Castro)
2 Sanchez St.
San Francisco, CA
415-934-9463
Cheese shop

Cowgirl Creamery at Ferry
    Building Marketplace
    (Embarcadero)
One Ferry Bldg., Embarcadero
San Francisco, CA
415-353-5650
Cheese shop

Farmstead Cheeses and Wines
(East Bay)
1650 Park St., inside Alameda
Marketplace
Alameda, CA
510-864-WINE
Cheese shop

Leonard's 2001 (Russian Hill)
2001 Polk St.
San Francisco, CA
415-921-2001
Cheese shop

Mollie Stone's Grand Central
(Pacific Heights)
2435 California St.
San Francisco, CA
415-567-4902
Store

Mollie Stone's Market (Peninsula)
164 S. California Ave.
Palo Alto, CA
650-323-8361
Store

Mollie Stone's Market (Peninsula)
49 W. 42nd Ave.
San Mateo, CA
650-372-2828
Store

Rainbow Grocery Co-Op (SOMA)
1745 Folsom St.
San Francisco, CA
415-863-0620
Store

San Francisco Ferry Plaza
Farmers Market (Embarcadero)
Foot of Market St. on the
Embarcadero; Ferry Building
Marketplace
San Francisco, CA
415-353-5650
Farmers' market

Say Cheese (Haight)
856 Cole St.
San Francisco, CA
415-665-5020
Cheese shop

Tower Market
(Westportal/Ingleside)
635 Portola Dr.
San Francisco, CA
415-664-1609
Store

24th Street Cheese Co.
(Noe Valley)
3893 24th St.
San Francisco, CA
415-821-6658
Store

Whole Foods
www.wholefoods.com/stores
Store

Woodlands Market (Marin County)
735 College Ave.
Kentfield, CA
415-457-8160
Store

Competition has heated up among the Bay Area's cheese sellers, with ever greater quality and variety the happy result. Here are some particularly good ones to watch out for, and some selected cheese stores. Note, though, that cheese has its seasons, so you won't find all cheeses mentioned below at all times.

Farmstead Cheeses and Wines, in the growing Alameda Marketplace, carries a small but select stock of wines (mostly from small and mid-size U.S. producers) and at least one hundred different cheeses, including an aged Brescianella served at French Laundry. The proprietors are eager to talk wine and cheese. In fall, they carry rigotte d'Echalas, similar to Epoisses with soft texture only not as pungent. Clarines is a runny cheese that is to be scooped out of its wooden container (theirs is very mild, but very good, reports *Michael*). Both are also available at Tower Market (which generally has an excellent selection).

A seasonal cheese to watch for is La Tur, a speciality of the Alta Lange region of Italy. It's hard to find in the United States, and while its flavor isn't complex, the texture's soft and luscious (creamy, slightly gooey, slightly cheesecakelike, says *babyfork*). Look for it at **Mollie Stone's** (which runs some excellent sales, by the way) or **Woodlands**.

24th Street Cheese Co. has a wide selection, including lots of soft washed-rind cheeses, and occasionally, raw milk products, but service can be gruff to new faces. **Leonard's** has good prices and selection of common cheeses, but they're precut and stored, which may compromise quality. **Coopers** can be pricey, but is a really nice independent store, says *laurie*.

One chowhound experienced rude service at **Say Cheese**, but most find the service helpful and friendly, with plenty of tastes offered. *SF Librarian* says that the "older guy with the beard who works there regularly can give you *great* wine/cheese pairing advice. He really knows his wine and cheese, and loves to talk about both." Go weekdays, late afternoon, or early evening when they're less busy and more able to provide extensive advice. **Artisan** is praised for its selection of hard cheeses, including Neal's Yard products from London and other hard-to-find varieties, as well as many local cheeses. Prices are high, though, and you won't find many French or Italian soft-rind cheeses.

Cowgirl Creamery, from Point Reyes, has a shop in the Ferry Building Marketplace with a huge selection of not only their own cheeses (St. Pat's, Red Hawk, cottage cheese, and more), but lots of others' (St. George from Matos, Point Reyes Blue, and Napa's Goat's Leap are just a few), including imports from Neal's Yard and Jean D'Alos. Lots of fresh cheeses in bulk (feta, cottage cheese, chevre, fromage blanc, crème fraiche, and ricotta), Straus milk and yogurt and some other go-with goodies like jams, olives, and honey. Add some bread from Acme Bakery, just next door, and you've got the makings of a picnic!

Soyoung Scanlan's **Andante Dairy** is another local favorite. Her cheeses, both cow and goat's milk, are sold at **Whole Foods** (which generally offers reasonable selection and user-friendly service), the **Cheese Board**, and the **Ferry Plaza Farmers Market** (Saturdays and Thursdays). For the best, freshest versions, including free tastes and advice, shop at the Ferry Plaza stand. Another plus to the Ferry Plaza stand: tastes of new cheeses that don't make it to the grocery stores. At **Rainbow Grocery**, staff gives advice, free samples, and free "Cheese Pride!" pins. Good prices, too.

Also see "*Sonoma: Provisioning* (Wine, Cheese, and Much, Much More)."

- **Cheese Board:** *see also* pp. 4, 198, 238.
- **Rainbow Grocery Co-Op:** *see also* p. 216.
- **San Francisco Ferry Plaza Farmers' Market:** *see also* pp. 2, 27, 79, 104.
- **Tower Market:** *see also* p. 55.
- **Whole Foods:** *see also* pp. 73, 230, 280.

CHEESE BOARD Favorites

Cheese Board (East Bay)
1504 Shattuck Ave.
Berkeley, CA
510-549-3183
Pizza bakery/Cheese shop/Pizzeria

If you can't afford to eat everything—moneywise and dietwise—at the wonderful but pricey East Bay gourmet store **Cheese Board**, here are some tips on where to start.

- cheese, of course—the staff is helpful even when busy and insists you taste before buying
- half-baked pizzas, for the ultimate take-out
- cheese rolls
- cheese bread, all flavors

- chocolate things
- wolverines
- shortbreads, especially ginger
- English muffins, but eat them right away
- crackers
- *zampano,* rolls with cheese and crushed red pepper
- granola
- baguettes, seeded or not
- mixed marinated olives

Pick up a copy of its cookbook (*Cheese Board: Collective Works: Bread, Pastry, Cheese, Pizza,* by Cheese Board Collective) and maybe you can learn to make chocolate things et al at home.

○ **Cheese Board:** *see also* **pp. 4, 51, 198, 238.**

CHEESECAKE Delights

Amici's East Coast Pizzeria
(Marina)
2033 Union St.
San Francisco, CA
415-885-4500
Pizza/Italian

J. M. Rosen's Cheesecake
(Sonoma County)
74 E. Washington St.
Petaluma, CA
707-773-4655
Bakery

J. M. Rosen's Waterfront Grill
(Sonoma County)
54 E. Washington St.
Petaluma, CA
707-773-3200
American

Tower Market
(Westportal/Ingleside)
635 Portola Dr.
San Francisco, CA
415-664-1609
Store

Zanze's Cheesecake
(Westportal/Ingleside)
2405 Ocean Ave.
San Francisco, CA
415-334-2264
Bakery

Stop! Put back that Sara Lee cheesecake and give **J. M. Rosen's** in Petaluma a call for New York–style cheesecakes. They don't come cheap; small cakes run $24, but hounds say they're worth it. Besides making a trek to Petaluma (the bakery's not set up for retail trade, but you can buy the cakes at **J. M. Rosen's Waterfront Grill**), they've been spotted at some local Sonoma County grocers. In San Francisco, **Amici's** on Union Street carries them. Also good: macadamia tart.

Zanze's makes a lighter, fluffier cheesecake than Rosen's. Sizes are 6-, 8-, and 10-inch and come in plain, mocha, and a few fruit flavors. **Tower Market** stocks them frozen, but they freeze beautifully.

○ **Tower Market:** *see also* **p. 52**

CHICKEN-FRIED STEAK

Alfred's Steakhouse
(Financial District)
659 Merchant St.
San Francisco, CA
415-781-7058
Steak house

The Van's Restaurant on the Hill
(South Bay)
815 Belmont Ave.
Belmont, CA
650-591-6525
American

Schellville Grille (Sonoma County)
22900 Broadway
Sonoma, CA
707-996-5151
American

○○○ Chowhound Tip:

Always ask whether CFS is assembled in-house,
or is the ubiquitous—and inferior—frozen Sysco
product, before taking the plunge

Hounds are always on the lookout for regional specialties like chicken-fried steak (CFS). **Alfred's** serves a fine CFS at lunch or dinner, along with soup or salad, garlic mashed potatoes, and rich white gravy. The meat at **Schellville Grille** is unusually thick (half an inch), but still tender and moist. White gravy, however, is marred by too many herbs, and the accompaniments are weak, says *Melanie Wong*. **Van's** also serves a good CFS, we hear.

○ **Alfred's Steakhouse:** *see also* p. 1.

CHIDVA (Indian Trail Mix)

Bombay Bazar (Mission)
548 Valencia St.
San Francisco, CA
415-621-1717
Indian store

Nilgiris (South Bay)
1187 W. El Camino Real
Sunnyvale, CA
408-746-0808
Indian store

India Foods (Peninsula)
650 San Bruno Ave. E
San Bruno, CA
650-583-6559
Indian store

Vik's Chaat (East Bay)
726 Allston Way
Berkeley, CA
510-644-4412
Indian

Indian Grocery & Spice
  (Peninsula)
2630 Broadway St.
Redwood City, CA
650-365-1832
Indian store

Indian trail mix, also known as chidva, namkeen, or chaat snack mix, is a salty snack made with rice puffs, dried nuts, sometimes raisins, and plenty of spices. You can find it at **India Foods** or **Nilgiris** in Foster City and at **Indian Grocery** in Redwood City. India Foods is the best: large, quite clean, with very friendly and helpful owners. Smaller and with slower turnover on food is **Bombay Bazaar** in the Mission, whose Hot Mix with soy and mung bean crunchies, raisins, nuts, and plenty of cayenne is, according to *Missy P*, very addictive. And then there's their ice cream selection, including fig, pistachio, saffron, cardamom, and more! In Berkeley, the king of Indian markets is Vik's Warehouse next to **Vik's Chaat**.

- ○ **Bombay Bazar:** *see also* p. 145.
- ○ **India Foods:** *see also* p. 142.
- ○ **Vik's Chaat:** *see also* p. 50.

○○○ Chowhound Tip:

Surf *www.thingsindian.com* to find Indian businesses around the Bay.

Sonoran-Style **CHILE VERDE**

Taqueria Mexican Grill (Marin County)
1001 Sir Francis Drake Blvd.
Kentfield, CA
415-453-5811
Mexican

Most Bay Area chile verdes are chock-full of tomatillos. **Taqueria Mexican Grill** serves a pure, green-chile based pork stew that *Michele Anna Jordan* calls close to perfection. Their rendition contains no tomatillos and no cumin, common in most local versions; it's pretty much just pork and roasted green chiles. Hot salsa verde adds extra spice if you want it.

CHINA VILLAGE Worship

China Village (East Bay)
1335 Solano Ave.
Albany, CA
510-525-2285
Chinese (Sichuan)

Chowhounds discovered and continue to worship **China Village**, where a Sichuan specialist chef trained at the Grand Hotel in Beijing hides in suburban anyonymity. There is much treasure here, requiring special esoteric knowledge to ferret out. We could have devoted half the book to strategies compiled on this one restaurant, but the following is the distilled essence of truly massive chowconnaisance.

You'll be offered a menu of mainstream Chinese and Chinese-American standbys (some of which are actually good). Hold out for the special menu, rife with Sichuan classics. John (the owner) is usually helpful with ordering advice, and in ensuring a balance of heat levels—you don't want to order everything spicy and blow out your taste buds! Quality can vary depending on which chef handles your order. One approach, if you've got a quorum, is to order a $198 set ten-course banquet for ten people. Chowhonds report loving all but the tea duck and buddha delight soup. But all courses (described below) can be ordered à la carte, as well.

- cold appetizers: sliced side pork with spicy garlic sauce, spicy combination (beef and tripe), cucumber with garlic sauce, ponpon chicken, jellyfish salad, and ribs. Best dish: pork with spicy garlic sauce.
- another appetizer: spicy combination (beef and tripe) sandwiched in a small round of sesame bread. It's not on the menu.
- sauteed calamari with scallops—not on the regular menu. Not spicy at all, very refreshing, very tender, not chewy at all.
- dry cooked shredded beef—beef jerky–like, very flavorful
- buddha delight soup with dry scallops, dry squid, quail eggs, Virginia ham, bacon, pork hock, bamboo shoots, and chicken. Not a favorite, also not on the regular menu.

- smoked tea duck—not a favorite
- *chen du* (aka *Chengdu*) style shrimp—addictively spicy, whole fried shrimp (including heads and tails). Favorite dish for those who *really* enjoy spicy.
- chili-sauteed mustard greens
- steamed Mandarin fish, or instead substitute spicy tofu with fish fillet (also known as "the red bowl of death"), which is perfectly cooked fish pieces, soft tofu, leeks, and more in a delicious chili oil broth, a real favorite
- sesame flat bread—good (sometimes perfect) but inconsistent (sometimes not cooked quite through)
- eight treasure rice cake—full of "treasures" (nuts and dried fruits)

Banquets aside, here are some more obsessively detailed tips.

- *shandong* (hand-shaved) noodles are really good, but available in only limited quantity (see below for more info)
- cold dishes are excellent, try them all; especially good is the small sesame bread filled with spicy combination (*fu qi fei pian*)—it's not on the menu but can be special ordered
- live mandarin fish (*gui yu*) is a must when available—it's served steamed or in various fillet preps
- vegetable and duck dishes aren't strong points
- combination hot pot is best ordered for more than one person
- there's a pickled cabbage side that's addictive, if you don't mind paying $1.95 for a small plate

Here are some favorite dishes (with menu numbers).

9 spicy combination—beef and tripe slices in spicy sauce
27 fire-busted pork loins—actually kidneys
29 (or is it 39?) dry-cooked tripe—actually intestines
31 hot and spicy pork feet—more likely shoulder
33 Village special lamb
35 west-style spicy fish—fish and bean thread noodles
37 Sichuan-style spicy boiled beef
70 spicy tofu with fish fillet—fish and tofu stew
79 eggplant with spicy garlic sauce
80 spicy sauce potato strips (good to order with spicy boiled beef)

89 dry sauteed slender bamboo shoots
97 river soft tofu flower—made in-house
106 sesame flat bread
121 lamb dumplings with green onions
129 spicy cold noodle with san si

We're not sure of menu numbers for these three.

- roasted whole prawns (which may only be available as a special)
- cumin lamb on skewers (different from 33), very gamey with a crusty exterior
- Village special seafood soup noodles (chao ma mian)—the only recommended dish on the Americanized menu

Melanie Wong dotes on excellent zha jiang mian (handcut, irregularly shaped chewy noodles, well-tuned bean paste and seasonings, minced pork, and slivered cucumbers). The noodles for this (per above) are made fresh before lunch and again before dinner with a mere twenty orders available for each seating no matter how much you beg. Sichuan spareribs are served with sauce that Melanie describes as lightly spicy with chilis, salty, a little sweet and a little sour; very intriguing and exotic flavor. Cumin lamb (grilled, seasoned lamb on skewers, like you'll find on the streets of Beijing) sounds good.

Pancho Chang suggests deep fried eel with Chinese celery—raved about by the owner—with fresh eel and scallionlike celery shoots to cut its oiliness; and watercress with *foo yee* (preserved bean curd). He also adds to the chorus of raves for pork shoulder simmered for eight hours, with great brown gravy and a bed of baby *gai lan* and Chinese mushrooms that raised the attention of surrounding tables.

There's a lunchtime special of three dishes for $15.99, but it's on a Chinese-language menu. If you can't read it, follow *SLRossi*'s lead and let your server choose for you. He ended up with spicy boiled beef (full of numbing Sichuan peppercorn heat), fish fillets in a spicy chili sauce, and fried chicken bits with chilis and fried garlic, all very good. Skip the peking duck, strangely not good.

○ China Village: *see also* pp. 77, 219, 267, 294.

CHINESE CHICKEN SALAD

California Cafe Bar & Grill
  (Peninsula)
700 Welch Rd., in Stanford Barn
Palo Alto, CA
650-325-2233
New American/Pan-Asian
  fusion

New Bamboo (Peninsula)
3130 Alpine Rd., Suite 300
Portola Valley, CA
650-851-1718
East Asian

Yank Sing (Embarcadero)
101 Spear St.
San Francisco, CA
415-957-9300
Chinese (Cantonese)/Chinese
  (Dim Sum)/Chinese
  (Hong Kong)

Yank Sing Restaurant
  (Financial District)
49 Stevenson St.
San Francisco, CA
415-541-4949
Chinese (Cantonese)/Chinese
  (Dim Sum)/Chinese
  (Hong Kong)

To experience the ultimate Chinese chicken salad—the kind with fried rice noodles and slightly sweet sesame dressing—check out **New Bamboo** (also good cabbage and grapefruit salad), a nice neighborhood café, close to Stanford. **Yank Sing**'s buffet version is pretty good, so *Melanie Wong* bets it's got to be even better prepped to order. And **California Cafe** does a good version, and there's an outdoor patio, too.

○ **Yank Sing Restaurant:** *see also* **p. 86.**

CHINESE of Many Flavors

Cafe Yulong (Peninsula)
743 W. Dana St.
Mountain View, CA
650-960-1677
Korean/Chinese

Dragon River Restaurant
  (Richmond)
5045 Geary Blvd.
San Francisco, CA
415-387-6698
Chinese (Hakka)/Chinese
  (Cantonese)

Shanghai (East Bay)
930 Webster St.
Oakland, CA
510-465-6878
Chinese (Shanghai)

Sun Wu Kong (Richmond)
5423 Geary Blvd.
San Francisco, CA
415-876-2828
Chinese (Shanghai)

Shanghai Dumpling House
   (Richmond)
3319 Balboa St.
San Francisco, CA
415-387-2088
Chinese (Shanghai)

Szechuan Trenz (Richmond)
294 8th Ave.
San Francisco, CA
415-752-8884
Chinese (Sichuan)/Chinese
   (Taiwanese)

The Bay Area is richest in Cantonese restaurants, but chowhounds have also found good representation from other regions such as Sichuan (known for spicy, numbing flavors from their magical peppercorns), Hakka (a migrant ethnic group from Canton and Fujian Provinces), Shanghai (which draws from the sweet saucing and alternately delicate and hearty cooking from Jiangsu and Zhejiang) and Shandong (in the north, best known for dumplings and noodles and interactions with Korean cuisine).

Szechuan Trenz is a trendy little café whose "flashy decor and kicked-back vibe reminds me of some little café in the shee-shee part of Taipei city," says *Charlie T*. The menu is a mixture of Sichuan, Taiwanese, and Shanghai. Sichuan dishes are particularly good. And the Taiwanese dishes include five different stinky (fermented) tofu dishes. Here are some items worth checking out: #3. Spicy Beef Bowl with Flaming Red Oil (*shui zhu rou pian,* aka "water-cooked substitute your choice of meat here"): includes all the right numbing-hot flavors, silky smooth pork and refreshing vegetable texture, but the oil lacks devastating intensity, as if it'd been Betty Crockerized. Nevertheless, immensely enjoyable, and also comes in a fish version. #44. Hot and Spicy Beef Combination (*fu qi fei pian*): beef shank/tripe with chili oil and cilantro, little garlic, with great textures, great beef flavor, and a good job with seasonings. #45. Spicy Chinese Bacon with Garlic (*suan ni bai rou,* aka "sliced side pork in spicy garlic sauce"). Presentation isn't as delicate as the rendition at China Village, and bacon is sliced a little thicker, and there's less garlic punch, but again, all flavors are right and portions are generous. #54. Vinaigrette Shredded Seaweed (*hai dai si*): shredded kelp—pretty bland, but very fresh-tasting, a nice counterpoint to the spices in the other dishes. And *chw yr fd* recommends numb and spicy tan tan noodles (ma la dan dan mian), fragrant eggplant (*yu xiang qie zi*), and numb and spicy cold cucumbers (*ma la huang gua*).

Hakka specialties are the best orders at **Dragon River** in San Francisco's Richmond neighborhood, according to *Han Lukito*, who says it's all about the three Hakka sauces: sweet green chilis, red chilis, and ginger and garlic. Huge portions and reasonable prices are just two more reasons to head here. Recommended dishes include salt baked chicken, *kao yuk* (pork bacon with preserved vegetables—not as good as Utopia Cafe's but still pretty darn good), fried tofu stuffed with ground fish, deep fried shrimp balls, jook, chow fun, tomato beef chow mein, and thick soupy noodles.

Then for Shanghainese, **Shanghai Dumpling House** in the Richmond neighborhood of San Francisco may have changed its name (it was Sweet Temptation), but food remains authentic and good. Vegetarian goose is lighter and less oily than most, with a nice roasted flavor. Broth in xiao long bao (soup dumplings) has a slightly bitter aftertaste, but they're good (crab version available if ordered twenty-four hours ahead). Tofu strips with soy beans and fresh Shanghai cabbage (mao dou qing cai bai ye) is excellent; deep flavor from chicken stock. Beijing-style pork and chive shui jiao are freshly made, delicious and juicy with thickish yet tender wrappers, says *Melanie Wong*.

Shanghai, in Oakland's Chinatown, has translated its "any three for $15" menu into English, making it more accessible. Claypot of chicken and chestnuts (redolent of garlic), herbal and moist rice with vegetables and salt pork, and dry-fried Shanghai spareribs aren't refined cooking, but are tasty in a rustic way, says *Ruth Lafler*. *1tonlover* recommends **Sun Wu Kong** (aka Sun Kunk) for damn good wonton soup with wontons filled with ginger and spinach. Great. Expensive, though. In a number of visits to **Cafe Yulong**, *Dee Glaze*'s experiences have varied from stellar to reliably good. Noodles are made in-house and "they care enough to warn customers about flavor-loss hazards of fresh noodles interacting with styrofoam containers for take out" (though not in those exact words, we presume). Service is pleasant, prompt, and they're happy to recommend dishes. Favorites include Yulong fish and leek dumplings, stir-fried spinach and mung bean thread in garlic wine sauce, Yulong

Chowhound Nametag: Celeste

○○○

Location: San Francisco

Occupation: Producer (video/web/multimedia/documentary)

Cholesterol Level: Better than it really should be for someone who has been eating straight butter and drinking half and half since the age of 7.

Farthest Out of the Way Traveled Just for Chow: I'm fairly certain that I went to New York (from San Francisco) one time just to try Totonno's pizza near Coney Island. And it was incredible.

Nabe Most Full of Explorable Unknown Chow: Richmond district in San Francisco

Underrated by Chowhounds: Alamo Square for seafood, Pauline's for pizza, Los Jarritos for mole enchiladas, Just For You in Dogpatch . . .

Weight Management Tip: Don't eat fake food.

Favorite Comfort Chow: I go to King of Thai noodles around the corner and order a Tom Kha Gai soup to go if I'm really down and out. For just a cheer-me-up, I go to Zuni, have a nice white by the glass and their house-cured anchovies.

Favorite Mail Order Chow: Harry and David Royal Riviera pears (*Harryanddavid.com*). And, thanks to Chowhound, Enstrom's toffee (*Enstrom.com*). Oh! And Jubilee chocolates (*Jubileechocolates.com*).

Favorite Chai: Cafe Cole—nice and spicy.

chicken (with roasted hot red peppers, black beans, and garlic-infused sweet and sour wine sauce), lemon pepper prawns, Yu-long shrimp (with garlic, ginger, and house tomato sauce), garlic and spinach noodles, Sichuan tea smoked duck (quality varies from great to average—sometimes skin's crispy but sometimes not. It's served with lotus flower buns, which can overpower the duck, so ask for mu shu wrappers instead). A hot and cold plate (for three to five people): uncut mung bean sheets, shrimp, calamari, scallops, pork, jellyfish, cucumber, carrots, and other veggies in Chinese-style mustard sauce. Toss well or risk wasabi-nose. Also see the Cuisine Index for more Chinese tips.

Neighborhood **CHINESE**

Chef Wang's Restaurant
(Peninsula)
5100 El Camino Real
Los Altos, CA
650-965-2689
Chinese (Beijing)/Chinese
(Sichuan)/Korean

Hon Lin Restaurant (Peninsula)
500 San Mateo Ave.
San Bruno, CA
650-872-2288
Chinese (Taiwanese)/Chinese

Hunan Home's Restaurant
(Peninsula)
4880 W. El Camino Real
Los Altos, CA
650-965-8888
Chinese (Hunan)/Chinese

Kwong's Seafood Restaurant
(Peninsula)
150 El Camino Real
Millbrae, CA
650-692-4465
Chinese (Hong Kong)/Chinese
(Cantonese)

Mings Restaurant (Peninsula)
436 San Mateo Ave.
San Bruno, CA
650-588-2375
Chinese/Korean

No fancy banquets, just good down-home neighborhood Chinese food at these spots. **Hunan Home's Restaurant** is a *Nancy Berry* favorite, especially for shrimp dishes and smoked pork with cabbage. Order live shrimp if available (expensive but really good). There are excellent lunch specials and "chef's selections" including tea smoked duck, sizzling eels, pork with dry bean curd, and a number of yellow chive dishes. While **Ming's** sign may tout Hunan, the chef is Cantonese but worked many years at San Wang (aka Sam Wong, a Korean-Chinese place known for hand-pulled noodles) in San Francisco's Japantown. Hand-pulled noodles in hot braised Mandarin lo mein (*zha jiang mian*) are lovely, silky, toothsomely elastic, and quite a treat. Xiao long bao are not quite right despite being made in-house—tender skins, good flavored filling, but a bit chewy and no soup at all. *Melanie Wong* thinks there are other gems to be found on the extensive menu of value-priced standards. Note: This Ming's may or may not be related to Ming's in Palo Alto, which is definitely not in the same class.

Hon Lin is a favorite Taiwanese weekend breakfast spot for *Yimster*. Soy bean milk made in-house and all sorts of Taiwanese snacks are available. For dinner try pig knuckles and hot and sour beef soup. **Kwong's** is open until midnight and close to SFO, serving fresh seafood from tanks. Melanie says salt and pepper oysters used to be the best, but she hasn't been in a while. Bargain and quality/value shine in a very competitive neighborhood for Hong Kong–style seafood.

Based on Melanie's preliminary look at **Chef Wang** in Los Altos, it's a step up in atmosphere and size from the old Mountain View location. Regular menu lists Shanghai, Sichuan, Mandarin/Shandong specialties and there's a supplementary menu in Chinese and English with Northern and Shanghai-style small eats. Good eats: spicy seafood and beef noodle soup (taso ma mien) is full of pleasing noodles, spicy conch salad (thin translucent slices of tender and slightly crunchy mollusk bathed in garlicky red chili oil with slivers of yellow leeks and scallions—very delicious and almost addictive). Do not order misshapen, stale, terrible xiao long bao.

Bargain (But Great!) **CHINESE**

China Tofu (East Bay)
1781 Addison Way
Hayward, CA
510-782-9728
Chinese (Cantonese)/Chinese
(Shanghai)

Koi Palace Restaurant (Peninsula)
365 Gellert Blvd. in Serramonte
Plaza
Daly City, CA
650-992-9000
Chinese (Cantonese)/Chinese
(Dim Sum)/Chinese
(Hong Kong)

Kong's Cafe (Mission)
4935 Mission St.
San Francisco, CA
415-333-8666
Chinese (Cantonese)/Chinese
(Hong Kong)

Legendary Palace (East Bay)
708 Franklin St.
Oakland, CA
510-663-9288
Chinese (Cantonese)/Chinese
(Hong Kong)/Chinese
(Dim Sum)

New Hong Kong Menu
(Chinatown)
667 Commercial St.
San Francisco, CA
415-391-3677
Chinese (Hong Kong)/Chinese
(Cantonese)

Queen's House Restaurant
(Peninsula)
273 Castro St.
Mountain View, CA
650-960-0580
Chinese (Beijing)/Chinese
(Taiwanese)

Shanghai Taste Delight
(Peninsula)
855 W. El Camino Real
Mountain View, CA
650-988-8820
Chinese (Shanghai)

Y Ben House Restaurant
(Chinatown)
835 Pacific Ave.
San Francisco, CA
415-397-3168
Chinese (Cantonese)/Chinese
(Dim Sum)

Yee's Restaurant (Chinatown)
1131 Grant Ave.
San Francisco, CA
415-576-1818
Chinese (Cantonese)

The clientele of mostly Chinese families and Taiwanese grad students testifies to the value found at **Queen's House**, whose well-priced menu includes fresh handmade noodle dishes and Taiwanese small dishes like rice cakes, stinky tofu and pork blood soup, as well as a $17.99 dinner special of three dishes plus rice or scallion pancake. *Melanie Wong* orders à la carte: fresh, housemade potstickers ($4.25) of the jumbo American style, though not as thick and filling as usual, are fresh and housemade, juicy and tasty, not greasy, and golden brown and crisped on one side with a well-seasoned pork and cabbage filling. Mix yourself some vinegar-soy sauce for dipping. Well-seasoned pork and cabbage is juicy. Five types of boiled dumplings are also available. Black bean paste noodles (zha jiang mian), $4.95, are much liked, and the sauce isn't pasty (like a blend of brown bean sauce with some hoisin or plum sauce), and the softish thick hand-pulled noodles on the bottom of the bowl are served hot and topped with a ladle of the sauce blended with slivers of pressed and smoked tofu, chopped raw onions, and seasoned ground pork. The knife work is unrefined, but it's delicious nonetheless. Claypots are on every table, and the eggplant and tofu claypot is, indeed, a winner with its meltingly soft caramelized Chinese eggplant, well-tuned sauce, and refreshing crunch from Napa cabbage. Less successful: inedibly tough oyster pancake and stir-fried greens don't seem to be a forte.

Y Ben House offers excellent dim sum value, especially on weekdays, when it's something like $1.70 per small plate. This place is no secret, packed with families and seniors by 9 a.m. on a weekday. Har gow are pingpong ball–sized babies, says *Bryan Harrell*. Soy milk skin rolls stuffed with ground pork and minced veggies are good, while crispy fried doufu pi (soy milk skin rolls) are even better, according to *Gary Soup*. Another goodie: baked flat pielike dumpling stuffed with whole shrimp.

New Hong Kong Menu is one of those hole-in-the-wall spots in Chinatown offering good solid Cantonese food at bargain prices. Chowhound *nja*, who admits to being a Chinese food novice, said of the feast: "The array of dishes we ordered comforted the gringo in me—familiar meats, vegetables, and presentation styles—but I'll admit the chowhound inside was a little disappointed at not being challenged." There are some homemade noodle dishes on the menu, look for *fook* (or foot) *mein,* or just ask for "wide noodles." Expect enormous portions when you order these recommended dishes: big dumpling in Supreme soup (pork dumplings in clear, simple, full-bodied broth), sugar snap peas with chicken, and salt and pepper shrimp

"I would not specially come to this place from afar, but if you happen to be nearby and a bit short on change it offers great value," says *Han Lukito* about **China Tofu**, which serves huge portions for unbelievably cheap prices. Recommendations: beef in claypot, kung pao chicken, fried pork chop, tofu with carrots and corn. *Yimster* says stinky tofu is one of the best versions his wife has had since leaving Hong Kong. Beef tendon soup was the best his son has ever had ("he kept saying 'this is what I have been looking for all my life and I have found it'"), good Shanghai rice cakes, pork chitterlings with pork blood, and best yet, the most expensive dish on menu is $5.99.

Check out **Yee's** $2 menu from 3 to 5 p.m. *Melanie Wong* picks: fried squid ("looked like pommes souffle in wedge shapes with greaseless light golden-brown batter puffed up around thick slices of giant squid, delicious with chili sauce") and soy sauce poached chicken. Sui gow (water dumpling soup) isn't recommended, though at $2, it's not shabby.

Kong's Cafe, a relatively new Chinese BBQ place, carries good duck, soy sauce chicken, wonton soup, and char siu with lunch specials at $3.95. Between 4 and 8 p.m., dinner specials offered for $2.88.

Legendary Palace has received some favorable reports; *miles* calls them a worthy contender in Oakland's Chinatown. It offers weekday dinner specials, 20 percent off weekday dim sum, an expanded menu with several banquet options (up to $1000!), separate menu for noodles and rice, and an all-Chinese house specials menu. Steer clear of Americanized dishes and opt for ge-oduck two ways (a good-not-great version with the proper sweet clammy crunch), Peking duck (with thin, crispy skin for only $9.99), bamboo pith seafood soup (a must-order), fried chicken with garlic (covered with deep fried chopped garlic), steamed red cod with scallions (goes very well with fried rice), *fook kin* fried rice (stir-fried rice with gravy full of minced shrimp, scallops, duck, mushrooms, and asparagus), crab sampan style (deep fried and then dry stir-fried with fried garlic and chilis and deep fried black beans—**Koi Palace** is the only place that might make a better version), yellow chive and sprouts x.o. beef dry chow fun (really fresh fun; light, fluffy, and chewy), and oyster/pork/tofu/mushroom claypot in garlic sauce (oysters deep fried in light batter, with BBQ pork bellies).

Shanghai Taste Delight has a $3.99 menu, including the delicious lion's head meatball dish. Spicy glass noodle claypot is also recommended.

- **Koi Palace Restaurant:** *see also* p. 82.
- **Legendary Palace:** *see also* pp. 42, 90.

CHOCOLATE News

Chocolate Affaire (South Bay)
603 E. Calaveras Blvd., in
    Milpitas Town Center
Milpitas, CA
408-945-1620
Chocolate/Candy shop

Chocolate Covered (Noe Valley)
3977 24th St.
San Francisco, CA
415-641-8123
Chocolate/Candy shop

Chocolatier Desiree (South Bay)
165 S. Murphy Ave., Suite C
Sunnyvale, CA
408-245-6090
Chocolate/Candy shop

Gandolf's Fine Chocolate, LLC
    (Sonoma County)
P.O. Box 367
Forestville, CA
888-800-0722
Chocolate/Candy shop

Joseph Schmidt Confections
    (Mission)
3489 16th St.
San Francisco, CA
415-861-8682
Chocolate/Candy shop

Joseph Schmidt Confections
    (Mission)
2000 Folsom St.
San Francisco, CA
415-626-7900
Chocolate/Candy shop

Joseph Schmidt Confections
    (South Bay)
356 Santana Row, Suite 1025
San Jose, CA
408-244-2553
Chocolate/Candy shop

Richart (Union Square)
393 Sutter St.
San Francisco, CA
1-888-RICHART
Chocolate/Candy shop

Santa Rosa Farmers' Market
    (Sonoma County)
1351 Maple Ave., in Veterans
    Hall
Santa Rosa, CA
707-522-8629
Farmers' Market

Gandolf's Fine Chocolates of Sonoma County sells year-round at the Saturday **farmers' market in Santa Rosa**, and also via their Web site, www.gandolfsfinechocolate.com. Gandolf's makes truffles in various flavors ($2 each or a box of 6 for $10), including an ultrasmooth cranberry truffle and terrific espresso truffle topped with chocolate-covered espresso bean, plus a signature confection called Nipples of Venus, using Guittard chocolates. *Melanie Wong* describes it as total lusciousness.

Super high-quality, super-expensive Lyon chocolatier **Richart** has its second US boutique in San Francisco in the Union Square area. Richart's small masterpieces look like art and are made from premium chocolates; some flavored with herbs and spices. **Chocolate Covered** is a small shop with a wide selection of packaged chocolates from premium producers (Valhrona, Cote d'Or, Michel Cluizel, Scharffen Berger, Dolfin, Vosges, Donnelly, and many more). The owner is determined to have the widest selection in the city, reports *nja*. No by-the-piece loose chocolates, but there are always several kinds open, and generous samples are offered. Large bars for baking aren't currently in stock, but they do special orders, and prices are fair.

For sweets in the South Bay, check out **Chocolatier Desiree**, which imports Belgian chocolates from Gartner in Antwerp. Minimum purchase is four pieces for $5. Their fresh cream flavors include vatel (fresh whipped cream, dark chocolate, crispy nut bottom), champagne (fresh champagne cream, white chocolate layered with marzipan), mocca cup (dark chocolate with fresh cream of mocca), and noir et noisette (dark chocolate with hazelnut praline), and they also carry Easter chocolates in bunny shapes and much more. Also in the South Bay is **Chocolate Affaire**. They do custom-decorated cakes and handmade chocolates priced to compete with See's, which means fresh, handmade chocolates for the price of mass-produced, says *Manuel*.

Also see "*Chocolate Ginger*" and "*Hot Chocolate* Heaven."

○○○ Chowhound Tip:

Gandolf's plans to start selling rich hot chocolate on cold days at the farmers' market.

CHOCOLATE GINGER

Scharffen Berger Chocolate Maker
(East Bay)
914 Heinz Ave.
Berkeley, CA
510-981-4050
Chocolate/Candy shop

See's
www.sees.com/seeshtm/shopframes
.htm
Chocolate/Candy shop

Trader Joe's (Regionwide)
www.traderjoes.com
Store

Whole Foods
www.wholefoods.com/stores
Store

Chocolate and ginger fans should know that **Scharffen Berger** now sells dark chocolate-dipped candied ginger. Buy it at their store at the Ferry Building Marketplace or their factory in Berkeley. It's pricey though: $12 for a 2.8 ounce package. Less expensive is **See's** version at $12.80 per pound. And for even more savings, Costco sells a package of two See's gift certificates ($18.99 for two 1-pound certificates) that will bring the per-pound cost down to $9.50. You can choose any combination of chocolates at See's stores. If you want to try your hand at making your own, *Windy* suggests starting with Australian candied ginger at **Trader Joe's** or **Whole Foods.**

- ○ **Scharffen Berger Chocolate Maker:** *see also* **p. 40.**
- ○ **Whole Foods:** *see also* **pp. 52, 230, 280.**

Dry-Style **CHOW FUN**

Gold Medal Restaurant (East Bay)
381 8th St.
Oakland, CA
510-268-8484
Chinese (Cantonese)/Chinese
(Hong Kong)

King Tin (Chinatown)
826 Washington St.
San Francisco, CA
415-982-7855
Chinese (Cantonese)/Chinese
(Hong Kong)

Two distinctive styles of chow fun (wide, flat fresh rice noodles with meat and veggies, usually bok choy or bean sprouts) are served at Bay Area Cantonese restaurants. "Wet," or "Hong Kong-style" is a base of noodles topped with meat and a generous amount of brown gravy. "Dry" or "dry-fried" is noodles, meat, and a thin veneer of savory sauce wok-cooked together, ideally, with a bit of brown char at the edges of the noodles. It's also the preferred style among many chowhounds, who caution that you should specify dry-fried when you order to assure the kitchen gets it right. **Gold Medal** serves a well-made chow fun with a higher beef-to-noodle ratio than usual, good wok flavor, and very neatly-trimmed bean sprouts.

○ **Gold Medal Restaurant:** *see also* pp. 42, 162, 167, 294.

Freshly Fried **CHURROS**

Dominguez Mexican Bakery
  (Mission)
2951 24th St.
San Francisco, CA
415-821-1717
Mexican bakery

Ricos Churros Cart (East Bay)
38th and International
Oakland, CA
Mexican street cart/Truck

Some of the best *churros* (fried Mexican crullers with cinnamon sugar) in Oakland can be found on the corner of 38th and International, most days from 4 to 8 p.m. They're delicious: lighter, crisper, and less doughy than your standard churro. **Dominguez Bakery** offers fresh-fried churros on Sundays only. Unfortunately, after they fry each batch, they dump them in a tray, where they sog, so hang around the fryer to score some fresh out of the oil. They are far better than the mass-produced churros you find at ball parks, carnivals, Costco, etc., with high doses of sugar and cinnamon and a lingering greasiness that makes *nja* suspect they are fried in lard. To find Dominguez's churros, walk through the retail area, past the baker's cooling racks, and into the kitchen.

Quick Bites Near **CIVIC CENTER**

Arlequin (Civic Center)
384b Hayes St.
San Francisco, CA
415-626-1211
French sandwich shop

Arlequin is a tiny takeout spot run by owners of Absinthe and Amphora Wine Merchant. It offers a good, quick bite if you're in the Hayes Valley area, e.g., before the symphony, opera, or ballet. It makes its own ice creams, including Guinness (yes, the beer) flavored. Addictive potato chips are thin, with a tiny waffle cut. All soups are good, Caesar salad is garlicky delicious, and crab cakes are wonderful. Don't miss polenta "oatmeal" on the breakfast/brunch menu. **Arlequin** offers a reasonable selection of wines by the glass and fresh-baked cookies, and there's patio seating out back.

○ **Arlequin:** *see also* **p. 123.**

My Darling **CLEMENTINE**

Chapeau! (Richmond)
1408 Clement St.
San Francisco, CA
415-750-9787
French brasserie

Clementine Restaurant
 (Richmond)
126 Clement St.
San Francisco, CA
415-387-0408
French bistro

Clementine is often compared with **Chapeau!**, since both offer French food in Richmond. Those who love Clementine praise its great French atmosphere, friendly, smooth, upbeat service, and classic bistro food. Also, its tables are set farther apart than those at Chapeau!, making for a nicer atmosphere. Items singled out: shrimp salad, great fries, poached pears, bitter chocolate cake, fourme d'ambert (blue cheese) tart, and lamb shanks.

Save room for pain perdu dessert that's "unbelievably delicious and deadly—we call it the artery clogger but it's totally worth it," says *Maya*.

- Chapeau!: see also pp. 24, 217.
- Clementine Restaurant: see also p. 24.

Mondrian Meets Miro at
CORTEZ

Bay Breads (Pacific Heights)
2325 Pine St.
San Francisco, CA
415-440-0356
French bakery

Cortez (Union Square)
550 Geary Blvd, in Hotel Adagio
San Francisco, CA
415-292-6360
French/New American

Cortez, a venture of the Bay Breads empire, has an interior that can be described as "Mondrian meets Miro" and a lounge serving excellent classic and creative cocktails. Result: instant hot spot. Food, at the bar or in the dining room, is excellent, though quite pricey given the tiny portions (a few bites per dish). Especially recommended: foie gras terrine, butternut squash ravioli, tuna tartare with fennel and herbs, hamachi croque monsieur, crab cake, halibut with saffron-vanilla sauce, date-and-mint-crusted Niman Ranch rack of lamb (with awesome cumin carrots), and sugar-and-spice beignets with Valhrona chocolate fondue. And don't pass up addictive rosemary popcorn served at the bar, cucumber-infused water, or excellent "sack" of breads from **Bay Breads**, all gratis. House cocktails $8, large wine-by-glass selection $6 to $9, reasonably priced bottles on the list. Service is accomodating and unobtrusive.

CRAB Grab

China Village (East Bay)
1335 Solano Ave.
Albany, CA
510-525-2285
Chinese (Sichuan)

Mama Lan's (East Bay)
1316 Gilman St.
Albany, CA
510-528-1790
Vietnamese

PPQ Vietnamese Cuisine
   (Richmond)
2332 Clement St.
San Francisco, CA
415-386-8266
Vietnamese

PPQ Vietnamese Cuisine (Sunset)
1816 Irving St.
San Francisco, CA
415-661-8869
Vietnamese

Dungeness crab season starts in mid autumn, when restaurants and local waters are teeming with 'em. (You can even catch your own!) At **China Village**, salt and pepper crab with fresh chilis is good-sized, with batter that's "very light and tasty, sauteed with small bits of green onion, red peppers, jalapeños, and sweet caramelized onions. I enjoyed the tasty and crunchy confettilike debris on the bottom of the platter, scooping it up and eating it from a spoon, as much as the crab itself," reports *Melanie Wong*. Steamed crab with ginger and scallions is also very good.

PPQ does popular crab-and-garlic-noodles combos; dinner for two ($42) comes with vinegary good chicken salad; cha gio; a

∘○∘ Chowhound Tip:

Recreational crabbing's not allowed in the San Francisco Bay, but you can go it alone from Pacifica's pier or with a hosted group on a party boat sailing beyond the Golden Gate.

crab, perfectly cooked; slightly sweet garlic noodles; and fried banana with ice cream, and it's all real good. One hound prefers spicy and salt-and-pepper preps here to the drunken crab. Roast Dungeness crab is tender and fresh, bathed in a very garlicky sauce that's sublime spooned on top of rice. A single crab without other courses runs about $32. Other hits: spicy salt beef ribs (very lightly fried) and lemongrass pork chop (permeated with sweetness and enough fat for flavor), spring rolls are light and crisp with interesting filling (all the frying here is very good, light, and greaseless). Crab (served several ways) is also a highlight at **Mama Lan's**.

○ **China Village:** *see also* pp. 59, 219, 267, 294.
○ **PPQ Vietnamese Cuisine:** *see also* p. 311.

Boil Your Own **CRAWFISH**

Concord Farmers' Market
   (East Bay)
Todos Santos Plaza, Willow Pass
   Rd. and Grant St.
Concord, CA
925-671-3464
Farmers' market

Housewives Market (East Bay)
907 Washington St.
Oakland, CA
510-835-4565
Store

Iselton Crawdad Festival (Delta)
Isleton, CA
www.isletoncoc.org/crawdad.htm
916-777-5880

Old Oakland Farmers' Market
   (East Bay)
9th St., between Broadway
   and Clay
Oakland, CA
510-745-7100
Farmers' market

Omega 3 Seafood Retail Market
   (Napa County)
1732 Yajome St.
Napa, CA
707-257-7674
Store

San Francisco Ferry Plaza
   Farmers Market (Embarcadero)
Foot of Market St. on the
   Embarcadero; Ferry Building
   Marketplace
San Francisco, CA
415-353-5650
Farmers' market

Ver Brugge Meat Fish Poultry
   (East Bay)
6321 College Ave.
Oakland, CA
510-658-6854
Store

Where to get fresh crawfish for your home crawfish boil? **Ver Brugge** in Oakland and **Omega 3 Seafood** in Napa can both special-order mudbugs. **Housewives Market** always has live ones (and everything else for Creole/Cajun cookery). And the little "bug"-gers have been spotted at various farmers' markets, like the Saturday **San Francisco Ferry Plaza, Concord**, and Friday **Downtown Oakland** markets. If you want someone else to do the work, head to **Iselton** in the Delta for its annual **Crawdad Festival**, usually held over Father's Day weekend.

○ **San Francisco Ferry Plaza Farmers' Market:** *see also* **pp. 2, 26, 52, 104.**
○ **Ver Brugge Meat Fish Poultry:** *see also* **p. 48, 230.**

Fragile, Chewy **CREPES**

Genki Crepes & Mini Mart
   (Richmond)
330 Clement St.
San Francisco, CA
415-379-6414
Japanese café

Sophie's Crepes (Pacific Heights)
1581 Webster St. #200
San Francisco, CA
415-929-7732
Japanese café

Laurel Street Cafe (Peninsula)
741 Laurel St.
San Carlos, CA
650-598-7613
French

Chowhound Nametag: Ruth Lafler

○◯○

Location: Alameda

Occupation: Editor

Cholesterol Level: Around 200

Number of Visits to McDonald's in Past Decade: Fifty? That sounds like a lot, but sometimes I just have to have a sausage biscuit, so five times a year isn't an unreasonable estimate.

Nabe Most Full of Explorable Unknown Chow: I'm still just scratching the surface on the Mexican and Vietnamese neighborhoods in Oakland.

Top Chinatown Pick: Two years ago I would have said San Francisco Chinatown was just a tourist trap. Now I know better, and go to Dol Ho for dim sum; Louie's for upscale; Great Eastern for seafood; Golden Gate Bakery for egg tarts. In Oakland Chinatown: Shanghai for xiao long bao; Legendary Palace for upscale; Chef Lau's for family dinners.

Underrated by Chowhounds: The entire city of Oakland: great food, no pretense, but still suffers from lack of glamour compared to San Francisco and Berkeley.

Favorite Comfort Chow: Barney's Burgers for a California burger (with bacon, green chile, and sour cream), fries, and a chocolate shake

Favorite Gelato Flavor: Fresh ginger

Chowhounding Rule of Thumb: Communicate! Ask questions of the server and other patrons. Looking back on my childhood, I realize my grandfather was a chowhound. He was a doctor and he'd get tips on places to eat from his patients. Then he'd schmooze the restaurant staff. Forty years ago he was getting the manager of a little hole in the wall in Oakland Chinatown to translate the specials off the Chinese menu for him. He made a personal connection with the restaurant (although I was always embarrassed when he'd introduce his family), and it paid off. Now I proudly follow in his footsteps.

"**Those of us who** have endured the cotton-woolly, watered-down pancakes that usually pass for crepes south of the Mission district finally have somewhere to go!" *Pia* exults at how **Laurel Street Cafe's** buckwheat galettes and crepes are fragile and chewy at the same time, made on proper inch-thick cast iron crepieres, and come in many flavors, including Hawaiian with pineapple and New Orleans with BBQ sauce. It might be best just to stick to traditional combos like ham, smoked salmon, or ratatouille ("vegetable stew" on the menu). Quebec crepe with apples, maple syrup, and walnuts makes for a great dessert. Also on the menu are sandwiches, tartines (open-faced sandwiches), platters of charcuterie and cheese, and salads (all crepes come with a green salad).

Japanese-style crepes, filled with sweet or savory fillings, are popular street food in Japan. You can now find these treats at **Genki**, where hounds recommend the almond-marshmallow, fresh fruit, and whipped cream, or nutella and banana crepes. Genki also offers eight flavors of Polly Ann ice cream plus a mini-market full of imported Asian snacks, candies, and drinks. **Sophie's** in Japantown also makes Japanese crepes, with prices about $1 higher than Genki's. Look for lots more crepes tips in the "Colossal *Farmers' Market* Round-Up"

Scientific **CROISSANT** Duel

La Farine Bakery (East Bay)
6323 College Ave.
Oakland, CA
510-654-0338
French bakery

Masse's Pastries (East Bay)
1469 Shattuck Ave.
Berkeley, CA
510-649-1004
French/American café

Croissants from East Bay French bakeries **La Farine** and **Masse's** were put to the test by the pastry loving staff at *Coolbean98*'s lab, where scientists (no joke) performed a blind tasting and observed critical differences. The results:

La Farine ($1.50): more pleasing shape, better-defined layers, saltier.

Masse's ($1.75): one ounce heavier, crisper, sweeter flavor; almost nutty in its butteriness.

Conclusion: Masse's has the edge.

○ **La Farine Bakery:** *see also* p. 4.
○ **Masse's Pastries:** *see also* p. 288.

DIM SUM in the Peninsula and South Bay

Fook Yuen Sea Food Restaurant
  (Peninsula)
195 El Camino Real
Millbrae, CA
650-692-8600
Chinese (Cantonese)/Chinese
  (Dim Sum)/Chinese
  (Hong Kong)

Hong Kong Flower Lounge
  (Peninsula)
51 Millbrae Ave.
Millbrae, CA
650-692-6666
Chinese (Cantonese)/Chinese
  (Hong Kong)/Chinese
  (Dim Sum)

Joy Luck Place (Peninsula)
98 E. 4th Ave.
San Mateo, CA
650-343-6988
Chinese (Cantonese)/Chinese
  (Dim Sum)/Chinese
  (Hong Kong)

Joy Luck Place (South Bay)
10911 N. Wolfe Rd.
Cupertino, CA
408-255-6988
Chinese (Dim Sum)/Chinese
  (Cantonese)/Chinese
  (Hong Kong)

Koi Palace Restaurant
  (Peninsula)
365 Gellert Blvd., in Serramonte
  Plaza
Daly City, CA
650-992-9000
Chinese (Cantonese)/Chinese
  (Dim Sum)/Chinese
  (Hong Kong)

Mr. Fong's Restaurant (Peninsula)
949 Edgewater Blvd.
Foster City, CA
650-573-9176
Chinese (Dim Sum)/Chinese
  (Cantonese)/Chinese
  (Hong Kong)

Seafood Harbor Restaurant (Peninsula)
279 El Camino Real
Millbrae, CA
650-692-9688
Chinese (Cantonese)/Chinese (Dim Sum)/Chinese (Hong Kong)

Some of the best Cantonese/Hong Kong style dim sum in the United States can be found in the Bay Area. After a rigorous series of regional dumpling face-offs, here are some of our top picks from the Peninsula and South Bay (note that several are very conveniently close to SFO airport, and the Millbrae places are a stone's throw from the BART Millbrae station).

Hong Kong Flower Lounge is very highly thought of. At their Millbrae Avenue location, all dishes are good, and would show well at any other dim sum joint in town, says *Ruth Lafler*. Service is a plus, and you'll generally enjoy fine value for the price. Best dishes: pan-fried turnip cake (best in its class), pan-fried rice noodle roll with XO chili sauce, duck with plum sauce, crispy tofu skin, braised tofu skin, spinach dumpling (vegetarian), sweet glutinous rice dumpling with black sesame paste, coconut and peanut rolls (weekends only), egg puff (weekends only—light, puffy, and greaseless balls of fried air and dough, a perfect ending). Controversial dishes at Hong Kong Flower Lounge: har gow (plump shrimp, but dough too thin and prone to breaking open, especially when eaten hot), pan-fried chives dumpling (some love the crispiness, others prefer more chives), small egg custard tart (pastry crust won't please cookie-style crust lovers).

Seafood Harbor would have been a contender if not for some service problems, says *Melanie Wong*. "The kitchen seemed unable to keep up with the demand, but for the patient, the food's well worth it, striking a happy medium between the refined delicacy of Harbor Village and the more robust flavors of **Koi Palace**. The crowds here are not as fierce as at its two neighbors in Millbrae, making it a good bet at busy times." Standouts: deep-fried taro dumplings, sharks fin dumpling, xiao long bao (best at any of the Cantonese dim sum houses), shrimp rice noodle crepes, deep-fried tofu skins filled with shrimp, scallop and shrimp dumplings, braised tofu skin rolls, har gow, pan-fried chive dumplings, and egg tarts. Just average dishes include: black bean spare ribs, BBQ pork rolls, braised chicken feet, *siu mai, teochew fun gor* dumplings.

Koi Palace offers many delicious dishes with creative flair in a robust easily appreciated style, says Melanie. "The key to satisfaction is to avoid the weekends and holidays when it will be more crowded, and bring ear plugs. Also, remember to call for a number or reservation before you arrive to cut down on waiting time." Prices are higher than other spots, at $2.40 to $3.90 per plate. Recommendations: pan-fried leek dumplings, rice noodle rolls, dau miu (pea shoots) sauteed in garlic, steamed spareribs over rice noodles, and especially roast suckling pig ($15 for small plate), which is "still the best example I've had on this side of the Pacific, even the soybeans that line the plate are special." Service isn't terrific here.

Fook Yuen makes excellent har gow and very good suckling pig (not as great as Koi Palace's, though). *Ruth Lafler* says the food's slightly less "refined" than Hong Kong Flower Lounge, but heartier and often more uniquely flavored. The atmosphere is warmer and richer (than HKFL) and the service is friendlier than average. Some believe fried foods aren't this kitchen's forte.

Here are the winners from the South Bay: **Mr. Fong's**, right on the Foster City Lagoon and boasting a pretty view, is a winner for happening dim sum in a nice atmosphere. There's also plenty of parking and even the cart ladies speak English! The BBQ pork appetizer is very succulent, like the version at Tai Wu (same owners). Dried scallop with assorted meat soup has perfect, nongloppy broth. Sichuan eggplant with shredded pork claypot is delightful, full of subtle sauce that mixes well with tomato and eggplant. Roast duck boasts perfectly crispy skin, and even steamed rice is great! A VIP card gets you one free dish off the special menu. Dim sum is served from 11 a.m. to 3 p.m. daily, and is worth a trip, especially for deep-fried shrimp stuffed with leeks and wrapped in bacon. Fried items are all well fried and crisp, and steamed items are plump with excellent fillings. It's not the most refined dim sum, but still really tasty. Good salty thousand-layer cake with a high proportion of salted ducks' egg, amazingly light radish cakes, and "mochi" with black sesame filling that's everything it's supposed to be: piping hot and oh-so-creamy/sandy (a nice texture combination), says *Peter Yee*. Skip microwave-reheated roast duck. Service is excellent, in the attentive-yet-not-too-formal Hong Kong style, and there's also a take-out spot next door. The combination of food, atmosphere, service, and lack of wait makes

Mr. Fong's a great alternative to the crowds and chaos of some of the more well known high-end dim sum places, says *Ruth Lafler*.

Joy Luck is near-perfect, especially for chicken feet in black bean sauce, taro fried dumpling, xiao long bao, fried crispy tofu skin, large and meaty chicken wings, Chinese donut, sweet black sesame dumplings (oozing wonderful smoky sweet flavor), mango pudding, and har gow (too much shrimp, a real embarrassment of riches). Just skip the spareribs and custard tarts. They have a good branch in San Mateo, too.

- **Joy Luck Place:** *see also* p. 42.
- **Koi Palace Restaurant:** *see also* p. 68.
- **Seafood Harbor Restaurant:** *see also* p. 130.

San Francisco **DIM SUM**

Dol Ho (Chinatown)
808 Pacific Ave.
San Francisco, CA
415-392-2828
Chinese (Cantonese)/Chinese
   (Dim Sum)

Garden Bakery (Chinatown)
765 Jackson St.
San Francisco, CA
415-397-5838
Chinese (Hong Kong)/Chinese
   (Cantonese) café

Gold Mountain Restaurant
   (Chinatown)
644 Broadway
San Francisco, CA
415-296-7733
Chinese (Cantonese)/Chinese
   (Dim Sum)/Chinese
   (Hong Kong)

Great Eastern Restaurant
   (Chinatown)
649 Jackson St.
San Francisco, CA
415-986-2500
Chinese (Cantonese)/Chinese
   (Dim Sum)/Chinese
   (Hong Kong)

Harbor Village (Embarcadero)
101 California St., at 4
   Embarcadero Center Lobby
   (second level)
San Francisco, CA
415-781-8833
Chinese (Hong Kong)/Chinese
   (Dim Sum)

Kan's Restaurant (Chinatown)
708 Grant Ave.
San Francisco, CA
415-982-2388
Chinese (Cantonese)/Chinese
  (Dim Sum)/Chinese
  (Hong Kong)

Louie's Dim Sum (Chinatown)
1242 Stockton St.
San Francisco, CA
415-421-2889
Chinese (Dim Sum)

Mayflower Seafood Restaurant
  (Richmond)
6255 Geary Blvd.
San Francisco, CA
415-387-8338
Chinese (Cantonese)/Chinese
  (Dim Sum)/Chinese
  (Hong Kong)

Ton Kiang (Richmond)
5821 Geary Blvd.
San Francisco, CA
415-387-8273
Chinese (Hakka)/Chinese
  (Dim Sum)

Wing Sing Dim Sum (Chinatown)
1125 Stockton St.
San Francisco, CA
415-433-5571
Chinese (Dim Sum) bakery

Yank Sing (Embarcadero)
101 Spear St.
San Francisco, CA
415-957-9300
Chinese (Cantonese)/Chinese
  (Dim Sum)/Chinese
  (Hong Kong)

Yank Sing Restaurant (Financial
  District)
49 Stevenson St.
San Francisco, CA
415-541-4949
Chinese (Cantonese)/Chinese
  (Dim Sum)/Chinese
  (Hong Kong)

Yet Wah (Richmond]
2140 Clement St.
San Francisco, CA
415-387-8040
Chinese (Cantonese)/Chinese
  (Dim Sum)/Chinese
  (Beijing)/Chinese (Hong Kong)

You's Dim Sum (Chinatown]
675 Broadway
San Francisco, CA
415-788-7028
Chinese (Dim Sum)

Chowhounds might consider the Peninsula a dim sum mecca, but they're also finding great dim sum right in San Francisco. Unless noted otherwise, the following tips come from *Melanie Wong*.

Mayflower Seafood's dim sum compares favorably with the top echelon of high-end dim sum houses, perhaps a notch below

Harbor Village, the trio in Millbrae (Fook Yuen, HK Flower Lounge, Seafood Harbor) and Koi Palace. Its food and friendly service put it ahead of Richmond neighbors like Yet Wah, Ton Kiang, Tong Palace, and Parc Hong Kong. On weekdays, you order from a check-off list and get the food hot from the kitchen. Dining room's a bit cramped and expect long lines, even on weekdays. Very good to excellent: har gow, shrimp rice crepe, salt and pepper fresh calamari, peanut powder-coated mochi balls with black sesame paste. Disappointing: cold soy-poached gooseweb on bed of candied soy beans, scallop dumpling.

Tiny barebones **Dol Ho** is a favorite San Francisco Chinatown dim sum spot for food a step above the other small, take-out places in Chinatown. It's no Harbor Village, but it offers great value for the price. There's no charge for tea and there's no time pressure, you can hang out as long as you'd like, as evidenced by the many seniors lingering over the paper and a pot of tea. You'll eat like a king for well under $10. Flavors are subtle, with no oversalting, no trace of MSG and a light touch, letting ingredients shine. Food's always hot and fresh and if you don't see what you want on the cart (there's only room for one!), go back to the kitchen and point at what you'd like. Don't miss the housemade chili sauce, with black beans and chopped pickled veggies. It's especially good on fried taro dumplings, and can be found on most tables along with soy sauce. Two standouts at Dol Ho: chicken, mushroom, and tofu wrapped in rice noodle vermicelli and steamed with gingery broth; and spareribs over rice (casserolelike, served in small metal bowls with rice topped with meat and steamed, then soy-based sauce—inflected with a bit of tangerine—poured over). Don't miss the warm chestnut sponge cake fresh out of the steamer. Avoid: egg custard tart, fried sesame ball, sweetened glutinous rice wrapped in banana leaves.

Harbor Village is the equal of Millbrae's HK Flower Lounge—that is, tops in the Bay Area—when the service staff is paying attention. *Yimster* says it's one of the best teahouses in San Francisco. They cook with refined delicacy, excelling at custard tarts, chicken feet, deep-fried taro balls, tofu skin vegetarian rolls, bao with pork and ginger filling, and roast duck with candied soy beans. Weakest links: shrimp rice rolls and har gow. *The ChowChild* offers this evocative report: "The chicken feet meat was juicy and tender. You could suck it through a straw! By the end of the meal I had a pile of toes and talons on my plate."

Ton Kiang is among the favorites of some, and its Hakka menu intrigues, but dim sum can be inconsistent. When the place is "on," you'll be stunned by see-through dumpling wrappers, perfect greens, shrimp with a little snap. But when it is "off" . . . be forewarned. We've devised some tips to minimize disappointment: (1) sit facing the kitchen and try to grab items as soon as they leave the kitchen, and (2) if you find one category lacking (i.e., greasy fried goods or overcooked shrimp) minimize ordering those dishes (different chefs handle different sorts of items). Chicken feet are cut into small maneagable pieces, braised in spicy red sauce till meat falls off bones. Don't miss their egg bombs (aka crullers), xiao long bao (no burst of juice, but very juicy thoughout), and, for dessert, nicely eggy custard tarts (very eggy, with just a hint of sweetness). There's no wait for a table at 11:30 a.m. weekdays. Service is pleasant and helpful, but many dishes are on the salty side, it's not a great value for the price, and there's street parking only (bring lots of quarters).

Yank Sing is a less traditional dim sum, using more California-style ingredients, and quality is excellent (*Ruth Lafler* raves over expert, light, greaseless frying, thin but not flimsy dumpling wrappers and delicate—sometimes overly so—tastes). Favorites include: minced chicken in lettuce cups, eggplant, soft shell crab, dumplings stuffed with leaves from snap peas, steamed lobster dumplings, egg tarts, and green tea custard. Warning: price per person will be $35 (lots of tourists go into sticker shock). Note that this refers to Yank Sing's Embarcadero location; we've not yet reported on the Financial District Yank Sing.

Kan's is a surprisingly good value, considering the above-average quality and ambience and low prices of this Grant Avenue landmark. Atmosphere is quiet and calm, with servers circulating with trays (not carts) carrying dim sum. Selection is adequate, nothing like Gold Mountain or Great Eastern. Negatives: stale tasting chicken feet and pasty and uninteresting shrimp dumplings. Best bets: steamed spareribs, har gow, crispy skinned fried soft tofu rolls.

Great Eastern serves dim sum at lunch from a preprinted menu (no carts). It's an outstanding value, costing not much more than low-end places, yet offering a setting that's much nicer and less chaotic and staff that speaks good English. Quality is better than at the more pricey City View, and it's recommended for good dim sum in Chinatown proper at a reasonable price. Favorite dishes: shrimp rice noodle crepe, soft black sesame-filled mochi balls. Tasty but not outstanding: siu mai, shrimp, dry scallop, snow pea shoot dumpling, deep-fried taro dumpling, thousand layer cake.

Yet Wah's Clement Street location holds its own in the mid-price level for dim sum, with a pretty nice room and good service as well. The quality of the dim sum is quite high, although more rustic in prep than the high-end places and assisted by some MSG. Har gau, siu mai, teochew fun gor dumpling, potstickers (more ginger than pork), and shark's fin dumpling in soup are all recommended. Braised tofu skin rolls are a particular favorite. And an important bonus in light of the local parking hell: validated parking across the street!

Finally, some San Francisco spots where you can grab good dim sum to go (Dol Ho, above, also sells to-go at a front counter, and will pack your order cold so it doesn't oversteam as you travel).

- **Garden Bakery** for baked BBQ pork bao, egg sponge cake, and other excellent savory and sweet filled buns. New owners account for an upswing in quality.
- **You's Dim Sum** for watercress and shrimp dumplings, *dou sa sou* (sweet bean paste-filled baked pastry), huge and savory potstickers. (Note: Both Garden Bakery and You's have small seating areas, so you don't *need* to take away.)
- **Louie's** for plain *mantou* (steamed white buns) and bok tong go (white sugar steamed rice cakes).
- **Wing Sing** for taro cakes and turnip cakes plus some unusual items not available at most other places.

○ Gold Mountain Restaurant: *see also* p. 294.
○ Great Eastern Restaurant: *see also* p. 41.
○ Wing Sing Dim Sum: *see also* p. 288.
○ Yank Sing: *see also* p. 62.

East Bay **DIM SUM** Picks

Legendary Palace (East Bay)
708 Franklin St.
Oakland, CA
510-663-9288
Chinese (Cantonese)/Chinese
  (Hong Kong)/Chinese
  (Dim Sum)

Lucky Palace Chinese Restaurant
  (East Bay)
34348 Alvarado Niles Rd.
Union City, CA
510-489-8386
Chinese (Dim Sum)/Chinese
  (Cantonese)/Chinese
  (Hong Kong)

New Hong Kong Seafood
  Restaurant (East Bay)
25168 Mission Blvd.
Hayward, CA
510-583-7898
Chinese (Hong Kong)

Restaurant Peony (East Bay)
388 9th St., #288 (2nd level of
  Pacific Renaissance)
Oakland, CA
510-286-8866
Chinese (Cantonese)/Chinese
  (Dim Sum)/Chinese
  (Hong Kong)

Chowhounds pick their favorite dim sum places in the East Bay: At **Peony,** weekdays are your best bet (weekends tend toward pandemonium). Choices are limited, so grab what you want the first time it circulates, for it may never your way come again. The kitchen's slow at processing special orders. As for dishes, you just can't go wrong, so grab away for your favorites. *Melanie Wong* says that the room's nice and food is of good quality for the most part—far better on both counts than Jade Villa, the other fave in Oakland Chinatown. Fried milk, a deep-fried cylinder of soft, sweet custard, is a rare treat you'll want to grab fresh and hot from the kitchen.

Dim sum at **New Hong Kong** is well worth a try. Usual dim sum fare (sui mai, shrimp goh, chicken feet, and pig intestines and turnips) is good and served steaming hot. Even better are specialty dishes such as black bean clams with red and green peppers, pan-fried veggies in bean curd, and perfect sticky rice (neither mushy nor bland). And off the regular menu: a delicious lobster with noodles.

The strategy with **Legendary Palace** is to (1) try and get a table in the downstairs dining room, preferably near the elevator where the food comes down from the kitchen, (2) check dim sum temperature (do you see steam rising?) on stuff in carts, which may overcirculate, and (3) skip dumplings and stick with BBQ and full dishes. The best dim sum choices include shrimp rice crepes, turnip cakes (less firm than most places, which is as the texture should be, according to our dim sum experts), tripe (could have been cut smaller though), suckling pig (very crunchy skin); panko fried sea bass (light and not greasy), song chow sweet rice (like Chinese risotto, good rice texture and bits of meat and veggies), Empress Chicken (steamed with scallion, ginger dipping sauce and properly cooked with red at the bone—the real Chinese preparation), fried soft shell crabs, flower tofu dessert (soft tofu with ginger syrup).

Lucky Palace is another favorite dim sum spot, especially for excellent sticky rice (with egg yolk and Chinese sausage), har gow with whole shrimp inside, chive dumplings, and siu mai. But *Yvonne* says food and service at Lucky Palace strive to emulate the more elegant Hong Kong–style palaces, but doesn't quite reach. She says to steer clear of high-end dishes and stick with more homestyle food. Also, pay attention to redundancies on set menus when ordering. Best bets: the BBQ combo platter (especially char siu or pork), scallops and squid stir-fried with sugar peas, and honey-glazed smoked sea bass.

○ **Legendary Palace:** *see also* pp. 42, 90.

DINER Survey

Alana's Cafe (Peninsula)
1408 Burlingame Ave.
Burlingame, CA
650-348-0417
Diner or Coffee shop

Albert's Cafe (East Bay)
1541 Webster St.
Alameda, CA
510-523-4600
Diner or Coffee shop/Mexican

Jeffrey's Hamburgers (Peninsula)
42 S. B St.
San Mateo, CA
650-348-8698
American

Lakeside Cafe
   (Westportal/Ingleside)
2529 Ocean Ave.
San Francisco, CA
415-337-0359
Diner or Coffee shop

Original Joe's (Tenderloin)
144 Taylor St.
San Francisco, CA
415-775-4877
Italian/American

Pork Store Cafe (Mission)
3122 16th St.
San Francisco, CA
415-626-5523
Diner or Coffee shop

Original Joe's is the home of the famous Joe's Special (eggs scrambled with ground chuck, spinach, and onion). Ingredients are good, and proportions right, but deliciousness varies depending on who's cooking. Ask for plenty of garlic, and add a splash of Worcestershire Sauce at table. Breakfast options here are limited—think bacon and eggs—but execution is excellent. Ten dollars buys three skillfully cooked eggs, half a dozen slices of thick, hand-cut bacon, good steak fries, and fresh French bread.

There's a second branch of the **Pork Store Cafe** in the Mission; it's missing the homey cafe vibe of the original on Haight, but the menu's the same. Food quality varies; things seem fresher and better in the morning, but breakfast dishes are your best bet at any hour. A favorite here is Georgia ice cream—two eggs over easy, served on grits. The grits are the real thing, slow cooked, with plump white grains. Also good: sausage gravy (but in afternoon, biscuits are tough from reheating), fresh lemonade (with free refills).

Lakeside Cafe has many winners on its menu, three meals a day. Look for quality egg dishes and pancakes, and excellent corned beef hash for breakfast. For lunch, they do excellent burgers—cooked as ordered and served on nice onion rolls—plus patty melt, grilled chicken pesto sandwich, salads, crispy spinach polenta. Early-bird dinners (5 to 7 p.m.) are $12 to $14 and include soup (housemade and very good) or salad (simple but very fresh); choice of about ten entrees, including comforting items like pot roast, chicken scallopine, and pork chops. On the regular dinner menu, broiled lamb chops are particularly recommended (and come with nice fried potatoes tossed with feta cheese).

Albert's Cafe is a real old-time place, with funky decor, a gravel-voiced, rainbow-haired grandmother presiding behind the counter, and a short-order cook with a twenty-year tenure, reports *Ruth Lafler*. Hash browns are excellent (but ask for them browned on both sides!), and scrambled eggs are perfectly cooked. The waitress recommends Mexican specialties (especially huevos Guillermo), and coffee comes in your choice of regular or Peet's French roast. Chicken fried steak is a definite miss, though. Lunchy things like burgers and sandwiches are also on the very inexpensive menu (topping out at $7.95 for steak and eggs). Open 7 a.m. to 2:20 p.m. (not 2:30!), seven days a week.

Alana's has good scrambles and housemade scones for breakfast or brunch. **Jeffrey's** is famous for hamburgers, but also has good soups, chicken caesar salad, and teriyaki chicken sandwiches in a diner atmosphere.

○ **Original Joe's:** *see also* **p. 161.**

DRAGON 2000 Menu Translation

Dragon 2000 Restaurant (East Bay)
1651 Botelho Dr., in Plum Court Shopping Center
Walnut Creek, CA
925-287-1688
Chinese (Shanghai)/Chinese (Sichuan)

While Dragon 2000's set menus all feature sweet and sour something and there are forks at every place setting, the hidden gem there is the chuan cai, Shanghai cai menu—in Chinese only—with over eighty Shanghainese specialties. Hound *chibi* (who likes their Eastern Chinese specialities like drunken chicken, tofu thread salad, ping-pan—assorted cold cuts—and chunks of braised pork leg) has partially translated it below, with tasting notes from *Melanie Wong*, who says Sichuan dishes are strongest here. Pay particular attention to the numbers next to the dishes so you can tell your waiter what you want.

Shanghai appetizers:

3 *liang ban gan si*—tofu strip salad
6 *yan xun ya tui*—smoked duck leg

7 *shang hai xun yu*—Shanghai smoked fish
8 *nan jing xian shui ya*—Nanjing style salt water duck

Sichuan appetizers:

10 *ma-la yao pian*—numbing hot kidney slices (thin, barely
  cooked sheets of kidney, meltingly tender and unctuous,
  with a foie gras–like texture; hot red oil is a bit sweet and
  blended with slivered scallions, cilantro, and lots of salt.
  Waiter says kidneys in garlic sauce are even better.)
12-1 *liang ban niu jin*—beef tendon salad

Sichuan dishes:

33 *san bei ji*—three cup chicken (braised in one cup each of soy
  sauce, wine, and sesame oil, plus garlic and basil. This
  version is homestyle, rustic, and thoroughly delicious. Also,
  it's actually more Taiwanese than Sichuan.)
49 *pao cai hue guo rou*—braised pork with preserved
  vegetables
63 *xue cai bai ye*—snow cabbage with tofu strips (proportion of
  ingredients is perfect; subtly flavored and executed with a
  light hand)
129 *gan bian si-ji dou*—dry-fried string beans (the beans
  should be fried twice, once to wrinkle them and then once
  with the seasonings. When it's good, it's heaven, but I have
  yet to find a really good version in the States. You can also
  get pork stomach (44), intestine (30), or rabbit (47) in this
  preparation.)

Shanghai dishes:

56 *jiu huang shan hu*—eels sauteed with yellow chives
63 *xue cai bai ye*—snow vegetable with tofu strips (since you
  guys are trying it everywhere)
69 *mei cai kou rou*—fatty pork braised with preserved
  vegetables
70–73 are all preparations of braised pork "foot"
137 *huang jin song zi*—literally "yellow gold pine nuts"
98 *yan du xian* (a traditional Shanghai soup with tofu strips,
  bamboo shoots, and ham; broth is delicious on its own,
  but other elements are a little washed out and not well
  knit)

99–101 are *ma-la* Sichuan style hot pots (large, medium, and small)

81–89-3 are various fish preps

94–45-1 are *lian guo* lamb dishes. I don't know what these are.

The next two sections are soups, dumplings, and noodles, which I think are on the English menu: #106 is xiao long tang bao (Shanghai-style little steamed dumplings—forgettable).

○ **Dragon 2000 Restaurant:** *see also* p. 167.

DUCK, DUCK, GOOSE

Happy Bakery & Deli
   (Westportal/Ingleside)
1548 Ocean Ave.
San Francisco, CA
415-337-8198
Chinese (Cantonese)/Chinese
   (Hong Kong) store

Happy Families (East Bay)
1009 Harrison St.
Oakland, CA
510-839-8871
Chinese (Hong Kong)/Chinese
   (Cantonese)

New Moon Restaurant
   (Chinatown)
1247 Stockton St.
San Francisco, CA
415-434-1128
Chinese (Cantonese)

Happy Bakery & Deli is a terrific Cantonese barbecue stand for soy sauce chicken, white blanched chicken feet, and tender roast duck with finely tuned spicing. Call ahead to check availability or to reserve. To help skin stay crisp in transit, ask for it to be packed whole, upright in an open top carton with a plastic bag underneath to catch dripping juices. **New Moon** is recommended, too. **Happy Families** sells a very tasty roast goose—similar to Chinese roast duck—with crispy skin. *Yimster* reminds hounds selecting roast ducks to look for one whose skin is not broken or burned.

∘○∘ Chowhound Tip:

An important message about duck juice, from
Melanie Wong, for anyone buying hanging ducks
from Chinese places.

Whenever you're getting roast duck, don't forget to
ask for an extra portion of the duck juices with your
order. It's liquid gold. At any of the places that sell
hanging roast ducks, there will be little condiment
cups filled with the juices that collect in the duck
cavity when its roasting. When the duck is cut open
for customers who want it hacked by the vendor, the
juices are drained into a bowl, vat, or gravy bucket
and then portioned into those little lidded cups. At
Happy Bakery & Deli (see below), the ducks don't
form much juice, so they'll only give you two of these
little cups at max. At other places that perhaps sew
their ducks up tighter and collect more, there's
usually a couple quarts or maybe a gallon of this stuff
by afternoon in the vat. My mom and my aunties,
and now I, bring a small glass jar and ask the counter
man to fill it with juice. If it's not too big a jar, they
usually will, and if it's a big one, they'll fill it partway.
The stuff is the essence of roast ducks and perfumed
with the magical rubs that season the bird. A
tablespoon of it can season a whole serving of noodles.

EASTER SWEETS

Acme Bread Co. (East Bay)
1601 San Pablo Ave.
Berkeley, CA
510-524-1327
Bakery

Acme Bread Co. (Embarcadero)
One Ferry Bldg. Embarcadero
San Francisco, CA
415-288-2978
Bakery

Liberty Cafe (Bernal Heights)
410 Cortland Ave.
San Francisco, CA
415-695-8777
American

Victoria Pastry Co. (Marin County)
292 Bon Air Shopping Ctr.
Greenbrae, CA
415-461-3099
Italian bakery

Victoria Pastry Co. (North Beach)
1362 Stockton St.
San Francisco, CA
415-781-2015
Italian bakery

The quest for hot cross buns has turned up one recommendation: **Liberty Cafe. Acme Bread Company** has sold kulich (Russian Easter bread) at farmers' markets (as small tea loaves) and at the bakery (as large cylindrical loaves) during Easter season. Watch for it! **Victoria Pastry** has La Colomba (a traditional Italian Easter bread, like panettone but with candied orange peel instead of raisins) shipped in each year, plus imported Perugina dark and milk chocolate Easter eggs, as well as their own hand-decorated chocolated eggs.

○ **Acme Bread Co:** *see also* **p. 3.**
○ **Liberty Cafe:** *see also* **pp. 8, 20.**

EASTERN European Survey

European Food Wholesale
  (Richmond)
3038 Clement St.
San Francisco, CA
415-750-0504
Central/Eastern European store

Food Warehouse (Russian Hill)
1732 Polk St.
San Francisco, CA
415-292-5659
Store

Moscow & Tbilisi Bakery
  (Richmond)
5540 Geary Blvd.
San Francisco, CA
415-668-6959
Russian bakery

New World Market (Richmond)
5641 Geary Blvd.
San Francisco, CA
415-751-8810
Russian store

Polkan (Russian Hill)
1806 Polk St.
San Francisco, CA
415-474-3940
Russian store

Quality Market (Sunset)
1342 Irving St.
San Francisco, CA
415-759-6500
Central/Eastern European store

Seakor Polish Delicatessen
  (Richmond)
5957 Geary Blvd.
San Francisco, CA
415-387-8660
Polish store

Winmart European Deli
  (South Bay)
833 W. El Camino Real
Sunnyvale, CA
408-736-3316
Central/Eastern European store

The Croatian Market, also known as **Food Warehouse,** once boasted all sorts of food and nonfood products from all over the world. It's been cleaned up a bit and the main emphasis is now on Eastern European foods. There's a front case with bolognas and meats, an olive bar, oils and vinegars in bulk (and clean bottles to fill), and shelves full of pickles, smoked fish, and other fun-to-discover treats. The proprietors also plan to serve sandwiches and salads soon.

According to *Stanley Stephan*, **WinMart European Deli** in Sunnyvale is worth a trip from San Francisco. It would do Chicago, Cincinnati, and Buffalo proud with its huge selection of Eastern European foods. It looks like a 7-Eleven from the outside, but inside it's clean, bright, and spotless. Over one hundred types of meats, lots of smoked fish, an astounding dairy case (six types of sour cream, dozens of butters), baked goods, half dozen types of horseradish, four kinds of salt pork, jars and jars of pickles, candies, cookies, biscuits, dried mushrooms from Poland, and it goes on and on. You can have lunch on the samples alone.

Stanley Stephan says **New World Market** is the best Russian store in San Francisco, but it's no WinMart. It carries a large selection of cold foods, smoked fish, cold cuts, horseradish galore, and even a liquor department with various flavors of Manischewitz wines. There's a salad bar with serve-yourself hot dishes like stuffed cabbage, stewed cabbage with chicken, and more, priced around $3.99 to $4.99 a pound. They sell, in huge bowls, seven types of caviar for all your party needs.

Moscow & Tbilisi Bakery is the best bet for freshly baked rye bread. It's like the Russian version of some of the North Beach bakeries. They also carry lots of cream cakes and huge yeasty donuts filled with custard or cherries, similar to Polish punski. **Seakor** has a large selection of Polish kielbasa, an unmatched selection of dried mushrooms and, on weekends, Polish cheesecake.

Quality Market is an unassuming store with an in-store bakery, making some of the best strudel in the city. Availability seems determined by the owner's whim; sometimes it's strudel, sometimes it's turnovers. Excellent blintzes are filled with ground beef and potatoes or mushrooms, eggs, and dill. They also have a nice cold cuts selection, Bobak sausages, and kielbasa imported from New York.

European Food Wholesale is packed with offbeat packaged foods from Russia, Poland, Latvia, and more. There is such variety of salamis, sausages, wursts, and other smoked meats that the refrigerated cases take up two walls ("my god, the flavor that comes pouring out when you open the refrigerated cases!" kvells *Zach Georgopoulos*). They also make marinated anchovies in-house. The owner of **Polkan** deli is slowly expanding the menu with homemade Russian items like borscht, piroshki, Russian chili, and more. The *piroshki* are way greasy but excellent.

○ **Moscow & Tbilisi Bakery:** *see also* **p. 48.**

EGGS: Unborn and Custard Tarts

Golden Gate Bakery (Chinatown)
1029 Grant Ave.
San Francisco, CA
415-781-2627
Chinese (Cantonese)/Chinese
    (Hong Kong) bakery

Yuen Yang Bakery (South Bay)
30 S. Park Victoria Dr.
Milpitas, CA
408-942-8088
Chinese (Hong Kong)/Chinese
    (Cantonese) bakery

Ocean Supermarket (South Bay)
2 S. Park Victoria Dr.
Milpitas, CA
408-942-3388
Vietnamese store

For years, *derek*'s been searching for unborn eggs (aka young chicken eggs) to add to chicken soup. **Ocean Supermarket** carries them! **Yuen Yang Bakery,** in the same shopping center, makes egg custard tarts that are almost as good as **Golden Gate Bakery's,** with a flakey crust and nice gently eggy custard—but not as sweet as GG's.

○ **Golden Gate Bakery:** *see also* **pp. 4, 288.**

ETHIOPIAN Exploration

Cafe Colucci (East Bay)
6427 Telegraph Ave.
Oakland, CA
510-601-7999
Ethiopian or Eritrean

Stylish and soothing Cafe Colucci has great curb appeal (with some sidewalk tables and a coffee), according to *Melanie Wong*, plus there's the predinner entertainment of trying to identify

Chowhound Nametag: Yimster

○○○

Location: Bay Area, California

Occupation: Civil engineer by training, retired maintenance manager federal government

Cholesterol Level: Normal with meds

Farthest Out of the Way Traveled Just for Chow: Vancouver, BC, Canada—fifteen years ago much better than the Bay Area, but now only a little bit better. Now we do not have to travel that far.

Nabe Most Full of Explorable Unknown Chow: Middlefield in Redwood City for Mexican food, San Jose for Vietnamese food, Santa Clara for Korean. We do not have time or space for me to list everything. My idea of a great weekend is to explore a new area and a new type of food.

Top Chinatown Pick: High end, Louie's; low end, Utopia

Weight Management Tip: Work out at least three times a week and cook your own meals. After cooking I do not want to eat that much.

Favorite Comfort Chow: Hong Kong Flower Lounge for sweet vinegar ginger pig trotters

Favorite Gelato Flavor: Mango

Chowhounding Rules of Thumb:
1. Watch the locals and order what they get
2. If having Mexican or Chinese food, check out the people there and see if they match up to the type of food
3. Do not believe what you read; try if for yourself

the legumes and grains in the compartments of the glass-topped tables. Preselected dinner combinations (vegetarian or meat) are a good way to sample a variety of dishes.

If ordering à la carte, these choices come recommended:

4 *atakilt*—fresh string beans, carrots, and potatoes sauteed with onions, fresh tomatoes, ginger, and garlic in turmeric sauce

5 *gomen*—collard greens sauteed with onions, tomatoes, garlic, and olive oil (jalapeños optional)

12 *buticha* (cold)—special fava bean powder, garlic, onions, jalapeño, olive oil, fresh lemon puree

7 eggplant tibs—eggplant sauteed with garlic, onions, bell pepper in turmeric (mild) or berbere sauce (hot)

13 *salata*—a salad with sparkling citrusy dressing (good counterbalance to all the starch)

16 *doulet*—an interesting (and incredibly rich) choice for offal lovers: minced lamb tripe and liver, lean top ground beef, sauteed onions, jalapeño in seasoned butter and mitmita

Least liked:

10 *shuro fitfit*—seasoned chickpea powder, onions, roma tomato, jalapeño, and olive oil

23 shrimp tibs—fresh sauteed shrimp with onions, bell pepper, jalapeño, fresh tomato in lightly spicy white wine sauce

Corkage is only $7, plus there's honey wine on the beverage list.

Colossal **FARMERS' MARKET** Roundup

Alemany Farmers' Market
(Bernal Heights)
100 Alemany Blvd.
San Francisco, CA
415-647-9423
Farmers' Market

Arizmendi (East Bay)
3265 Lakeshore Ave.
Oakland, CA
510-268-8849
Bakery

Campbell Farmers' Market
(South Bay)
East Campbell Ave. between
Central and 1st St.
Campbell, CA
510-745-7100
Farmers' market

Daly City Farmers' Market
(Peninsula)
Serramonte Mall
Intersection of Hwys. 1 and 280
Daly City, CA
Farmers' market

Evergreen Farmers' Market at
Mirassou Vineyards
(South Bay)
3000 Aborn Rd.
San Jose, CA
510-745-7100
Farmers' market

Fillmore Farmers' Market
(Pacific Heights)
Fillmore and Eddy
San Francisco, CA
Farmers' market

Heart of the City Farmers' Market
(Civic Center)
1182 Market St. #415
San Francisco, CA
415-558-9455
Farmers' market

Jack London Square Farmers'
Market (East Bay)
Broadway and Embarcadero
Oakland, CA
800-949-FARM
Farmers' market

Los Gatos Farmers' Market
(South Bay)
Montabello Way and Broadway
Los Gatos, CA
408-353-4293
Farmers' market

Lunardi's
www.lunardis.com
Store

Marin Civic Center Farmers'
Market (Marin County)
Civic Center at Hwy. 101 and
San Pedro
San Rafael, CA
800-897-FARM
Farmers' market

Menlo Park Farmer's Market
(Peninsula)
Crane and Chestnut
Menlo Park, CA
831-688-8316
Farmers' market

Napa Chefs' Farmers' Market
(Napa County)
1st St. and Main
Napa, CA
707-252-7142
Farmers' market

Oakland Grand Lake Farmers'
Market (East Bay)
Grand Ave. at Lake Park Way
Oakland, CA
800-897-FARM
Farmers' market

Old Oakland Farmers' Market
(East Bay)
9th St. between Broadway and
Clay
Oakland, CA
510-745-7100
Farmers' market

San Francisco Ferry Plaza
Farmers Market (Embarcadero)
Foot of Market St. on the
Embarcadero; Ferry Building
Marketplace
San Francisco, CA
415-353-5650
Farmers' market

San Jose Blossom Hill Farmers'
Market (South Bay)
Princeton Plaza Mall at Koozer
and Meridian
San Jose, CA
800-806-FARM
Farmers' market

San Mateo Farmers' Market
(Peninsula)
1700 W. Hillsdale Blvd., in
parking lot at College of
San Mateo
San Mateo, CA
800-949-FARM
Farmers' market

Santa Cruz Community Farmers'
Market (Santa Cruz County)
Lincoln and Cedar
Santa Cruz, CA
831-454-0566
Farmers' market

Santana Row Farmers' Market
(South Bay)
400 S. Winchester Blvd.
San Jose, CA
408-551-4600
Farmers' market

S. F. Produce Wholesale Market
(Potrero Hill)
2095 Jerrold Ave.
San Francisco, CA
415-550-4495
Farmers' market

The following is, by far, the guide's longest entry. Farmers' market strategy takes great experience to accumulate, and mostly involves knowing which vendors are the good ones, and which specific items to watch for from which vendors. Avid market-going hounds have pooled copious experience to provide this amazing and authoritative cheat sheet.

San Francisco

The year-round **Saturday Ferry Plaza** Market (8:00 a.m. to 2:00 p.m.) is one of the Bay Area's largest. In the same location, there's a smaller Tuesday market (10:00 a.m. to 2:00 p.m.) and seasonal ones on Thursday afternoon, and Sunday (the latter is a Garden Market, featuring nurseries and plant vendors). Happy Quail Farms sells a wide assortment of fresh peppers and finely ground habanero and cayenne peppers (a great alternative to pepper flakes), and pricy Pimientos de Padron peppers in season (mostly quite mild, especially early in the season, but you do hit really hot ones sometimes). Happy Quail is one of the few US farms growing these Spanish tapas favorites. Saute in olive oil until skins blister, then season with coarse sea salt. Andante Dairy is a small cheesemaking operation run by Soyoung Scanlon. She's usually at the Saturday market selling her fresh, seasonal cheeses. Look for her summer Figaro cheese (fresh cow and goat cheese, wrapped in fig leaves, soaked in white wine). Note that the asterisks next to cheese names indicate extra good ones that week. Capricious Cheese (www.capriciouscheese.com) makes goat feta, goat sausages, and aged goat cheese that is marvelous on pasta, grated over white bean and roasted garlic soup, or just eaten out of hand. Marshall's Honey has many seasonal varieties available. Their beeswax candles are amazing, burn forever, and smell great. If you don't see what you're looking for, be sure to ask, as they're willing to bring special items to the market for you. Brickmaiden Breads (Sunday market): try their sesame bread ("I took a bite and said with much passion 'oh my.' It stopped someone else in their tracks who had the same reaction!"—*Stanley Stephan*). Small loaves run $1.50. Other favorites: Swanton Berry Farms (strawberries), Zuckerman's (potatoes, asparagus), Balakian (zucchini and squashes), Hamada (dried fruits, citrus, Asian pears), Blossom Bluff (peaches, cherries, blueberries), Iocoppi (fresh and dried beans, artichokes, greens), Cap'n Mike's Holy Smoke (smoked fish, try the salmon dip), Bariani Olive Oil, Van Mourick (nuts), and June Taylor Jams.

○○○ Chowhound Tip:

The market's Web site (*www.ferryplazafarmersmarket .com*) includes a regularly updated roster of vendors.

Heart of the City Farmers' Market, Sundays, is the one for Asian veggies, fresh fish, and some organic produce (though not as much as other San Francisco markets). There are usually a few dried nut and fruit vendors; *Thea* especially likes Francesca's Almonds for organic almonds (and ground ones for baking). Worthy prepared foods options include All Star Tamales, with many flavors of homemade tamales, and Artisan Breads, for tender fruit pastries (strawberry cream cheese is really good). Some of the Ferry Plaza vendors (see above) sell here, as well.

The **Alemany Farmer's Market,** held on Saturdays from 6 a.m. to 5 p.m., has lots of nearby parking and rock-bottom prices even for organic produce (most of the organic stands are at the end nearest the entrance.) There's also lots and lots of Asian produce and "exotic" items like squash leaves. Point Reyes Oysters sells oysters (and clams) by the dozen, ranging from extra small to large. There's an egg vendor with salt-pickled duck eggs, quail eggs, duck eggs, balut (fertilized duck or chicken eggs, a Filipino delicacy), and more. Live poultry is available across the street in the small annex next to the main parking lot. Seafood and egg vendors are in same vicinity. Medrano Flowers sells only at this market, and carries absolutely stunning flowers at bargain prices, says *Stanley Stephan*. All Star Tamales (see above) also sells here.

Fillmore Farmers' Market is located behind the Safeway on Geary, and gets somewhat of a late start, with vendors still setting up around 9 a.m. on Saturdays. Pricing is somewhere between Ferry Plaza and Alemany. Best vendors include: Happy Boy Farms (expensive, but worth it for salad greens, melons, fingerling potatoes, and great lettuce including romaine and "little gems"—like a cross between romaine and butter—also salad mix with flowers, cukes, tomatoes, melons, and more, depending on the season); Peter Chan Nursery (the best flower bargains and the freshest cut flowers); and Crepes by Antoine, from Los Gatos. Many regular vendors from the Ferry Plaza Market (see above) are here.

The **San Francisco Produce Wholesale Market** is open to the general public, but it's not like your basic farmers' market. The hours are 1 a.m. to 8 a.m. (regulars suggest arriving by 2 a.m. for the best selection), and you must buy by the case. Perfect for ambitious jam makers!

Oakland

Grand Lake Market is under the freeway near Lake Merritt on Saturdays. It's only a couple of blocks from **Arizmendi** bakery, a hound favorite for thin, crisp-crusted pizza with daily-changing toppings, and bread and pastries. There are some Ferry Plaza (see above) regulars here, including Marshall's Honey, Zuckerman's, Swanton Berries, Hamada, and Balakian. *Stanley Stephan*'s favorite vendors include Neufeld Dried Fruits (selling the most amazing dried fruit); Big Paw (an olive oil and vinegar vendor from Napa; their balsamic bread dipper makes excellent salad dressing; lots of samples offered; their fig balsamic is pretty good straight out of the bottle); and Octoberfeast (selling Eastern European baked goods, many made with organic flours, including a crusty dark rye and some wheat-free varieties), which also has a shop in San Francisco (more info at www.October feast.com).

Sundays, check out the market at **Jack London Square** from 10 a.m. It's larger than Grand Lake, with a nice location right on the waterfront, plus live music. Tends to be less expensive than Ferry Plaza and you can park free at the garage under Barnes & Noble (just pick up a sticker at the organizer's booth right off the square). *Ruth Lafler* says this market has some of the best qualities: fine variety and quality but not as chichi and expensive as Ferry Plaza, and a nice, laid back setting, plus it has a great view and is very handicapped accessible, with plenty of benches. Lots of small farmers are represented, and many of the South Bay farmers' market vendors (see below) are here. Good vendors include John Spenger Foods (for oils and vinegars, including eighteen-year-old balsamic, Thai sesame ginger blend, Bistro blend with garlic infused extra virgin olive oil, balsamic vinegar, spices, chilis and parsley—info at www.spenger.com); Stackhouse Brothers Orchards (for nuts, including many flavored nuts); Nina's Kitchen (for fabulous Russian baked goods like poppy seed rolls, moist tea cakes, and piroshki with just right ratio of filling to pastry, also buckwheat crepes); Joe Gotelli & Sons (cherries); Reno Xeiri (eggs); Happy Boy (see above); Bariani (see above); Cap'n Mike's Holy Smoke (see above); Blossom Bluff (see above); and Iocoppi (see above).

Old Oakland Farmers' Market, on Fridays, is like an extension of adjacent Chinatown: more serious shopping and less of a carnival/street fair atmosphere, according to *Ruth Lafler*. There's some organic, lots of Asian veggies, excellent bread from Crepe and Brioche Boulangerie. Don't miss the street food (tamales, sausages, coffee, and more). Vendors here include: Lizzie's Cookies (www.lizziescookies.com, with amazing chocolate pecan coconut and other flavors); Big Paw (see above); and RoliRoti (www.roliroti.com) sells chickens from their rotisserie truck—whole $10, half $5. They smell amazing and have lots of salty herby flavor.

Peninsula

Peninsula hounds point out the high points at the **San Mateo Farmers' Market**, held Wednesdays and Saturdays from 8:30 a.m. to 1:30 p.m. in the College of San Mateo parking lot: Kashiwase Farms (peaches and nectarines); Tecklenburg (melons only, but oh, what melons!); Happy Boy (see above); Crepe and Brioche Bakery (apple tart, walnut levain, pumpkinseed levain, brioche, asiago bread, and mixed fruit bread, but skip the pain au chocolat—too light on the chocolate).

Daly City Farmers' Market, Thursdays, has over fifty vendors (some organic), selling fresh seafood, sausage, and much more. Lots of the same vendors as the Ferry Plaza market (see above), but lower prices. *Nancy Berry* warns not to miss really good organic Asian veggies at the stand near the entrance. Also nice fish and prepared items.

Sundays (9:30 a.m. to 1:30 p.m.) at the **Menlo Park Farmer's Market**, look for Pietro, selling fresh-caught salmon from Half Moon Bay.

South Bay Farmers' Markets

There are some notable vendors at the **Santana Row Farmers' Market**, held Sundays in an upscale shopping plaza: Morganic Hill Top Crop Honey (this honey can hold its own with Marshall's (see above) at a third of the price, says *Stanley Stephan*—varieties include lotus, sage, blueberry blossom, buckwheat, echinacea, tanbark, star thistle, wildflower mixes, and much more); Santa Maria (great-tasting raspberries and strawberries); Alonsso's Bakery (interesting bread varieties, including blue cheese, and $2 tamales); Fabrique Delices (www.fabriquedelices.com—an artisanal charcuterie, selling a selection of their more than one hundred products, including pâtés and mousses); and don't miss the incredible Russian blini makers (who *Judith Hurley* says can really cook). Also, the Hurdy Gurdy Italian Ice Cart, with lemon, mango, passion fruit, and chocolate ices.

Outstanding vendors on Sundays at the **Los Gatos Farmers' Market** include Lathe House Nursery (fresh medicinal and culinary herbs, including wormwood to make your own absinthe); Country Essences (beautiful flowers, and flower arranging classes on Tuesdays and Thursdays, followed by lunch; call 831-722-4549 for info); and Nina's Kitchen Russian pastries (see above).

Evergreen Farmers' Market at Mirassou Vineyards is held Sunday mornings (9 a.m. to 1 p.m.) from May to October. While it may not be a destination market, it's a fine place to spend a Sunday morning. There are around twenty-five vendors, including some familiar from other area markets, like Happy Boy and Zuckerman's (see above). Also look for La Fleur de Lyon (out of El Cerrito, selling strawberry, apricot, apple, and cranberry breads plus savory tarts and turnovers) and Whole Bean of Santa Cruz (with a mellow brewed coffee and organic, shade grown and/or fair trade beans). Just around the corner is a Lunardi's with quite an impressive meat and seafood counter and decent wine department with tasting counter.

San Jose Blossom Hill Farmers' Market, a Sunday market, boasts great parking and easy access from any number of directions; there are about thirty booths, including the Tomato Lady, who sells many varieties for planting.

The Sunday **Campbell Farmers' Market** has lots of vendors, heavy on baked goods, plus the same vaunted Russian blini makers as at the Santana Row Farmer's Market. There are lots of places here just to sit, have a coffee, and watch the world go by.

Santa Cruz Community Farmers' Market is held Wednesday afternoons. After a morning at the beach you could put together a very satisfying picnic dinner, go back to the boardwalk, spread out your goodies and watch the sun set, says *Stanley Stephan*. Expect to hear a little live music and a lot of political talk among the marketgoers. Many of the Santana Row and Los Gatos market vendors, like Morganic Hill Top Crop Honey and Lathe House Nursery (see above) are here as well, plus Donnelly Fine Chocolates (www.donnellychocolates.com) and Sweet Elana's Bakery with lovely quichelike tarts filled with grilled veggies and goat cheese, breads, and cookies. There's also a vendor serving fresh oysters on the half shell.

North Bay Farmers' Markets

Marin Civic Center Farmers' Market is the most fun market, and it has many of the Ferry Plaza vendors, says *Stanley Stephan*. Watch for Triple T Ranch (hydroponic and naturally grown produce and free-range eggs, including beautiful pastel Ameraucana chicken eggs); M&CP Farms (blue cheese and Parmesan/Romano-stuffed olives, lots of other olives, pickles, canned veggies, and sweet-hot gherkins—West Coast pickles with that gherkin crunch and a hot jalapeño kick); De Santis Farms (outstanding citrus, including Tarrocco Sicilian blood oranges, Morro blood oranges, Valencias, navels, Seville, Cara Cara, and sweet limes—which make great limeade—plus the market's least expensive mulberries); Leon Day's Condiments (huge selection of chutneys, jams, jellies, sauces, dressings, glazes, salsas, mushroom pate, and more); Sante Fe (handcrafted microwave tortilla warmers and nontraditional tortillas in flavors like black bean garlic, chipotle, habenero, spinach and onion, green chili garlic, and more); Calio Groves (olive oils and vinegars, and a Persian lime olive oil made with whole crushed fruit) and RoliRoti's rotisserie chickens (see above).

Napa Chefs' Farmers' Market is a seasonal (spring through fall) Friday evening market that's quite the party, with live music, lots of prepared foods, Napa Valley Vintners Association wine booth, and beer stands run by various civic groups.

○ **Alemany Farmers' Market:** *see also* p. 207.
○ **Arizmendi:** *see also* pp. 3, 238.
○ **Heart of the City Farmer's Market:** *see also* p. 26.
○ **Menlo Park Farmers' Market:** *see also* p. 230.
○ **San Francisco Ferry Plaza Farmers Market:** *see also* pp. 26, 52, 79, 104.

FILIPINO (with an Emphasis on Crispy Pata)

Neneng's Restaurant & Catering
(Solano County)
1030 Tennessee St.
Vallejo, CA
707-643-8617
Filipino

Penoy Parin (Solano County)
1601 Marine World Pkwy., #135
Vallejo, CA
707-554-3835
Filipino

Ongpin Noodles (Peninsula)
73 Camaritas Ave.
South San Francisco, CA
650-615-9788
Filipino

Crispy (or krispy, as some spell it) pata is made by boiling a pork haunch, freezing it, then plunging the icy pork into hot fat. It puffs up into the world's largest pork rind; a *great* dish when done right. At **Ongpin Noodle House**, crispy pata comes with or without garlic. The meat's tender and crispy in areas exposed to the frying oil, but remains moist. There's minced garlic and oil slathered over the meat, which *Pia* tells us Filipinos slather all over their rice, calories be damned. The only issue here is inconsistently crispy skin. Try to request crispier parts. Also unequivocally delicious here is *daing na bangus* (fried marinated milkfish). The atmosphere, though, is unequivocally basic.

Penoy Pa Rin is a small Filipino grocer in Vallejo carrying some fresh vegetables, seafood (cleaned and fried at no charge), basic Filipino staples, video rentals, and a three-item steam table (with indoor seating for four). Crispy pata, with thin, crispy skin and firm meat, is served everyday, not just weekends like most other spots. Opa squash with garlic, tomato, and beef bits is also a good bet there.

Neneng's steam table stands out among Vallejo's Filipino spots with its fresh and light hand without the fattiness and excess sodium so often found in Filipino steam table food. The sauces are more like unthickened pan juices, with no heavy layer of oil floating on top (*Melanie Wong*). They're open for breakfast and lunch, with takeout offered throughout the afternoon. Go for late lunch if you're craving noodles *(pancit)*; it takes them a while to get them on the steam table. Lunch rice plate special runs $4 for two items, steamed rice, dessert, and canned soda.

See the Cuisine Index for a few more Filipino choices.

FIREFLY: Comfort Food with Flair

Firefly Restaurant (Mission)
4288 24th St.
San Francisco, CA
415-821-7652
New American/Pan-Asian fusion

Old standby Firefly still delivers, and offers one of the best deals in town: Sunday through Thursday, get appetizer, main course, dessert, and coffee or tea for just $25. Order freely from anything on their menu. Rack of lamb is full of flavor and delicious, *jen maiser* reports, pot roast is wonderfully tender, and has great gravy, and appetizers of romano beans and potstickers are big hits, too. The peach tart is killer. Expect comfort food with flair; *amalia* says chef Brady Levy takes the plebeian to a new level. The menu changes seasonally, and usually includes vegetarian or vegan choices. Here's an interesting tip: Around the Jewish high holy days, Firefly adds some great Jewish-inspired dishes that are more interesting than your grandmother's.

○ **Firefly Restaurant:** *see also* **pp. 118, 217.**

FISH-AND-CHIPS

Bab's Delta Diner
(Solano County)
770 Kellogg St.
Suisun City, CA
707-421-1926
Diner or Coffeeshop

Barbara's Fish Trap
(Peninsula)
281 Capistrano Rd.
Half Moon Bay, CA
650-728-7049
Seafood

Edinburgh Castle (Tenderloin)
950 Geary St.
San Francisco, CA
415-885-4074
British pub

Foley's Inn (Union Square)
235 O'Farrell St.
San Francisco, CA
415-397-7800
American/British

Lucas Wharf Restaurant
(Sonoma County)
595 S. Hwy. 1
Bodega Bay, CA
707-875-3522
Seafood/American

Moss Beach Distillery Restaurant
(Peninsula)
140 Beach Way
Moss Beach, CA
650-728-5595
American

Old Chelsea (Tenderloin)
932 Larkin St.
San Francisco, CA
415-474-5015
British

Yorkshire Fish & Chips (East Bay)
248 Grand Ave.
Oakland, CA
510-251-0622
British

Hound favorites for fish-and-chips cravings: **Foley**'s version has light and crispy batter with medium-cut fries. *Missy P* also recommends chicken potpie and crab cakes. Plus, plenty of scotch and whiskey choices and they pour a decent Guinness. For impeccably authentic fish-and-chips—greasy and wrapped in newspaper—you can't beat the atmosphere at **Edinburgh Castle**. Order at the bar and they'll send someone over to **Old Chelsea** around the corner for your order. *Yuzo Watanabe* says that it's really more about the selection of beer and the authenticity of arriving in newspaper than about the quality of the food.

North of San Francisco, **Lucas Wharf Restaurant** is right on the water and has killer views, reports *svL*. Style is similar to

Barbara's (see below) but the fries are crisper and thinner. The scenery is not as good (you'll be sitting on a deck next to the takeout building and it often gets quite windy) but the fish is really fresh. Fish-and-chips is the Friday special at **Bab's Delta Diner** (skip the gloppy clam chowder). *Kent* says it's a steal for $6.95.

Yorkshire Fish & Chips, which seems mostly a lunch operation, does fried fish right. Three-piece servings of tilapia, catfish, cod, or snapper are generous portions. Crab cakes (four to an order) are excellent. *Shepherd B. Goode* says there's more on the menu, including an intriguing stuffed veg-and-meat-of-your choice Korean chimichanga. Coleslaw is very basic with just the right amount of mayo for a hint of creaminess—more alluded to than delivered—and nothing else. And for your shopping pleasure, check out their eclectic selection of used books.

Barbara's Fish Trap for extremely fresh, huge, lightly battered chunks of fish, and thick-cut fries; *svL* prefers the takeout shack to the dining room. If you choose the former, bring your own wine or go over to the brewery pub across the street and bring back some excellent draft beer to have with your meal. **Moss Beach Distillery** is, hands down, the best fish-and-chips *Azuki* has ever had. Huge pieces of perfectly prepared fish in a super-light batter served with a very generous amount of fries. Hounds generally prefer the view to the menu here, but hope runs high that Azuki's found the one good dish!

Flowers Plus Flours Equals
FLOWER FLOUR

Flower Flour (South Bay)
896 Willow St.
San Jose, CA
408-279-0843
Café

Combo florist shop and bakery, **Flower Flour** is for anyone who's bored of Starbucks, tired of standardized experience, and happy to support independent, creative businesses. This is baking as art, *Judith Hurley* tells us. Seating is at garden tables, surrounded by plants, orchids, and flowers. Don't miss the butter cookies and gorgeous cakes.

Late Night Drinks and **FONDUE** in North Beach

Golden Gate 303 (North Beach)
303 Columbus Ave.
San Francisco, CA
New American/Swiss

Golden Gate 303, a cool spot in North Beach, serves fondues (cheese with crab meat, chocolate, etc.), desserts, and lots of urbane cocktails till late. *BDA* says it's swank yet inexpensive (plus they show James Bond movies for added flair). Upstairs is art deco, while the downstairs lounge has a speakeasy feel.

FOODS FROM EVERYWHERE

South Seas Market (Peninsula)
612 San Mateo Ave.
San Bruno, CA
650-873-2813
Eclectic store

Look for the the storefront painted with flags of many countries and the window display of hot sauces and you'll know you've found **South Seas Market**. "Wander the aisles and see so many of the food products that I've read about on Chowhound from desperate folks seeking the taste from home," says *Melanie Wong*. Their business card says "Foods from your Homeland—Ireland, Brazil, South Africa, Argentina, Polynesian, Caribbean, and more!"

FRENCH CLASSICS in Hayward

A Street Cafe (East Bay)
1213 A St.
Hayward, CA
510-582-2558
French bistro

A Street Cafe is like a very delicious time warp says *Melanie Wong*, who tells us its cooking brings back memories of how French food used to be. Entrees hover around $18 and include choice of soup or salad. Cream of asparagus soup's wonderfully silky and smooth, Quenelles are tender and featherlight in creamy and intensely flavored sauce Nantua studded with juicy and succulent shrimp. Entrees, all winners, include *entrecote marchand de vin* (perfectly cooked with veggies that are just a little more than al dente to bring out flavors); fettucini primavera (full of shiitakes, snow peas, aspargus tips, broccoli florets in cheese cream sauce); sauteed prawns (perfectly cooked, served with mustard tarragon cream sauce and pasta); and duck breast with red wine and ginger sauce. Maine scallops in beurre blanc are the best of the entrees and worth the extra charge.

Desserts are even better than entrees: chestnut sundae is a scoop of housemade vanilla ice cream in chestnut sauce, garnished with creme Chantilly and bing cherries macerated in brandy, served in cookie tuile cup. Strawberry Napolean (served only in season) is thin, delicate phyllo pastry layered with pastry cream and fragrant, ripe strawberry slices, and is worth traveling for.

Presentations are simple, portions are generous, service is friendly and professional, and corkage is $15. Twilight dinners are offered from 5:30 to 6:15 p.m. for just $13.

FRIED CALAMARI Options

Betelnut (Marina)
2030 Union St.
San Francisco, CA
415-929-8855
Pan-Asian fusion/New American

Bistro Aix (Marina)
3340 Steiner St.
San Francisco, CA
415-202-0100
French bistro

Cha Cha Cha (Mission)
2327 Mission St.
San Francisco, CA
415-648-0504
Spanish/Cuban

Chilli Cha Cha Thai Noodle
   (Haight)
494 Haight St.
San Francisco, CA
415-552-2960
Thai

Duarte's Tavern (Peninsula)
202 Stage Rd.
Pescadero, CA
650-879-0464
American/Portuguese/Seafood

Kelly's Mission Rock (SOMA)
817 China Basin
San Francisco, CA
415-626-5355
New American

Picaro Cafe (Mission)
3120 16th St.
San Francisco, CA
415-431-4089
Spanish

Scala's Bistro (Union Square)
432 Powell St.
San Francisco, CA
415-395-8555
New American/Italian

Thirsty Bear Brewing Co.
   (Financial District)
661 Howard St.
San Francisco, CA
415-974-0905
Spanish

Yuet Lee Seafood Restaurant
   (Chinatown)
1300 Stockton St.
San Francisco, CA
415-982-6020
Chinese (Hong Kong)/Chinese
   (Cantonese)

Where to get fresh, crisp, greaseless, tender fried calamari.

   Mission Rock: lightly breaded and lightly fried, served with a
      sweet sauce
   Picaro: breading is not too heavy and it's fried to perfection,
      (*Yanira*)

Chilli Cha Cha Thai Noodle has good fried calamari, as does **Cha Cha Cha**—(always meaty, juicy, and perfectly fried, (*sunny*)

Yuet Lee: roast salt and pepper squid is amazing, (*Shreesh Trakar*)

Bistro Aix: fresh and very tender, tempura-fried (*MikeW*)

Betelnut: spicy, tossed with pieces of fried chili

Scala's: earth and surf includes fried calamari and vegetables

Thirsty Bear: crunchy, with tasty sauce

Duarte's: "the best I have ever tasted," says *DavidT*

○ **Duarte's Tavern:** *see also* **pp. 232, 294.**
○ **Scala's Bistro:** *see also* **p. 179.**

FRIED CHICKEN

Albertson's
www.albertsons.com
Store

Caesar's Chicken (East Bay)
19450 Hesperian Blvd.
Hayward, CA
510-786-9755
Southern

Chenery Park Restaurant
(Noe Valley)
683 Chenery St.
San Francisco, CA
415-337-8537
New American

The Cosmopolitan Cafe
(Embarcadero)
121 Spear St.
San Francisco, CA
415-543-4001
New American

Estrada's Mexican Restaurant
(Peninsula)
7440 Mission St.
Daly City, CA
650-755-1282
Mexican

Firefly Restaurant (Mission)
4288 24th St.
San Francisco, CA
415-821-7652
New American/Pan-Asian fusion

Jodie's (East Bay)
902 Masonic Ave.
Albany, CA
510-526-1109
Southern/Diner or Coffee shop

Merritt Restaurant & Bakery
(East Bay)
203 E. 18th St.
Oakland, CA
510-444-8680
Diner or Coffee shop

Porky's Pizza Palace (East Bay)
1221 Manor Blvd.
San Leandro, CA
510-357-4323
Pizza/American/Italian

Purple Plum (East Bay)
4228 Park Blvd
Oakland, CA
510-336-0990
New American/Southern

Willie Bird's Restaurant
   (Sonoma County)
1150 Santa Rosa Ave.
Santa Rosa, CA
707-542-0861
American

Willie Bird's is known for fine turkeys (their motto is "Turkey always and turkey all ways"), but the restaurant also serves perfect, simple fried chicken and great, homey sides. **Estrada's**, a Mexican restaurant, makes really tasty fried chicken (with Mexican-style macaroni). **Jodie's**, just off Solano, serves excellent fried chicken (choice of white or dark) on weekends only, with good, spicy fries on the side. We don't know about the pizza at **Porky's Pizza Palace**, but *Shep* calls their fried chicken the best in the East Bay, hands down. Opens at 3 p.m. Sunday through Friday, 1 p.m. Saturdays. **Chenery Park** has a $14 Monday night fried chicken special that not everyone raves over, but at least one hound describes perfect fried chicken and mashed potatoes. **Firefly**, known for homey comfort food staples, serves a half chicken that's very flavorful, with terrific texture, along with veggies and a biscuit for around $15 (*ChowFun*). The best fried chicken of his life at **Purple Plum**, *marzipan* reports, and great sides (e.g. mashed potatoes, green beans, and mac and cheese), too. There's always a wait, but it's well worth it. Fried chicken at the **Cosmopolitan**, when it's a special, is excellent. **Merritt** is an old favorite for quality East Bay fried chicken. It's crisp and juicy, and less expensive when ordered at Merritt's takeout counter. (Throwing a mega-bash? Get the 500-piece special!) Someone at **Albertson's Marina Village** store knows how to fry chicken; theirs ain't your average supermarket bird; its crispy crusted, well cooked and not at all dry. **Caesar's** garners kudos for flavorful and crisp crust, but occasionally turns out dry pieces. The fried chicken comes with a side of spaghetti plus bread. No seating, but there's a park across the street with picnic tables and kiddie train.

○ **Chenery Park Restaurant:** *see also* p. 10.
○ **Firefly Restaurant:** *see also* pp. 112, 217.

FROZEN CUSTARD Found!

Bec's Frozen Custard (Nevada)
670 Mt. Rose St.
Reno, NV
775-322-9332
Ice cream or Gelato

Willow Glen Frozen Yogurt Co.
 (South Bay)
1098 Lincoln Ave.
San Jose, CA
408-292-5961
Ice cream or Gelato

Frozen custard is much craved by Midwestern and East Coast expats, but the real thing hasn't previously been found in the Bay Area. Good news: **Willow Glen Frozen Yogurt Co.** (which also sells Treat ice cream) has it—though only in vanilla and only on Saturdays and Sundays (we hear they might serve it midweek on occasion, too). It seems to be the real deal: egg based, with 10 percent butterfat, silky and dense texture, and no iciness. The flavoring is a bit muted, but you can choose from several toppings for extra oomph. Another choice: Reno is a bit off the map for Bay Area chowhounds, but who wouldn't drive a few hours for real frozen custard? **Bec's Frozen Custard** in Reno has several flavors available each day (mango is intense) and also sells pints packed to go, reports *janet*.

Oh, FUDGE!

The Candy Jar Outlet
 (Potrero Hill)
2065 Oakdale Ave.
San Francisco, CA
415-550-8846
Chocolate/Candy shop

Z Cioccolato (North Beach)
474 Columbus Ave.
San Francisco, CA
415-395-9116
Chocolate/Candy shop

Z Cioccolato not only makes 20-plus varieties of fudge but carries every type of classic penny and hard candy you can imagine (including a large selection of Italian candies), chocolates, and even sugar-free candies. It's a fun store to visit, with super-friendly help and toys to play with! Fudge sells for $9.95 a pound and free samples are offered. The fudge at **The Candy Jar** outlet store is very creamy and since it's at the factory the prices are extremely reasonable—also, great truffles, toffee, peanut brittle, and loads more.

GREEK Roundup

Alekos (East Bay)
2 Theatre Sq. #105
Orinda, CA
925-254-5290
Greek

Estia Greek Eatery (North Beach)
1224 Grant Ave.
San Francisco, CA
415-433-1433
Greek

Mediterranean (East Bay)
1847 Willow Pass Rd. #B
Concord, CA
925-825-0608
Middle Eastern/North African

O'Mythos Greek Tavern
  (Russian Hill)
2424 Van Ness Ave.
San Francisco, CA
415-749-0341
Greek

Simply Greek (East Bay)
4060 Piedmont Ave.
Oakland, CA
510-428-0588
Greek

Estia has some intriguing dishes on the menu, and a wine list devoted to premium indigenous Greek grape varieties. When last we checked, the owner was doing the cooking, eager to share his cuisine: cold appetizers ($3) including unctuous and delicious baked eggplant and slightly mild taramosalata; *avgolemono* (lemony chicken soup) is very chickeny and grandmotherly, with the texture of Chinese rice porridge; *souzoukaki* (grilled lamb and beef meatballs that are braised in thick tomato sauce and served at room temperature) are tasty; and lavender and fig ice cream with sour cherries is sensational. They also do charbroiled whole fish and charbroiled *sheftalia* (Cypriot sausages of minced pork, lamb, and beef wrapped in lamb caul fat). Real good lamb chops.

On weeknights, **O'Mythos** offers little ethnic color or ambience (aside from a clean and pleasant dining room), but there's live music on weekends. Good pastitsio and generous portions; *chowhoundX* likes chicken souvlaki. And they deliver. **Simply Greek** is a casual little spot with friendly service. Fluffy, warm pitas are filled with moist and tender chicken souvlaki or gyro with delicious tzatziki sauce. Fries and salads are pretty standard. Dessert options: yogurt with honey and *risogalo* (rice pudding).

Two picks from *Bung*: **Alekos** for gyros, grilled meat wraps, stews, roast chicken, and great french fries; and **Mediterranean**, though not really Greek, makes good gyros, hummus, fasouli gigantes, and great lamb shwarma. See the Cuisine Index for more Greek tips.

GREENS Strategies

Greens Restaurant (Marina)
Fort Mason Bldg. A
San Francisco, CA
415-771-6222
Vegetarian/New American

The legendary vegetarian restaurant **Greens** might be overpriced and way past its prime these days, but *god of cookery* says the best strategy is to go on a Monday afternoon, and head straight to the Greens-to-Go counter where the soup's always good, sandwiches can be hit or miss, salads pretty good, and pastries, pies, and scones are great. Since the main restaurant is closed Mondays, you can enjoy the same gorgeous view for a fraction of the usual cost, agrees *Melanie Wong*. Greens-to-Go counter opens at 8 a.m. (for pastries and drinks only) with more items available as the kitchen stocks up for lunch. When the restaurant's open, there are some bar tables with bench seating inside or you can eat outside on a park bench with the seagulls. Dinner advice: stick with appetizers, salads, and desserts.

Multinational **GRILLED CALAMARI**

Delfina Restaurant (Mission)
3621 18th St.
San Francisco, CA
415-552-4055
Italian

Ramblas Tapas (Mission)
557 Valencia St.
San Francisco, CA
415-565-0207
Spanish

Kokkari (Financial District)
200 Jackson St.
San Francisco, CA
415-981-0983
Greek

Zarzuela (Russian Hill)
2000 Hyde St.
San Francisco, CA
415-346-0800
Spanish

Many nationalities make grilled calamari. Here's a world tour (around the Bay): **Delfina's** Italian take on fried calamari is a signature dish, sometimes served with white bean salad. Many hounds consider it definitive. **Ramblas** offers a Spanish spin, with squid a regular on their tapas menu. **Kokkari** makes a classic Greek calamari. Grilled cuttlefish, similar to squid and octopus, is a frequent special at **Zarzuela**, where it's tender and sweet with satisfying charry flavor, served with a creamy and very garlicky aioli (*Melanie Wong*).

- **Delfina Restaurant:** *see also* pp. 219, 294.
- **Zarzuela:** *see also* p. 210.

GRILLED SANDWICHES

Acme Chophouse (SOMA)
24 Willie Mays Plaza
San Francisco, CA
415-644-0240
Steak house

Arlequin (Civic Center)
384b Hayes St.
San Francisco, CA
415-626-1211
French sandwich shop

Il Massimo Del Panino
(Financial District)
441 Washington St.
San Francisco, CA
415-834-0290
Italian café

Palio Paninoteca (Sunset)
500 Parnassus Ave., on UCSF
campus
San Francisco, CA
415-681-9925
Italian café

Palio Paninoteca
(Financial District)
505 Montgomery St.
San Francisco, CA
415-362-6900
Italian

Zax Tavern (East Bay)
2826 Telegraph Ave.
Berkeley, CA
510-848-9299
New American

Acme Chophouse serves a Cubano with lots of tasty pork, cheese, and pickles. It's not the same as being in Miami but good, nonetheless, says *runningman*. **Zax** offers two grilled sandwiches as one of their lighter options (fillings vary with the changing menu). **Il Massimo** does a fine Italian sandwich pressed in a traditional Italian sandwich grill. Open weekdays from 11 a.m. to 3 p.m. **Arlequin** has a trio of sandwiches on its menu, mainly variations on Croque Monsieur. Big, cheesy, and cheap. At **Palio Paninoteca**, the café offshoot of Palio d'Asti, they grill the whole sandwich—filling and all—rather than running it open-faced under a broiler like Quizno's. They also have terrific soups. Their sandwiches are really large, so you'd probably want to order a half the first time to test your appetite, says *mcchowhound*.

○ **Arlequin:** *see also* **p. 75.**

HABANA: Better Than Havana?

Habana Bar & Restaurant (Russian Hill)
2080 Van Ness Ave.
San Francisco, CA
415-441-2822
Cuban

Chowhound Nametag: Limster

∘◯∘

Location:
North End, Boston (formerly San Francisco)

Occupation:
Molecular biologist

Cholesterol Level:
Excellent

Number of Visits to McDonald's in Past Decade:
1 or 2, maybe

Farthest Out of the Way Traveled Just for Chow: Never travel just for chow (because there's great chow everywhere waiting to be found).

Nabe Most Full of Explorable Unknown Chow:
Excelsior

Weight Management Tip:
Eat far away, walk home.

Guilty Pleasure:
Pleasure is never guilty.

Favorite Gelato Flavor:
Soursop at Marco Polo Gelato

Current Chow Obsession: Chocolates from single bean varietals and single regions or estates. Complex woods, smoke, and earth from Ecuadorian chocolates are current favorite.

Habana's theme is Havana, circa 1948, with three rooms decorated in Hemingway-period Cuban style, but it's subtle enough to work. The food's got lots of bright, tangy flavors; ceviche (shrimp and mango, jicama, papaya mint sauce), mango-glazed ribs, and duck with tamarind chile glaze were winners. Wonderful banana flan and even better lemon cream tart finish up the meal. Lots of Spanish wines on the wine list, many in the $22 range. Excellent service. Owner Sam DuVall boasts that "Havana [the real Havana, in Cuba] is great, but it doesn't have food as good as mine," and *mcchowhound* thinks he may actually be right.

Chow-Worthy **HAPPY HOURS**

El Rio (Mission)
3158 Mission St.
San Francisco, CA
415-282-3325
Eclectic pub

Fume Bistro (Napa County)
4050 Byway East
Napa, CA
707-257-1999
New American

Naked Fish (Marina)
2084 Chestnut St.
San Francisco, CA
415-771-1168
Japanese

Zinsvalley Restaurant
  (Napa County)
3253 Browns Valley Rd.
Napa, CA
707-224-0695
New American

It's easy to find happy hours with cheap drink deals. But here are top choices for that plus cheap—yet high-quality—eats.

In San Francisco, **Naked Fish** offers drinks (beer, sake), items from the *robata* (grill) and "sushi tinis" at half price from 5 to 7 p.m. every night. Recommended by *kate*: lamb and bacon-wrapped shrimp from the robata. **El Rio** serves free oysters on the half shell on Fridays from 5 to 7 p.m. In Napa, **Fume Bistro** serves free appetizers and $2 drinks 4:30 to 6 p.m. weekdays (also: the Five Buck Chuck at the bar on Monday nights, a terrific $10 burger for half price). **Zinsvalley** has half-price appetizers 5 to 7 p.m. daily. You'll have a hard time finding a better deal than smoked salmon or goat cheese and caviar for $5, or

calamari for $4 at Zinsvalley, says *rich*. It's easy to make a
light meal from their appetizer menu.

○ **Zinsvalley Restaurant:** *see also* **p. 317.**

The Mighty (Delicious)
HIMALAYAS

Little Nepal (Bernal Heights)
925 Cortland Ave.
San Francisco, CA
415-643-3881
Nepalese

Taste of the Himalayas
 (Sonoma County)
464 1st St. E.
Sonoma, CA
707-996-1161
Nepalese

Little Nepal fills a dining niche in Bernal Heights. It's a charming
and impeccably clean space, with friendly and knowledgable
service, so expect a crowd. Prices are a bit higher than usual for
San Francisco Indian food (Nepali is similar to Northern Indian), but the food's superior. Favorite appetizers include special chhoila (BBQ lamb or pork marinated in special spices),
samosa (veggie or lamb, deep fried but not greasy), mismass
pakauda (fried spinach and onion). The meat curries, *felice*
says, are winners—tender, not too oily, and each tastes quite
different. Best: *kukhurako ledo* (tandoori chicken cooked in
light cream cashew sauce, a little like chicken tikka masala)
and *jhinge machhako tarkari* (shrimp curry cooked in garlic,
ginger, tomato, onion, fish curry spices; slightly spicy, complex
flavor). Good vegetarian choices include *sabjiko tarkari* (potato
and cauliflower), sagko tarkari (mustard greens lightly sauteed
and slightly bitter with vibrant sauce), tofuko tarkari (tofu and
green beans in yellow curry; very rich, best to share with a
large group), and *chhyauo tarkari* (mushroom in traditional
spices; slightly spicy). Best from the tandoor is *poleko jhinge
machha* (tandoori shrimp, large, juicy, cooked just right); beware that *poleko khasi* (lamb tandoori) can be overcooked and
tough. Care is taken with sides: fragrant, whole-grain basmati,
great-textured naan, very spicy tomato chutney, beaten rice

and popped soybeans that taste like rice cakes, and have a texture like Grape Nuts add a sprinkle and texture to whatever dish you wish. Small wine and beer list and no corkage fees.

Taste of the Himalayas is a rare Nepalese restaurant in the heart of Wine Country, run by the same folks who used to own Sherpa restaurant in Glen Ellen. Outdoor tables are popular, so call ahead to try to reserve one. All dinners come with daal (souplike version) and naan (airy and nicely charred) *or* basmati (not so good). Beef momo (thin-skinned dumplings bursting with juice) are terrific. Kukhura ra saag (boneless chicken and spinach curry), made with moist thigh meat, is a great combination of long-simmered flavors; "the sauce infuses the chicken along with the barely cooked freshness of the spinach and green heat of the chilis," drools *Melanie Wong*. The eggplant curry is also real good, and a small wine list (including many by the glass) is well matched to the food (plus there's a decent beer selection). Atmosphere is warm.

Melanie Wong, who's been to both spots, offers this comparison: Taste of the Himalayas is tops for momo, tomato condiment, and chicken. Little Nepal excels at naan, basmati, mango lassi. But overall, she likes both places.

HISPANIC MARKETS

Casa Lucas Market (Mission)
2934 24th St.
San Francisco, CA
415-826-4334
Latin American store

La Palma Mexicatessen (Mission)
2884 24th St.
San Francisco, CA
415-647-1500
Mexican/Salvadoran store

La Carreta Store (East Bay)
4425 Treat Blvd. #M
Concord, CA
925-609-8208
Latin American store

Mercado Del Valle (East Bay)
1651 Monument Blvd.
Concord, CA
925-687-7032
Mexican store

Mercado Del Valle is a very clean, well-organized grocery store where produce is beautifully displayed and the meat counter offers quail, oxtails, tripe, goat, *every* part of the pig, and more.

Seafood includes tilapia and baby octopus. There's also a take-out counter with al pastor (pineapple properly perched atop the spit), fried whole tilapia, and your basic burritos, tacos, yummy horchata, good salsas, and even birria on weekends. **La Carreta** offers homemade tamales on Sundays, a meat counter with all those cuts you won't find at Safeway, and almost every chile you could imagine.

In San Francisco, **La Palma Mexicatessen** is always a great stop for takeout items (particularly carnitas, which you can buy by the pound), salsa, beans, rice, and prepared hot items. It not only sells fresh masa (made in back of the store) for tortillas or tamales, but fresh, thick, handmade tortillas. And if it has potato chips (or anything else fried), pick up a bag or two! There's some produce, chiles, spices, and canned goods, and quesos, too. For a larger selection of produce and dry goods, go to **Casa Lucas** on the next block.

○ **La Palma Mexicatessen:** *see also*

p. 214.

HOG ISLAND OYSTER BAR

Hog Island Oyster Bar (Embarcadero)
One Ferry Building, #11-1; Ferry Building Marketplace
San Francisco, CA
415-391-7117
Seafood

Hog Island Oyster Bar in the Ferry Building serves oysters fresh from the farm in a small room with a wall of windows overlooking the bay and ferry docks. Assorted raw oysters are $20 a dozen or $37 for two dozen, and come with mignonette, cocktail sauce, and lemon and lime wedges. Cooked dishes such as oyster stew are also available. Wine prices are very reasonable, and staff is quirky, friendly, and enthusiastic.

HONG KONG Worth a Trip to Millbrae

Hong Kong Pavilion (Peninsula)
1671 El Camino Real
Millbrae, CA
650-588-9972
Chinese (Hong Kong)/Chinese
    (Cantonese)/Chinese
    (Dim Sum)

Seafood Harbor Restaurant
    (Peninsula)
279 El Camino Real
Millbrae, CA
650-692-9688
Chinese (Cantonese)/Chinese
    (Dim Sum)/Chinese
    (Hong Kong)

Millbrae's quite the Hong Kong restaurant nexus; it's well worth a trip (especially now that BART runs to Millbrae). And, for those taking longer trips, Millbrae is an essential chow fueling area for flights out of SFO. *Melanie Wong* reports on her two favorite Hong Kong venues: Seafood Harbor and Hong Kong Pavilion.

Seafood Harbor is praised for interesting items (e.g., fried milk), good value set menus, and an admirably consistent kitchen. House special cold appetizers include superb jellyfish, almost crunchy little red octopi with a great dried-seafood texture (you want a bowl of these things next time you watch a baseball game), and uncommonly good stewed beef tendon. Best entries include crispy fried milk with crystal prawns (heartbreakingly delicious breaded blobs with sweet, light-green (from honeydew), custard inside, like the perfect custard donut), geoduck clams cooked two ways with yellow chives (a light touch preserves the sweet flavor and softly crunchy texture), salt and pepper style clam bellies with crispy tofu cubes (terrific plate of crunchy texture food, perfectly crunchy, excellent party snacks), smoked filet of cod (this dish actually originated in Vancouver, but is now ubiquitous at Hong Kong–style seafood restaurants. Since it takes approximately thirty minutes to cook to order, a multicourse banquet is the ideal time to try it), sauteed sugar snap peas with fresh scallop and dried conch (actually fresh conch, not dried, and so juicy and tender—and the kitchen does beautiful knife work, as evidenced by finely filigreed garnishes), and fresh taro with tapioca pearl dessert soup. One negative: some dishes can be very salty. For info on dim sum at Seafood Harbor, see *"Dim Sum* in the Peninsula and South Bay."

Melanie Wong also highly recommends **Hong Kong Pavilion**, especially for fabulous roasted squab with garlic soy sauce (at special weekday prices; juicier and larger than your average squab), Queen's clam (clear steamed with lightly seasoned soy sauce, served in the half shell, an amazing rendition), sauteed frog with minced pork and salted duck egg (a perfect oily-rich, garlicky, salty snack that'd be perfect with beer at a ballgame; best to share since it's intensely flavored). Even the complimentary flower tofu with ginger sauce is good, smooth and flavorful with a strong gingery bite.

HK Pavilion offers a special set dinner Monday through Friday only, with many choices. Especially good (as summarized by *Cynthia*): fried abalone supreme (braised in oyster sauce, with mustard greens; slightly smoky flavor, meaty texture), chiu chow preserved vegetable (lan cai), minced pork, and crisp-fried green beans, XO lean pork slices with celery and chili pepper flakes, garlic and supreme soy sauce frog (silky and falling from its tiny bones), honey pepper-chili oysters and broccoli ("deeply flavored yumminess, served with hot and crisp edges"), and claypot of chicken and chestnuts (deeply flavored and redolent of garlic). The set menu is in Chinese only, but we offer this translation, courtesy of *Limster* and *chibi*: Cost is $30.88 per person, which includes a choice of soup (chicken velvet bird's nest soup or fish swim bladder five snake), one individual abalone, and one choice from the following:

Secret sauce garlic fragrant ribs (made with pork chops)
Chiu chow preserved vegetable (lan cai), minced pork, string beans
Some kind of pepper and mustard pickle stir-fried minced fish
Salt fish, minced chicken, eggplant claypot
XO pork neck bones (but no bones)
Garlic and supreme soy sauce frog
Honey pepper-chili oysters
Japanese-style eggplant and beef short ribs
"Earth covered in gold" (salt baked shrimp)
Fish and kai lan (not sure which kind of fish—it translates as "big land")
Chestnut and chicken claypot
Dried scallops, prawns, and napa cabbage claypot
"Gold sign" fried spareribs (this is a sweet-and-sour dish)

French-style beef stew

Silver and gold (salted and preserved) eggs, pork strips, seasonal veggies

Scallop and tofu in black bean sauce

○ **Seafood Harbor Restaurant:** *see also* **p. 83.**

HONG KONG–STYLE COFFEE SHOPS (Weird, Delicious Amalgams)

ABC Bakery Cafe (Chinatown)
650 Jackson St.
San Francisco, CA
415-981-0685
Chinese (Hong Kong)

Cutlet House Cafe (Sunset)
3560 Taraval St.
San Francisco, CA
415-566-9035
Chinese (Hong Kong)

Hong Kong is full of casual restaurants serving dishes that are an amalgam of Chinese and Western flavors—macaroni with Spam, rice porridge with roast beef, pork with sweet corn—which have become homegrown comfort food for locals. Several places in San Francisco serve such dishes (best known: **ABC Bakery Cafe**), and most also offer old-fashioned American standards like roast beef, plus Chinese noodle soups and dumplings. *John* finds **Cutlet House** the best of the lot. His favorites: beef rice, curry chicken rice, and ketchup chicken rice.

HOT CHOCOLATE Heaven

Cafe Madeleine (Union Square)
43 O'Farrell St.
San Francisco, CA
415-362-1713
French café

Cafe Society (Napa County)
1000 Main St.
Napa, CA
707-256-3232
French café

Fleur De Cocoa (South Bay)
39 N. Santa Cruz Ave.
Los Gatos, CA
408-354-3574
Café

Tartine (Mission)
600 Guerrero St.
San Francisco, CA
415-487-2600
French café

When the weather turns cool, houndly thoughts turn to hot chocolate, preferably the thick, rich, melted-chocolate-bar-in-a-cup European variety. These are favorite spots for a serious hot chocolate fix: **Tartine** always has deep, rich hot chocolate on tap, and **Cafe Madeleine** makes what's essentially a chocolate ganache melted down with hot milk and topped with chocolate whipped cream (also great brown-sugar shortbread, personal-size pastries), reports *David Kaplan*. **Fleur de Cocoa** makes a great cup, as does **Cafe Society** in Napa, which serves the famous hot chocolate from Angelina in Paris in a pitcher containing two cups' worth. They also sell pricey French antiques here, so the atmosphere is tres chic, says *Jennie Sheeks*.

For decadent home consumption, try melting Valhrona 71 percent chocolate in milk, whisk in some Valrhona cocoa and a bit of sugar, cinnamon, and ground Sichuan pepper.

○ **Tartine:** *see also* **pp. 5, 8.**

HOT DOG!

Bongo Burger (East Bay)
2154 Center St.
Berkeley, CA
510-540-9014
Middle Eastern/North
 African/American

Bongo Burger (East Bay)
2505 Dwight Way
Berkeley, CA
510-540-9147
Middle Eastern/North
 African/American

Bongo Burger (East Bay)
1839 Euclid Ave.
Berkeley, CA
510-540-9573
Middle Eastern/North
 African/American

Colonel Mustard's Wild Dogs
 (East Bay)
3208 Grand Ave.
Oakland, CA
510-835-9281
American

Colonel Mustards Wild Dogs
(East Bay)
74 Moraga Way
Orinda, CA
925-258-0864
American

Gourmet Franks (Peninsula)
199 Stanford Shopping Ctr.
Palo Alto, CA
650-327-7246
American

Gumbah's Italian Beef
(Solano County)
138 Tennessee St.
Vallejo, CA
707-648-1100
Italian/Pizza/American

Happy Hound (South Bay)
15899 Los Gatos Blvd.
Los Gatos, CA
408-358-2444
American

Jimbo's Hot Dogs (Marin County)
4288 Redwood Hwy.
San Rafael, CA
415-472-7707
American

K & L Bistro (Sonoma County)
119 S. Main St.
Sebastopol, CA
707-823-6614
French bistro

Kasper's (East Bay)
4521 Telegraph Ave.
Oakland, CA
510-655-3215
American

Marvin Gardens (Peninsula)
1160 Old County Rd.
Belmont, CA
650-592-6154
American

Rosamunde Sausage Grill
(Haight)
545 Haight St.
San Francisco, CA
415-437-6851
American/German

Royal Frankfurter (Marin County)
811 4th St.
San Rafael, CA
415-456-5485
American

Sac's Tasty Hot Dogs
(Solano County)
2445 Springs Rd.
Vallejo, CA
707-642-2442
American

Stoddard's Brewhouse & Eatery
(South Bay)
111 S. Murphy Ave.
Sunnyvale, CA
408-733-7824
New American

Top Dog (East Bay)
2503 Hearst Ave.
Berkeley, CA
510-843-1241
American

Top Dog (East Bay)
5100 Broadway
Oakland, CA
510-601-1187
American

Top Dog (East Bay)
2534 Durant Ave.
Berkeley, CA
510-843-5967
American

Top Dog No 5 (East Bay)
2235 Milvia St.
Berkeley, CA
510-845-1660
American

Hot dogs, tube steaks, sausages . . . call them what you will.
They are most at home at baseball games, and, indeed, local
ballparks offer good options (available at the game or via mail
order). SBC Park's Chicago hot dog stands use Skinless Big
City Reds, which are beefy, smokey, and assertively spiced but
not particularly hot (more info at www.bigcityreds.com). SBC
Park's other stands serve the skinless Giants Dog, made by
Alpine Meats, available at local supermarkets under the Giants
label, along with Polish sausage and hot links (Alpine also now
has a premium line of natural casing sausages and hot dogs
sold under its own name, which are also excellent—more info at
www.alpinemeats.com). Oakland's Network Associates Coliseum
serves dogs made by Miller's, with more snap but subtler flavor
than Big City Reds (more info at www.millerhotdogs.com). The following are some hound-recommended hot dog home runs outside the ballpark, arranged by region.

In San Franciso, **Rosamunde Sausage Grill** is the natural favorite
for all things sausagey. In the North, **Gumbah's** Chicago dogs are
Vienna Beefs, but they're skinless, which isn't very authentic.
Vienna Beef's Polish sausage does have a natural casing,
though, and you can order it with "the works": mustard, relish,
chopped onions, a quarter spear of dill pickle, two slices of
Roma tomato, celery salt, and two whole sport peppers. The
sausage is unfatty yet moist and has a slight sweet edge to the
cure, and fries are excellent. Note their weird hours: Gumbah's
is open Monday through Saturday from 11 a.m. to 2:20 p.m. (no,
that's not a typo!). And definitely call ahead—the owner keeps
threatening to retire. Also in Vallejo, *Steve N* prefers the Tasty
Dog at **Sac's**, which resembles the signature dog at Oakland's
much-beloved Kasper's (see below). Cheese, chili, and saurkraut

are available, and chili dogs are so generously topped that you'll want to take knife and fork to them. Sac's closes around 5 or 6 p.m., earlier on Sundays. **Jimbo's** in San Rafael is good for franks, Polish, hot sausages and an ungodly assortment of stuff to pile on top. According to *rich*, **Royal Frankfurter** is pure hot dog heaven. And *ed k* likes **K & L Bistro** in Sebastopol for housemade boudin blanc and frites—not exactly a hot dog, but definitely a sausage. Don't expect a burger joint, it's tres French. Also recommended there: fresh fish, small but innovative wine list. Closed Sundays and Mondays.

South of San Francisco (in the Peninsula and South Bay), **Gourmet Franks'** dogs in Palo Alto are pricey but worth it, according to *claire*, who especially recommends Frank's Chicago Vienna dog. **Stoddard's** in Sunnyvale is a favorite for excellent hot sausage sandwiches. **Marvin Gardens** in Belmont serves wicked flame-grilled Louisiana hots, says *Bung*, and **Happy Hound** in Los Gatos is a big *Ken Hoffman* fave. And, with a few branches in the East Bay, **Top Dog's** the big favorite, but **Bongo Burger** in Berkeley is a fine alternative, and *Bung* recommends **Colonel Mustard**'s in Orinda. If **Kasper's** has reopened by the time you read this (give them a call), definitely make a pilgrimmage!

○ **K & L Bistro:** *see also* p. 244.
○ **Rosamunde Sausage Grill:** *see also* pp. 17, 236.

Asian Fusion at **HOUSE**

House (North Beach)
1230 Grant Ave.
San Francisco, CA
415-986-8612
Pan-Asian fusion/New American

House serves up Asian fusion foods like fried halibut with garnish of glittering, neon-orange pearls of tobiko and spicy tartar sauce, top notch asparagus with sweet Asian-style sauce and deep-fried salmon rolls with Chinese mustard. All meals start with an Asian-style amuse-bouche of delicious marinated cucumbers, says *Stanley Stephan*. Great drinks include a food-friendly wine list, beers, nonalcoholic offerings like Navarro grape juices, lichee black iced tea, and brewed Chinese teas (monkey picked ti kwan yin, jasmine pearl, keemum mao feng, pu erh, lapsang souchong, dragonwell, green rice flower, chrysanthemum and peppermint). Loud, bustling atmosphere.

Fragrantly Spicy **HUNANESE**

Chili Garden Restaurant
 (East Bay)
3213 Walnut Ave.
Fremont, CA
510-792-8945
Chinese (Hunan)

Hunan Gourmet (South Bay)
163 S. Murphy Ave.
Sunnyvale, CA
408-739-8866
Chinese (Hunan)/Chinese
 (Shanghai)/Chinese (Sichuan)

Hunan's cuisine is "xiang-lah" (fragrant-spicy), vs. Sichuan's "mah-lah" (numbing-spicy). The former's not as common, but hounds have come up with two alternatives. **Chili Garden Restaurant** serves authentic Hunanese, and *tanspace* reports on three especially toothsome dishes. House special Chili Garden Beef is red-roasted (hong-shao) whole beef shank, sliced, then stir-fried with red and green peppers and onions in hot-chili oil. Dry-fried beans are stir-fried to perfection with not an additional drop of oil to be found on the large plate, nonspicy, yet flavorful. And sour cabbage bamboo pork is spicy and great with rice. As usual, there are two menus, one in English and one in Chinese, and most of the "authentic" dishes are on the Chinese menu. So ask for help with translations!

Hunan Gourmet serves good, traditional, regional Chinese. Again, authentic dishes are, alas, in Chinese. Lunch recommendations from *Dynos*: beef with caraway seed, pork with pickled mustard green, tofu with homemade pickled mustard green, hunan stir-fry, and dried-cured pork belly with green garlic. For dinner, they make a good fishhead stew in claypot. Cooking is authentically oily.

HUNGARIAN Find

Bistro E Europe (with Gypsy
    Flavor) (Mission)
4901 Mission St.
San Francisco, CA
415-469-5637
Hungarian

DJ's Bistro (East Bay)
1825 Sutter St.
Concord, CA
925-825-3277
Czech/Central/Eastern European

DJ's Bistro makes much better Hungarian food than better-known **Bistro E Europe**, insists *VDP*, including great schnitzel and very beefy goulash rich in paprika. They also serve the original Czech Budweiser (called Czechvar in the US). But Quirky Bistro E Europa has its devoted fans for homey Romany-inflected dishes cooked to order from scratch by a lone chef. That means waits can be long and service slow, and like most home cooking, many dishes never come out quite the same way twice. An open mind and patience will be repaid with terrific food and good cheer. Mushroom paprikash varies in style from night to night, but is always excellent. Dishes tend to need salt at the table. The improvisatory mood can be an unexpected boon; chef Julia coped with an unexpected power outage by cooking delicious organic vegetables and marinted lamb on a propane grill. Food here is cooked with love that extends to the dining experience; slow down, suspend expectations, and you can find yourself transported to another time, another continent. "Maybe you will find that there's a little Gypsy in your soul," says *Cynthia*. There's live Roma music on Fridays and Saturdays, and if you stay late enough, *RedRob* reports that you might even get to party down and dance in the aisles with the person who cooked your food.

Bay Area Monster **ICE CREAM** Survey

A-Lot-A Gelato & More
   (Peninsula)
1301 Old County Rd., #4
Belmont, CA
650-594-0540
Ice cream or Gelato

A-Lot-A Gelato & More (SOMA)
635 8th St.
San Francisco, CA
415-487-1530
Ice Cream or Gelato

Bombay Ice Creamery (Mission)
552 Valencia St.
San Francisco, CA
415-431-1103
North Indian ice cream or Gelato

California Gold Rush (North
   Beach)
Union, between Columbus and
   Powell
San Francisco, CA
Ice cream or Gelato

Ciao Bella Gelato (SOMA)
685 Harrison St.
San Francisco, CA
415-541-4940
Ice cream or Gelato

Fiorello's Italian Ice Cream
   (Marin County)
3100 Kerner Blvd.
San Rafael, CA
415-459-8004
Ice cream or Gelato

Gelato Paradiso
   (Santa Cruz County)
26 Hangar Way # B
Watsonville, CA
831-761-3198
Ice cream or Gelato

Joe's Ice Cream (Richmond)
5351 Geary Blvd.
San Francisco, CA
415-751-1950
Ice cream or Gelato

Marco Polo Italian Ice Cream
   (Sunset)
1447 Taraval
San Francisco, CA
415-731-2833
East Asian ice cream or Gelato

Mitchell's Ice Cream (Mission)
688 San Jose Ave.
San Francisco, CA
415-648-2300
Ice cream or Gelato

Pizzelle (Financial District)
50 Post St., in Crocker Galleria
San Francisco, CA
415-362-2228
Pizza/Italian

Real Ice Cream (South Bay)
3077 El Camino Real
Santa Clara, CA
408-984-6601
Indian ice cream or Gelato

Rick's Ice Cream (Peninsula)
3946 Middlefield Rd.
Palo Alto, CA
650-493-6553
Ice cream or Gelato

Tango Gelato (Pacific Heights)
2015 Fillmore St.
San Francisco, CA
415-346-3692
Argentinian ice cream or Gelato

Straus Family Creamery
(Marin County)
5600 Petaluma Marshall Rd.
Marshall, CA
415-663-5464
Farm or Farmstand

Treat Ice Cream Co.
(South Bay)
11 S. 19th St.
San Jose, CA
408-292-9321
Ice cream or Gelato

Swensen's Ice Cream
(Russian Hill)
1999 Hyde St.
San Francisco, CA
415-775-6818
Ice cream or Gelato

Tucker's Super Creamed
Ice Cream (East Bay)
1349 Park St.
Alameda, CA
510-522-4960
Ice cream or Gelato

Where to satisfy your ice cream cravings? Here's a region-by-region breakdown of your best options.

In San Francisco, **Bombay Ice Creamery** is a Chowhound mecca—even New Yorker *Jim Leff* makes a beeline to this spot for saffron milkshakes. Other favorite flavors are cardamom, fig, saffron pistachio, and rose. You'll find interesting tropical flavors at much loved **Mitchell's**, as well as at **Marco Polo. California Gold Rush** features Mitchell's ice cream, smoothies, shakes, and "made to orders" (sundaes maybe?). For gelato, **Tango Gelato** is a huge favorite, and **Ciao Bella Gelato** has a small shop South of Market (hours are unpredictable, so call ahead). **Pizzelle**, hidden in the food court at the Crocker Galleria, carries Ciao Bella gelato in at least seven flavors (skip their pizza, though). **A-Lot-A-Gelato & More** sells addictive gelato truffles called "truffelatos." The filling's ice cream–like with bits of fruit. In the perpetually foggy Richmond District, **Joe's Ice Cream** makes its own version of It's Its (ice cream cookie sandwich), and there's always a flavor of the month (pumpkin's a fave in the fall). For low fat parlor ice cream, **Swensen's** original location can't be beat, and the ice cream making equipment is right in the front window for extra entertainment value.

In the Peninsula, South Bay and Santa Cruz: **Real Ice Cream** is a South Bay favorite for Indian chaat and ice cream. Go for exotic flavors like cardamon and mango. **Tucker's** makes great ice cream plus astounding ice cream sauces in two flavors, caramel and bittersweet chocolate that don't harden when applied to ice cream. (*Ruth Lafler* says it's "simply the best jarred chocolate sauce I've ever had. Better to my taste than Scharffen Berger or Michael Recchuiti.") For traditional ice cream in seasonal flavors, head to **Rick's** in Palo Alto. His cranberry walnut ice cream is zingy and tart; egg nog is rich and well spiced (with a shot of rum flavor); toasted almond and kulfi have terrific, deep flavor (though marred by soggy nuts—perhaps better when fresher). Rum raisin for the holidays features plump alcoholic raisins soaked in rum. Mango ice is pulpy with fresh fruit puree, and orange ice is very intense with good acid balance. Look for the much loved **Gelato Paradiso** brand, in stores and restaurants in the Watsonville/Santa Cruz area. **Treat Ice Cream** is actually the secret behind Palo Alto Creamery, Tucker's, Sweet Retreat and Lunardi's house brand, where it's sold under the store's label in one-gallon tubs. *Oceanlover* says their low fat version is the best you can do for supermarket ice cream. Also check out "truffelatos" (see above) from A-Lot-A-Gelato & More in Belmont.

In Marin, **Fiorello's** supplies Ravenous with gelato (coffee and ginger are among the wonderful flavors). **Straus Family Creamery**, the organic dairy in Marin, is rolling out certified organic super premium ice cream in three flavors: vanilla bean, Dutch chocolate, and raspberry. Look for it at Whole Foods, Wild Oats, and other local markets (more info at www.strausmilk.com).

○ **Joe's Ice Cream:** *see also* pp. 26, 285.
○ **Mitchell's Ice Cream:** *see also* pp. 20, 26, 285.

Enchanting **INCANTO**

Incanto Italian Restaurant & Wine Bar (Noe Valley)
1550 Church St.
San Francisco, CA
415-641-4500
Italian

Incanto has racked up awards for its wine cellar, and the kitchen's putting out food to match. Bean alert: it does a fantastic job with legumes. Other winners, according to *Windy*: sand dabs with capers, escarole salad (with ricotta, almonds, and grapes), squid ink pasta ("the absolute juiciest squid I've ever tasted"), tomato and cheese pasta (with the texture of gnocchi but none of the heaviness), and campari grapefruit sorbetto (a perfect dessert for someone who could not have stood another bite). Twenty-five wines are available by the half glass, glass, or half liter, plus several hundred bottles. Good quality stemware comes labeled to help you keep selections straight. The bar offers wine flights, including a dessert flight and mystery flights. They do a special wine program weeknights, 5:30 to 6:30 p.m

○ **Incanto Italian Restaurant & Wine Bar:** *see also* p. 294.

Superior **INDIAN GROCERIES**

Bazaar (Solano County)
1601 Marine World Pkwy., #250
Vallejo, CA
707-644-1294
S. East Asian store

Chaat Paradise (Peninsula)
165 E. El Camino Real
Mountain View, CA
650-965-1111
Indian

India Cash & Carry (South Bay)
1032 E. El Camino Real
Sunnyvale, CA
408-735-7383
Indian store

India Foods (Peninsula)
650 San Bruno Ave. E.
San Bruno, CA
650-583-6559
Indian store

Nilgiris (Peninsula)
1058 D Shell Blvd.
Foster City, CA
650-212-0608
Indian store

Novelty Indian Grocery & Spices
  (Peninsula)
1469 El Camino Real
  (next to Mustang City)
Belmont, CA
650-596-0707
Indian store

Stores with a nice selection of fresh Indian ingredients and prepared foods: **Bazaar** in Vallejo carries fresh herbs and produce, kosher chickens, fresh-baked Afghan bread on Thursdays, many freshly made sweets, an array of ice creams, halal meats, vast bags of frozen goat stew meat, buttery yellow vats of ghee, a huge selection of Indian frozen foods, and a mind boggling selection of packaged snacks, all overseen by an anxious-to-please owner. **India Foods** offers extra freshness and variety—a large place with deep selection, but **India Cash & Carry** is truly massive and adjacent to several quality Indian restaurants. **Novelty Indian Grocer** is tiny (with commensurately small inventory), but advertises "the only chaat in Belmont," including pani puri. Both **Chaat Paradise** and **Nilgiris** bake fresh roti every day.

○ **India Foods:** *see also* p. 57.

A Comparison of Berkeley
INDIAN LUNCH BUFFETS

Indian Supermarket (East Bay)
Shattuck Square, between 21 and
   48 Shattuck Sq.
Berkeley, CA
Indian Store

Kamal Palace Indian Cuisine
   (East Bay)
2175 Allston Way
Berkeley, CA
510-848-9907
Indian

Khana Peena Indian Cuisine
   (East Bay)
2136 Oxford St.
Berkeley, CA
510-849-0149
North Indian

Priya Indian Cuisine (East Bay)
2072 San Pablo Ave.
Berkeley, CA
510-644-3977
Indian

There are a number of Indian restaurants near UC Berkeley offering lunch buffets. None are great, but that doesn't mean it's not worth obsessing over which is best. **Khana Peena** is around $6.00 and throws in a soda, plus it offers three chutneys and pickles. Stick with the veggie dishes as chicken can be very disappointing and lamb curry is just decent, says *philosopher*. KP's

Chowhound Nametag: Chowfish

○◯○

Neighborhood:
Lafayette

Occupation:
Financial advisor

Cholesterol Level:
Before or after I discovered Chowhound?

Number of Visits to McDonald's in Past Decade: Zero; did go fourteen years ago when my son was young and liked to play in the balls.

Weight Management Tip:
If you saw me you wouldn't ask.

Guilty Pleasure:
Potato chips

Favorite Mail Order Chow: Harry and David pears: harryanddavid.com; otherwise we're so spoiled in the Bay Area we don't need to mail order—it's all right here!

buffet is available late, at least until 3:30, and staff was even replenishing it at 3 p.m. **Kamal Palace**, just around the corner from Khana Peena, produces very stewy flavors, almost like Indian leftovers in a good way. **Priya**'s buffet is head and shoulders above the pack, insists buffet buff *Kathleen Mikulis*. Lunch buffet runs $6.99 (check the East Bay Express for dinner buffet coupons). Here, for your consideration, are the six reasons *Alexandra* insists that Priya's best: (1) all-you-can-eat free naan is good, and they also offer fresh masala dosa; (2) great chicken tikka masala; (3) large salad/vegetable selection; (4) best onion pakora ever; (5) really large selection of dishes; (6) very attentive service (taking away old dishes, bringing more bread).

Indian Supermarket in downtown Berkeley has perhaps the cheapest buffet in the area: $3.99 for lunch or dinner. Quality's not great, but there's an intriguing fried item resembling hush puppies—golf ball-sized pieces of savory dough fried to a golden brown which taste a lot like long, tubular Chinese crullers, but with a hint of curry taste and a bit on the greasy side, so they're best fresh out of the hot fat. They're very interesting and worth checking out, says *the jealous sound*.

INDO-PAK Treasure

Amber India (Peninsula)
2290 El Camino Real, #9
Mountain View, CA
650-968-7511
North Indian

Amber India (South Bay)
1140 Olsen Dr., in Santana Row
   Mall
San Jose, CA
North Indian/S. East Asian

Annapoorna (Peninsula)
2299 S. El Camino Real
San Mateo, CA
650-345-4366
South Indian

Bombay Bazar (Mission)
548 Valencia St.
San Francisco, CA
415-621-1717
Indian store

Bombay Gardens (East Bay)
5995 Mowry Ave.
Newark, CA
510-774-6945
North Indian/South Indian

Bombay Gardens (Peninsula)
172 E. 3rd Ave.
San Mateo, CA
650-548-9966
Indian

Chaat Cafe (East Bay)
1902 University Ave.
Berkeley, CA
510-845-1431
North Indian

Chaat Cafe (East Bay)
3954 Mowry Ave.
Fremont, CA
510-796-3408
North Indian

Chaat Cafe (SOMA)
320 3rd St.
San Francisco, CA
415-979-9946
S. East Asian

Chutney (Tenderloin)
511 Jones St.
San Francisco, CA
415-931-5541
North Indian/Pakistani

Coconut Hill (East Bay)
39207 Cedar Blvd.
Newark, CA
510-742-8704
Indian store

Darbar (Russian Hill)
1412 Polk St.
San Francisco, CA
415-359-1236
Pakistani/North Indian

Favorite Indian Restaurant
 (East Bay)
1235 A St.
Hayward, CA
510-583-7550
North Indian

Ganesh Restaurant (Mission)
2700 16th St.
San Francisco, CA
415-437-9240
North Indian/Indian

Pakwan Restaurant (Mission)
3182 16th St.
San Francisco, CA
415-255-2440
Pakistani/North Indian

Shalimar Restaurant (Tenderloin)
532 Jones St.
San Francisco, CA
415-928-0333
Pakistani

Sue's Indian Cuisine (South Bay)
895 Willow St.
San Jose, CA
408-993-8730
North Indian

Sultan (Tenderloin)
339 Taylor St., in Ramada Hotel
San Francisco, CA
415-775-1709
Pakistani/North Indian

A huge round of Indian/Pakistani feasts: **Darbar** cooks Pakistani and Punjabi specialties to order, with spiciness adjusted to taste. The following are recommended: plain paratha, tandoori prawns, chapli kebab (pan-fried patties of beef and lamb, lentils, herbs, and spices), achar gosht (goat curry with peppers, mango pickles, and spices), daal makhani (mild lentils with creamy sauce—a real down-home preparation), nargisi kofta (boiled eggs wrapped in minced beef, in creamy yellow curry sauce; a special order), sarson ka saag (mustard greens and spinach pureed with spices), makke ki roti (corn roti, similar to corn tortillas; a special order traditionally eaten with sarson ka saag), palak paneer, lamb samosas, a thin fried lamb and lentil cake, nicely spiced biryani, and—a hazy but intriguing tip—the first chicken curry dish on the menu, "which is similar to a tikka masala, centered around tandoori chicken pieces, but with a smokier, somewhat less creamy sauce," according to *JohnnyP*.

Pakwan's Mission location does a nice job with both vegetable and meat curries. Recommended: seekh kebab (well spiced and juicy), chicken achar (excellent sauce), lamb kofta vindaloo, malai (vegetarian) kofta (with deep, smoky tomato yogurt curry sauce), and peppers in tamarind curry sauce.

Shalimar can be inconsistent, but when it's on, it's an all-around favorite. Its curries are usually on the hot side. Outstanding dishes include: lamb chops, seekh kabob (juicy and well-spiced beef), murgh tikka sultana (grilled whole chicken leg), lamb brains masala (brains finely minced—texture likened to tofu—with much black cardamom), nihari (braised beef curry with intricate, subtle flavor—not too spicy—and deeply beefy sauce), goat curry (Thursday special; not on menu, must ask for it), daal masala (made with larger yellow lentils, some left whole), mili jubi sabzi (vegetable curry, not strongly flavored, but vegetables extremely fresh), plain naan (best reordered throughout meal so you always get it hot and fresh), galub jamun (deep-fried dough balls in sweet syrup). Ask to have it reheated.

Sultan cooks each dish to order (so specify your spice level). Decor and service are several steps up from neighborhood standards like Shalimar, but prices are just as low. Food here is almost always cooked with care, made with fresh, high-quality ingredients, and full of flavor. Recommendations from the lunch menu: prawn curry (mild, deeply flavored sauce redolent of shellfish; a special order), palak paneer (spinach, tomato, and fresh pressed cheese; each element retains its flavor), lamb kofta (well spiced and moist, in cashew-yogurt sauce; listed on the menu under chicken dishes, but now made with lamb), seekh kabob (made with lamb, not beef; well seasoned and juicy), charga chicken (fried, spice-coated white-meat chicken is moist), boondi raita (chickpea-flour puffs in yogurt; "a lot of fun to eat," says *nja*), boori, samosas (meat samosas wrapped in crackly, crunchy filo dough that retains its crunch well), makhani chicken (aka butter chicken; buttery and tomatoey, more refined than most versions), and housemade kulfis (milk chocolate with bits of chocolate and pistachio, and keser pista— intense saffron flavor with pistachios) Other recommendations: chicken korma, mutton dum pukhta (in a creamy curry sauce with tomato, made from housemade yogurt), dal palak (soupy moong dal with spinach; homey and full of flavor) Sultan is open daily, 7 a.m. to 10:30 a.m., 11 a.m. to 3 p.m., 5 p.m. to 11 p.m.

At **Chutney**, *squid-kun* recommends tandoori fish, "great with plain naan . . . be sure not to skip the onion, orange with spice-laden ghee." **Chaat Cafe** has a burgeoning empire. The Berkeley location makes great chicken tikka masala and naan plus much loved strawberry lassi. Opinions differ on whether the large San Francisco branch matches others in the chain, and several hounds feel the Fremont location is best—perhaps because it serves a large Indian immigrant population. Buffet selection at **Bombay Gardens** in Newark is huge, with three rows of buffet tables displaying at least twenty-five hot dishes, plus soups, dosai, salads, chutneys, sauces, desserts, and drinks. Especially good are lamb and spinach curry, spinach pakoras, and mango ice cream (*Han Lukito*). Naan is brought fresh to the table; plates are removed and water glasses refilled promptly; and the restaurant is beautifully turned out. It's much larger than the San Mateo Bombay Gardens location.

Annapoorna offers complex and well-spiced versions of standard South Indian vegetarian dishes. Recommended: mixed vegetable pakoras, onion and spinach vada (intense and complex flavors and lot of heat), mysore masala dosa (tender, crisp crepe with potato-veggie blend and a layer of intensely flavored, very, very hot chutney), onion and chili utthappam, channa bhatura (complexly spiced, soft and luscious chickpeas topped with a puffy fried bread), and carrot halwah (fresh taste, lightly sweetened), plain halwah (made with ground almonds and cashews and a heavy does of saffron, served warm).

Amber in Mountain View has been on a downhill slide, but its newer sister restaurant in San Jose's swanky Santana Row shopping center is much better, though more expensive. The menu's been tweaked to appeal to locals, but serious cooking shines through. Goat cheese aloo kebab (fried potato patties with mint chutney and a little goat cheese inside) works well; papdi chaat is formed in a cylinder and drizzled with tamarind chutney, but tastes like what you'd find at a good chaat shop; and butter chicken is subtly flavored but satisfying. Ambience is slightly over the top, with simulated night sky and techno music.

Judith Hurley says the Willow Glen location of **Sue's Indian Cuisine** is much improved. "We had a lovely visit with the owner, came away feeling almost as if we had visited someone's home." Samosas are especially good. Mixed tandoori grill and matter paneer are excellent with good-size portions. Dinners include naan and raita.

Optimistically named **Favorite Indian Restaurant** had flown under chowhound radar, but *WLA* found that this great little place lives up to its name. Everything sampled has been good: starters of samosas (both meat and potato-pea), chili pakora, naan stuffed with onions or fruits and nuts, really excellent butter chicken (shredded roast chicken in tomato-butter-saffron cream sauce), tandoori chicken, and an interesting sounding tandoori eggplant stewed with tomato cream sauce.

Ganesh's husband-wife team make pretty darn good Indian food, says *Liz*. Excellent samosas have well-seasoned filling and were still crispy even as takeout, and lamb vindaloo and wonderful mango pickles were among other winners. Evening business is pretty slow, so getting a table's no problem.

If you're cooking at home and don't have time to make your own paneer (it takes a day or so for the whey to drain, leaving firm cheese curds), **Bombay Bazaar** in San Francisco and **Coconut Hill** in Newark both carry vacuum-packed paneer in their refrigerator cases.

Also see "Alhamra Vs. Pakwan: *South Asian* Chow-Off," and the Cuisine Index for lots more South Asian chow.

○ **Chutney:** see also **p. 49.**
○ **Darbar:** see also **p. 49.**
○ **Shalimar Restaurant:** see also **p. 50.**

ISLAMIC CHINESE

Darda Seafood Restaurant
  (South Bay)
296 Barber Ct.
Milpitas, CA
408-433-5199
Chinese (Muslim)

Fatima (Peninsula)
1208 S. El Camino Real
San Mateo, CA
650-554-1818
Chinese (Muslim)

Fatima (South Bay)
1132 S. De Anza Blvd.
San Jose, CA
408-257-3893
Chinese (Muslim)

Old Mandarin Restaurant (Sunset)
3132 Vicente St.
San Francisco, CA
415-564-3481
Chinese (Muslim)/Chinese
  (Beijing)

If you're in the mood for something different, Islamic Chinese, heavy on lamb and noodles and heavy, satisfying preparations, isn't quite like anything else. Both locations of **Fatima** earn a big thumbs up from *Melanie Wong* for its Islamic Chinese dishes, best of which seem to be lamb with pickled cabbage warm pot (a homey prep of thin-sliced lamb blanched in hot broth with winter napa cabbage in a soup tureen, with a surprisingly delicate taste for a preparation that also feels so homey), mu shu beef with egg topping (way different from Americanized mu shu, it's an intensely flavored stir-fry of slivers of beef with red and green peppers, onions, scallions, and pressed and smoked tofu shreds, crowned with a browned, fluffy, and moist, thick omelet—a messy, but delicious dish), lamb with leek (dusky and exotic spicing and the flavor of a hot, well-seasoned wok made it special), three flavors dough slice chow mein (which turns out to be housemade knife-shaved noodles, tossed with slivers of beef, chicken, and prawns for the three flavors), water spinach with garlic sauce (seasonal, not on menu), bean curd with spicy sauce, sesame bread with green onion, and for dessert, red bean pancake. Sole clunker: sliced fish (fresh, not fried) with spicy sauce. All meats are halal and no pork is served, of course.

Darda calls itself a seafood restaurant but also does great things with meat. There are three set banquet menus: one is $98, two are $168, but most of the banquet dishes are available on the regular menu, as well. Recommended from the $168 set menus: lamb with pickled cabbage warm pot (just the right amount of sour—a real treat on a cold day, says *Yimster*), braised oxtail (outstanding, with good texture and a red date flavor), shrimp with candied walnuts (not in a mayonnaise-based sauce), lamb with green onions, sea cucumber with ox tendon (tendon cooked just right), sliced sea bass with fried garlic (served on fire plate to keep it hot without overcooking). Dishes are served with terrific sesame bread studded with green onions.

At **Old Mandarin Restaurant,** *YinShiNanNu* reports that excellent hotpots are really close to those once tried in Beijing. A wide variety of meats (including organs) and vegetables are available for simmering in the broth, and lamb and pickled cabbage (add the latter in at the end) are particularly recommended.

Celebrate with **ITALIAN**

Acquerello Restaurant (Russian Hill)
1722 Sacramento St.
San Francisco, CA
415-567-5432
Italian

When hounds are looking for a celebration-type restaurant in San Francisco, **Acquerello** is often mentioned. *Victoria Libin*, who puts the restaurant in a league with La Folie, describes the consistently good food as "high-end Lombardian" with an excellent wine list which includes some rare great wines like Moroder Dorico Ross Conero from the Marche. Service is formal but not stuffy. Favorite dishes: made-to-order risotto finished with aceto tradizionale twenty-five-year-old balsamic vinegar, cured raw swordfish and veal with radicchio and taleggio.

Good Neighborhood **ITALIANS**

Bella Restaurant Trattoria
 (Richmond)
3854 Geary Blvd.
San Francisco, CA
415-221-0305
Italian

Bertucelli's La Villa Gourmet
 (South Bay)
1319 Lincoln Ave.
San Jose, CA
408-295-7851
Italian deli

Capellini Ristorante (Peninsula)
310 Baldwin Ave.
San Mateo, CA
650-348-2296
Italian

Dopo (East Bay)
4293 Piedmont Ave.
Oakland, CA
510-652-3676
Italian

Mangia Bene (East Bay)
1170 Arnold Dr., #116
Martinez, CA
925-228-9123
Italian

Mezza Luna (Peninsula)
459 Prospect Way
Princeton-by-the-Sea, CA
650-728-8108
Italian

Pasta Moon (Peninsula)
315 Main St., C
Half Moon Bay, CA
650-726-5125
Italian

Prima Trattoria e Negozio di Vini
 (East Bay)
1522 N. Main St.
Walnut Creek, CA
925-935-7780
Italian

Ristorante Bacco (Noe Valley)
737 Diamond St.
San Francisco, CA
415-282-4969
Italian

Ristorante Il Porcino (East Bay)
1403 Solano Ave.
Albany, CA
510-528-1237
Italian

Sociale (Pacific Heights)
3665 Sacramento St.
San Francisco, CA
415-921-3200
Italian

Warm neighborhood fixture Bacco is worth a special trip when you want terrific Italian with no California spin. It feels like an Italian restaurant in Italy, with a predominately Italian staff and homey, comfortable atmosphere. This is allegedly the only San Francisco restaurant that makes risotto from scratch to order. Recommended: figs and prosciutto, risotto quattro formaggi (creamy, toothsome, very well cooked), tagliata with broccoli rabe and cannelini beans. Also, specials of buckwheat polenta with whipped baccala; pappardelle with pork and green beans; puff pastry with mascarpone cream. Do not by any means miss their very rare special of fava bean crostini (two batard-sized slices of bread spread with a hummuslike mixture bursting with the flavor of the beans and garlic topped with Sardinian pecorino and a drizzle of truffle oil).

Dopo, a tiny place, offers only a limited menu and boasts just a few tables and bar seats, but it has a big heart. Friendly service, relaxed atmosphere, and flavorful Italian cooking made this place an overnight sensation. It doesn't hurt that the chefs worked with Paul Bertolli of Oliveto! Recommended: sauteed calamari with bacon, white beans, and spinach, pizza (great crust), lasagne, pasta with spicy ragout, pasta puttanesca (with tuna, fishy, in a good way, describes *Bung*), pork loin tonnato, and panna cotta. Food and wine are very reasonable (pastas around $10), and wines complement food very well. Go early or late, or be prepared to wait.

Prima delivers elegant food and exemplary service in their noisy dining room or covered patio. Heirloom tomato salad with pecorino Toscano features large chunks of several varieties of tomatoes with perfect texture and excellent sweet/acid balance (*nestorius*). Gnocchi (with mussels and sausage) and tagliatelle (with rabbit ragu) are pasta highlights; for heartier fare, try lamb shanks.

At **Bella**, pastas are best (especially anything with porcini or duck), though roasted wild boar (cinghiale) is a *Limster* favorite. Warm service, relatively quiet, and affordable prices.

Sociale's got a very pretty patio/courtyard and cozy interior, and *babyfork* says it's in a great neighborhood for a postdinner stroll "past all the huge houses with perfect spring landscaping—one even had a topiary Easter bunny." Italian flavors win: chicken cooked under brick, fried olives appetizer, any ravioli in marinara or in mushroom walnut cream sauce. Their special salad of the day "looked like something from the cover of *Gourmet*," and artichoke potato soup and the braised baby artichokes which come with petrale sole and parsnip puree are awesome. Don't miss the fried olives. Here's a tip from *Lydia*: "if you go later on a Saturday night you may get free cookies at the end of your meal.

On the coast, **Mezza Luna** is strong all around, but *Wendy-san* particularly loves their linguini ala toto (with clams, mussels, and white sauce), which tastes exactly like what she had in Florence. **Pasta Moon** is friendly, quiet, and casually elegant, says *tom in sf*, who raves about fritto misto, mussels in marinara, duck confit–frisee salad, smoky wood-roasted chicken, pizza, and boozy tiramisu. **Capellini Ristorante** is all about classics done well, like their spectacular housemade ravioli con fungi and veal scallopini. Tasty lemon tart with raspberry sauce for dessert. Very good salad with beets, candied pecans, feta and greens. High quality (and strong) drinks and friendly service.

Relaxing, low-key **Il Porcino** may not be a great restaurant, but from bread basket to dessert, food and service can perfectly satisfy a craving for hearty, traditional Italian comfort food. Focaccia is soft and has great texture and flavor. Insalata il porcino (mixed greens with melon and orange) is refreshing, and red lentil soup (with a pronounced but gentle lentil flavor and a dab of cream) is a must-order. Entrees have well-defined flavors; penne with sausage has a multidimensional sauce, and scallopini al porcini is made with flavorful meat and a sauce tasting of reduced veal stock. Sauteed squid doused in red sauce is fresh and not rubbery, veal main courses are served with fresh veggies, and pasta is under $15. Housemade chocolate mousse and tiramisu are top-notch.

You'll eat well indeed at **Mangia Bene**, where you feel as if you've been transported to the old country. Wood-roasted meats are the best entrees and the fresh pasta of the day (e.g., gnocchi with nettles and chanterelles) is always great, says *Victoria Libin*. You can get half orders of pasta for starter or middle course, and everything's reasonably priced.

La Villa's not a restaurant; it's an Italian deli with tons of character, the type of neighborhood destination where first names are tossed around. Ravioli is its speciality, but it also carries dozens of other hot and cold deli items, made-to-order sandwiches and much more. Preheated lasagnas available for parties. There's always a line, so take a number.

○ **Ristorante Bacco**: *see also* **pp. 202, 217.**

JAI YUN

Jai Yun (Chinatown)
923 Pacific Ave.
San Francisco, CA
415-981-7438
Chinese (Shanghai)/Chinese (Hunan)

Jai Yun, a one-man Shanghai/Hunanese operation, intrigues hounds with its prix fixe menus, ranging from $35 to $100 per person. While prices have risen, food quality is also better than ever, with flavors more intense and spicing more assertive. *Bryan Loofbourrow* says "a sense of care is taken with each dish, subtleties rule, knife work is notable; what a wonderful, variegated food experience. I'd go again in a heartbeat." Six people is a good size group to experience most dishes, and weekday nights are much less busy and more enjoyable. Standouts include spicy cubes of fish with pine nuts (sort of like a Chinese tandoori fish), edamame braised in spicy wine, squirrel fish, shrimp with ginko nuts, crispy eggplant, and a dry-fried spiced beef with sneaky spiciness.

JAM AND OIL

Frog Hollow Farm Kitchen
  (Contra Costa County)
Hwy. 4
Brentwood, CA
925-634-4660
Store

June Taylor Company
  (Embarcadero)
Ferry Plaza Farmers Market
San Francisco, CA
510-548-2236
Farmers' market vendor

Lagier Ranch (Central Valley)
16101 S. Murphy Rd.
Escalon, CA
209-982-5618
Farm or Farmstand

Lou Lou's Conserves (East Bay)
  Berkeley Farmers' Market,
  Center St. and Martin Luther
  King Way
Berkeley, CA
Farmers' market vendor

Mendocino Specialty Vineyards
   Tasting Room
   (Mendocino County)
17810 Farrer La., at Hwy. 128
Boonville, CA
707-895-3993
Winery

Pasta Shop (East Bay)
1786 4th St.
Berkeley, CA
510-528-1786
Store

Pasta Shop (East Bay)
5655 College Ave., at Rockridge
   Market Hall
Oakland, CA
510-655-7748
Store

Swanton Berry Farm
   (Santa Cruz County)
25 Swanton Rd.
Davenport, CA
831-469-8804
Farm or Farm stand

Yorkville Cellars
   (Mendocino County)
25701 Hwy. 128
Yorkville, CA
707-894-9177
Winery

Recommendations for jam, preserves, and conserves for slathering on sandwiches, or toast, topping on yogurt, or anything else you need to make sweet and fruity:

June Taylor ("Queen of Jams") is the brand to look for, with favorite flavors like bing cherry and Meyer lemon. Frog Hollow Farm makes wonderful Meyer lemon preserves and *Patrick Nolan* says their naval orange marmalade is a must-eat. Lagier Ranch for Arapaho berry preserves (avoid other berry varieties, urges *Stanley Stephan*). Lou Lou's Conserves is a jam maker who's been spotted at the Berkeley Thursday (2 p.m. to 6 p.m.) and Saturday (10 a.m. to 3 p.m.) farmers' markets. Conserves are a bit tart but full of fruit. Swanton may have great strawberries, but *Stanley Stephan* has been less than impressed with their preserves.

Winning oils: Wente Vineyards (www.wentevineyards.com) makes an organic olive oil from olive trees over 100 years old, while Da Vero makes three kinds of oil from trees in Healdsburg and also imports one from Tuscany (order online at www.davero.com or find it at most local markets). Up in Boonville, Stella Cadente (www.stellacadente.com) is making delicious olive oil. Three extra virgins (estate blend, early harvest mission, and everyday late harvest mission) and a Meyer lemon oil are all worth a trip. Buy Stella Cadente oils in bulk at the **Mendocino Specialty Vineyards Tasting Room** in downtown Boonville (across from the Boonville Hotel, open daily from 10 a.m. to 6 p.m., bring your own jars or buy pint and quart jars for a nominal charge), and also sell fancy prepackaged bottles at some spots in the Valley (including **Yorkville Cellars**) and at the **Pasta Shop** markets in Berkeley and Oakland. More than one hound has expressed disappointment with McEvoy's olive oils.

- ○ **Pasta Shop:** *see also* **p. 47.**
- ○ **Swanton Berry Farm:** *see also* **pp. 232, 273.**

JAPANESE Gems

Ariake Japanese Restaurant
(Richmond)
5041 Geary Blvd.
San Francisco, CA
415-221-6210
Japanese

Chika (Sunset)
841 Irving St.
San Francisco, CA
415-681-5539
Japanese

Ebisu Japanese Cuisine (Sunset)
1283 9th Ave.
San Francisco, CA
415-566-1770
Japanese

Kabuto Sushi (Richmond)
5121 Geary Blvd.
San Francisco, CA
415-752-5652
Japanese

Kui Shin Bo (Pacific Heights)
22 Peace Plaza, in Japan Center
San Francisco, CA
415-922-9575
Japanese

Kyo-Ya Restaurant
(Financial District)
2 New Montgomery St.
San Francisco, CA
415-546-5090
Japanese

Maki Restaurant (Pacific Heights)
1825 Post St.
San Francisco, CA
415-921-5215
Japanese

Ozumo Restaurant (Embarcadero)
161 Steuart St.
San Francisco, CA
415-882-1333
Japanese/Pan-Asian fusion

Toshi's Sushiya Restaurant (Peninsula)
211 El Camino Real
Menlo Park, CA
650-326-8862
Japanese

Here is a selection of Japanese restaurants much loved by chowhounds but still relatively unknown by most local diners.

Maki is a sweet little dining spot just around the corner from the huge Kinokuniya Bookstore in the Kinokuniya building. Reservations are highly recommended. Chowhound *jen maiser* reports an excellent meal of tuna sashimi appetizer (very good tuna, beautiful presentation), wappa meshi with Japanese mountain vegetables (a rice basket with assorted veggies and lots of mushrooms served with wonderful miso soup, kobachi [seaweed] dish and small tsukemono dish), and steak teriyaki dinner (generous serving of steak, no hint of sweetness in teriyaki sauce). Even the rice is good!

Kyo-Ya is reportedly recommended by Japanese conglomerates to their (well paid!) traveling salesmen. *Wendy-san* considers this "probably the best and most authentic Japanese restaurant in San Francisco. It is *very* expensive and more suited to a special occasion or to diners with generous expense accounts." It's worth the tab, agrees *Paul H*, who was "blown away by the service and quality of the food. Each table has an Ikebana flower arrangement, and the wasabi is grated from fresh wasabi root. This place is pure gold."

A big fan of **Chika** is *chowhoundX*—for serious sushi (it's not **Kabuto**, but better then **Ebisu**), and, especially, for cooked dishes like buta no kakuni (simmered pork belly), agedashi dofu (lightly battered fried tofu in broth), and just about any grilled fish. And, unlike Ebisu around the corner, Chika doesn't make you wait!

Ariake's chef Jin was formerly at Ebisu. *Kevin Yu* likes Ariake better for food quality, but the atmosphere may not be as "fun" as Ebisu's—it's rather plain and traditional and quiet. Large portions, exceptional quality fish.

Kui Shin Bo offers home-style Japanese food that makes a very generous lunch for around $10. Five or six daily specials round out a menu of standards (tonkatsu, nabeyaki, chicken teriyaki, etc.). *Celeste* praises a special of whole crab cracked open and steamed (served with tonkatsu-style vegetables, chawan mushi, and perfectly cooked sticky rice). Tuna donburi, ginger pork (thinly sliced pork with onions in a miso-ginger-soy sauce), and fresh fish specials are recommended—along with more of that great sticky rice. This isn't dazzling cuisine, just "rather perfect in its simplicity," says *Celeste*. Find Kin Shin Bo in the uppermost pod of the mall, next to the five-and-dime-ish Japanese store.

Ozumo bills itself as "contemporary Japanese." To *pavement2112*, it's carefully made Japanese with clean Western accents: fusion that works. Vegetable robata are expertly grilled (each comes with its own sauce). Excellent hamachi rolls are better than sushi with bland rice. The general approach is deftly executed traditional preparations with interesting little twists. Staff handles off-menu requests (e.g., ochazuke [tea with rice]) with aplomb, and the presentation's impressive, as is the view over the Embarcadero and Bay Bridge.

Of **Toshi** in Menlo Park, *grow power* says: "Don't go for the bento box, go for the sushi and the amazing cooked dishes." House special of thinly sliced potato in plum sauce with avocado is "visually stunning, a fluffy mound of white potato, against a backdrop of salmon-colored sauce contrasting with the cool green of avocado. Divine." Other fine nonsushi dishes: agedashi nasu (similar to agedashi tofu but made with eggplant); grilled tofu; parboiled and sliced baby squid in sweet sesame dressing. And then the sushi: toro, shiro maguro, atlantic sockeye salmon, uni, black sea bass, hamachi, spicy tuna, and more. Toro is "sooo good, so rich and creamy it was hard to believe it was fish." See the Cuisine Index for many more Japanese tips.

○ **Maki Restaurant**: *see also* p. 224.

High Swank at **JARDINIERE**

Jardiniere (Civic Center)
300 Grove St.
San Francisco, CA
415-861-5555
French/New American

Jardiniere is swanky and expensive, popular with opera and symphony goers. A luxurious six-course tasting menu runs $75, plus $45 for matching wines. *Paul H* tried it and reported that dinner included roast lobster with corn puree and rich and caramelized lobster jus; duck pâté (with Dijon aioli, capers, cornichons) and rabbit rillete with plum moustarde; halibut with heirloom tomatoes and salsa verde; lamb chop with heirloom haricots (fresh beans of many colors and types) and olive jus; cheese plate; and chocolate-mint napoleon with mint parfait and mint syrup. Similarly luxurious ingredients and preparations pepper the à la carte menu, as well. Service is professional and helpful, and wine pours are generous. We loved Paul's fish-out-of-water account:

> If I had been born to old money instead of young love, or had I not procrastinated so much when contemplating an application to Harvard things may have turned out differently, and I might feel more at home in Jardiniere. It's not that I felt out of place or that someone thought I was out of place; it's that Jardiniere is so upscale, so refined, so expensive. When I go to Jardiniere, I take a look at the menu, gulp, and rationalize that I eat there, on average, once every 540 days. Then I look around at my company at the bar and realize that they must eat here once a week, or at least every time they attend the opera or the symphony.

In conclusion, "I think that Gary Danko provides the best value in an upscale tasting menu in San Francisco, but Jardiniere is also a top-notch spot and its pull is hard to avoid when in the City Hall/Cultural District."

○ **Jardiniere:** *see also* **p.10.**

Eat at **JOE'S**

Joe's at Woodlake (Peninsula)
856 N. Delaware St.
San Mateo, CA
650-401-5637
Italian/American

Joe's of Westlake (Peninsula)
11 Glenwood Ave.
Daly City, CA
650-755-7400
Italian/American

Marin Joe's Restaurant
  (Marin County)
1585 Casa Buena Dr.
Corte Madera, CA
415-924-2081
Italian/American

Original Joe's (Tenderloin)
144 Taylor
San Francisco, CA
415-775-4877
Italian/American

Original Joe's Restaurant
  (South Bay)
301 S. 1st St.
San Jose, CA
408-292-7030
Italian/American

Original Joe's is a step back in time to the classic Italian-American joints of 1940s San Francisco. Huge menus, huge portions, classic food: steaks, lamb chops, osso buco, sweetbreads, roast chicken, veal marsala or picatta, eggplant Parmigiana, and much more. Plus the legendary Joe's Special, a concoction of ground beef, spinach, onion, and egg. Don't bother with pastas (too mushy) or salads. There are other Joe's restaurants—which we understand to all be independently operated—but we'd like to focus on the Tenderloin Joe's, which *crimson* says has an art deco bar area "where the drinks are always doubles." Favorites from this location include a half chicken that's flour-dredged and sauteed in lots of olive oil, then sauced with caramelized onions, wine, and mushrooms (or in your choice of many variations on the theme). Thin-sliced roast lamb served in jus is tasty and well balanced once it's perked up with a squeeze of lemon (ask for a wedge). Osso bucco, a Wednesday lunch special, is made with a shank that's more young beef than veal, affording a nicely chewy texture and a wide bone full of delicious marrow. Sweetbreads are crisp outside and soft inside, sauteed in a tomato and wine sauce. Large, juicy burgers are made with house-ground beef and served simply on firm grilled and buttered rolls. All entrees come with choice of spaghetti, plump meat ravioli, steak fries (plum and potatoey, but limp—so ask for well done), or vegetables (tasty if freshly cooked, but limp and tired if in the steam tray; you can see for yourself if you sit at the counter). Food here is anything but haute, but what Joe's lacks in finesse it makes up for in generosity and reasonable quality, promises *Zach Georgopoulos*, most likely sending you home with a doggy bag and a rosy outlook for around $10 to $13 per entree.

○ **Original Joe's:** *see also* **p. 92.**

Jonesing for **JOOK**

Gold Medal Restaurant (East Bay)
381 8th St.
Oakland, CA
510-268-8484
Chinese (Cantonese)/Chinese
   (Hong Kong)

New Hong Kong (East Bay)
389 8th St.
Oakland, CA
510-465-1940
Chinese (Cantonese)/Chinese
   (Hong Kong)

Jook is the hip word for congee. We haven't received many tips for specific destinations, possibly because some people fail to appreciate the simple pleasures of rice gruel. Note that many better Chinese restaurants make good jook (in the morning) as a badge of honor (barbecue places, with meats hanging in the window, often do double duty as jook joints). Here are a couple of quick tips: **Gold Medal** is a godsend to hounds jonesing for jook—*Joel Teller* is particulary fond of the versions with pork, liver, and kidney; pork and preserved egg; or seafood; good to know for early morning and late night noshing is **New Hong Kong**, which serves a happening jook from 9 a.m. to 3 p.m. and 9 p.m. to 3 a.m.

○ **Gold Medal Restaurant:** *see also* **pp. 42, 73, 167, 294.**

Chowhound Nametag: David Boyk

○◯○

Location: Berkeley

Occupation: I study history and cognitive science at UC Berkeley.

Cholesterol Level: Lower than it should be, considering the way I eat.

Number of Visits to McDonald's in Past Decade: Three, maybe? Some friends in high school used to drag me occasionally. I have no shame about In 'N' Out, though.

Farthest Out of the Way Traveled Just for Chow: I went to Bombay from Hyderabad, 440 miles, largely to eat Parsi food. The food was great. Other than that, my family made the hundred-mile trip to Santa Barbara from LA pretty often when I was a kid (and even when I'm home now, we still go), just to go to La Super Rica. They have the best horchata possible, and the Tuesday special, chicken sopes, is almost obscene in its deliciousness.

Favorite Comfort Chow: The Apple Pan in Los Angeles, where I get a Hickoryburger, well-done fries (you gotta eat 'em within about five minutes, before they get nasty) and an IBC root beer, served in those infuriating paper cones gripped in the red plastic holders.

Guilty Pleasure: I really kind of like Mother's pink and white circus animal cookies.

Favorite Gelato Flavor: When I was a kid, I really loved the gianduia from Al Gelato in West LA. Now, I think my favorite is crème brûlée.

Favorite Mail Order Chow: Everything Zingerman's (Zingermans.com) sells is terrific. I can't imagine a better pastrami than theirs; it's not the standard pink salt lick.

Chowhounding Rules of Thumb:
1. Soccer posters on the wall are a good sign at taquerias.
2. Pizza places should not have tablecloths.

Favorite Place to Get Abused by the Counterman, Jostled by Drunks, and Eventually Served a Brilliant Butterflied Calabrese: Southside Top Dog, Berkeley.

Ode to **JOY**

Joy Restaurant (Peninsula)
1495 Beach Park Blvd.
Foster City, CA
650-345-1762
Chinese (Taiwanese)

Chowhound *ed k* gushes over dinner at **Joy**, a Taiwanese chow mecca in Foster City, where he doted on amazing (and beautifully presented) befong tang shieh (fried whole crab with garlic salt and chili pepper, served with rice noodle soup), simple but awesomely flavorful ming tsu xiao chow (famous chef stir-fry or Joy special stir-fry, including chopped tofu, greens, and much more), stewy, strong-flavored *wu gung chung wong* (intestine blood and tofu) eaten over rice, and very tender hong xao yuan ti (braised pork butt). Boneless Eight Treasures duck stuffed with sticky rice was another winner. It helps to understand Mandarin to get the full experience here, and corkage runs around $3 a bottle.

JUST FOR YOU: Beignets, Breads, Breakfast, Catfish, Etc.

Mabel's Just for You (Potrero Hill)
732 22nd St.
San Francisco, CA
415-647-3033
Cajun/Creole/New American/Diner or Coffee shop/Mexican

Many hounds love beignets at homey **Mabel's Just for You**, but they're only one of many reasons to visit. House-baked breads, used for sandwiches and toast, are also available by the loaf. A full breakfast and lunch menu offers an eclectic variety, including New Orleans classics like oyster po' boys, plus Mexican and European flavors. Hounds recommend: blackened catfish with eggs; huevos rancheros (with green sauce); biscuits and gravy;

and the amazing Creole crabcake breakfast. For lunch, try a cheeseburger (tasty and meaty with crisp bacon and good cheese, reports *vespaloon*) or a rich croque monsieur, both on quality house-baked bread. Fries are fresh and hand cut. Open daily for breakfast and lunch; cash only.

KABUTO'S Bargain Sushi Lunch

Kabuto Sushi (Richmond)
5121 Geary Blvd.
San Francisco, CA
415-752-5652
Japanese

Kabuto, a big sushi favorite, has bargain-priced lunches. Check out $8, $10, or $12 specials including special salad or appetizer of the day; choice of grilled fish, tempura or tonkatsu; miso soup; rice; and ice cream. Pricier specials come with better starters and maybe one more dish. *Celeste* raves: "The tonkatsu was the best I have had since living in Japan. For the sublime quality of the food, this was a great deal for lunch." Note that at dinner, the sushi specials aren't necessarily maki, but ramekin-sized piles of rice with the ingredients on top— good, but maybe not what you'd expected.

KEBABS, Kabobs, Kebaps

Chopan Kabob (East Bay)
2699 Monument Blvd.
Concord, CA
925-671-7955
Afghan/Central Asian

Kabob House (South Bay)
1590 Berryessa Rd., at the
    Berryessa Flea Market
San Jose, CA
408-453-1110
Middle Eastern/North
    African/Farmers' market
    vendor

Leila (Financial District)
50 Post St., third floor, Crocker
    Galleria
San Francisco, CA
415-217-0099
Middle Eastern/North African

Rihab's (Peninsula)
1504 El Camino Real
San Carlos, CA
650-631-3739
Iraqi

Roya (South Bay)
1253 W. El Camino Real
Sunnyvale, CA
650-962-8007
Afghan

Shalizaar Restaurant (Peninsula)
120 W. 25th Ave.
San Mateo, CA
650-341-2600
Persian

Shoma Deli (Sonoma County)
177 Dry Creek Rd.
Healdsburg, CA
707-433-5529
Persian

Sinbad Mediterranean Cuisine
    (Peninsula)
150 E. 4th Ave.
San Mateo, CA
650-347-6060
Lebanese

It doesn't matter how they're spelled—kebabs, kabobs, kebaps. If they're juicy and well seasoned, we want some! Tiny **Rihab's** (just one table, though lots of takeout), specializing in Iraqi cuisine, is a true find. Handmade pita is continuously produced, homey dishes are skillfully crafted, and there's a generous selection of good quality Middle Eastern groceries. Laham belajeen ($3) is delectable with diced tomato, ground meat, roasted onions, and herbs melding with a chewy, blistered, puffy base. Also available: a plain cheese topping, and feta'ar—bread stuffed with spinach and cheese. Lamb kebab is served with yogurt on deeply flavored rice (at $6.99, the most expensive item). Dolma are tender, with luscious minted rice stuffing. Baklava with pistachios is crisp and not oversweet.

Chopan is a hole-in-the-wall with a very brief kabob-heavy menu. Best is chapli kabob, a very thin ground beef patty oven-fried to a crusty sheen on both sides, made even crunchier by the chopped onions and lots of whole coriander seeds worked into the mix—*heidipie* finds it memorably tasty, though says the keema (tender, herbed ground beef) and chicken kabobs are tasty but mild, and require a dose of chatni (a mild cilantro sauce on the table) to perk them up. With advance notice, the kitchen will make a variety of Uzbeki specialties, including salads and pasta dishes; call to arrange.

Sinbad is a very good Lebanese grocery-cum-restaurant. Order an adana–shish kebab combination plate with hummus and tabouleh, and then some baklava and mint tea for dessert, suggests *Malik*. At **Persion Shalizaar**, koobideh and joojeh (on the bone), are the kabobs of choice. **Afghan Roya**, formerly of Walnut Creek, has resurfaced in Sunnyvale. Juicy, tender chicken and lamb kabobs come with flavorful basmati rice, and kaddo (baked pumpkin), meaty noodle soup, and steamed dumplings are also recommended. **Kabob House**, a vendor at San Jose's massive Berrysessa flea market ("a self contained village of commerce with named streets and addresses to tame its out of control vastness"), serves chicken kabobs rolled in grilled pita, "dripping with paprika-stained juices that make mopping up a real pleasure" (*Ken Hoffman*).

Shoma supplements standard deli offerings with Persian dishes Fridays through Sundays. Falafel is fried to order from housemade batter and served in sesame-studded pita with yogurt-lemon sauce and very fresh veggies. Aggressively flavored doogh (a yogurt drink with fresh and dried herbs) really wakes up the palate. We've had one report of an underseasoned chelo kebab (served with overcooked wet rice, no less), though. There's a pretty patio with fountain, plus indoor seating and a wide selection of sodas and local wines and beers.

Order lamb kabob at **Leila**, and ask for it medium rare. Also excellent: saffron-heavy rice, hummus, dolma. Bad news: dry, bland beef and lousy commercial pita.

Krazy for **KIDNEYS**

Dragon 2000 Restaurant
  (East Bay)
1651 Botelho Dr., in Plum Court
  Shopping Center
Walnut Creek, CA
925-287-1688
Chinese (Shanghai)/Chinese
  (Sichuan)

Gold Medal Restaurant (East Bay)
381 8th St.
Oakland, CA
510-268-8484
Chinese (Cantonese)/Chinese
  (Hong Kong)

Happy Cafe Restaurant
 (Peninsula)
250 S. B St.
San Mateo, CA
650-340-7138
Chinese (Shanghai)

Utopia Cafe (Chinatown)
139 Waverly Pl.
San Francisco, CA
415-956-2902
Chinese (Hong Kong)/Chinese
 (Cantonese)

Shanghai Gourmet (East Bay)
1291 Parkside Dr.
Walnut Creek, CA
925-256-6869
Chinese (Shanghai)

Vien Huong Restaurant (East Bay)
712 Franklin St.
Oakland, CA
510-465-5938
Vietnamese

Hate cooking kidneys at home (all that coring, scoring, and smelling 'em raw), but hate it when they're overcooked? Hounds like these spots for kidneys done right. **Vien Huong** serves kidneys sauteed with ginger and green onions—a very popular dish. They close early (around 5 p.m.), so no dinner. **Happy Cafe** boils and mixes kidneys with ginger, sesame oil, and soy for a simple and authentic dish. **Shanghai Gourmet** in Walnut Creek does a good job with kidneys (as well as a bunch of interesting and unique Shanghai dishes, all worth exploring; the Walnut Creek location's hidden in an auto parts strip mall). **Dragon 2000**, also in Walnut Creek, makes unbelievable kidneys ("the texture of foie gras and bathed in a Sichuan ma la sauce that tastes of sesame and lots of chilis," says *Melanie Wong*). **Utopia** has a pork kidney and liver dish, but you can ask them to hold the liver and specify the doneness of the kidneys (so they're not overcooked). **Gold Medal's** jook with kidney and liver is popular, perfectly tender, and never overcooked. They add thin raw slices to the jook to cook. This dish has a generous (some feel overly so) dose of fresh ginger. They also serve a kidney stir-fry with scallions and ginger. Good service at takeout counter, especially if you speak Chinese. Tasty roast duck and Gold Medal's preserved vegetable stew with overnight roast whole pig are big favorites of *Yimster*.

○ **Dragon 2000 Restaurant:** *see also* **p. 93.**
○ **Gold Medal Restaurant:** *see also* **pp. 42, 73, 162, 294.**
○ **Utopia Cafe:** *see also* **p. 288.**

∘◯∘ Chowhound Tip:

Joel Teller suggests using lamb kidney for home cooking, since it's milder and easier to clean and prepare than veal.

KOREAN Favorites: San Francisco and Oakland

Chick n' Deli (Sunset)
2001 Taraval St.
San Francisco, CA
415-566-9221
Korean

Dong Baek (Tenderloin)
631 O'Farrell
San Francisco, CA
415-776-1898
Korean

Koryo Wooden Charcoal BBQ
  (East Bay)
4390 Telegraph Ave., J
Oakland, CA
510-652-6007
Korean

Lee's Tofu House & Korean BBQ
  (East Bay)
6050 Mowry Ave.
Newark, CA
510-790-8989
Korean

Pyung Chang Tofu House
  (East Bay)
4701 Telegraph Ave.
Oakland, CA
510-658-9040
Korean

Sam Won Barbeque House
  (East Bay)
2600 Telegraph Ave.
Oakland, CA
510-834-5757
Korean

Seoul Gom Tang II (East Bay)
3801 Telegraph
Oakland, CA
510-597-9989
Korean

Wooden Charcoal Barbecue House
  (Richmond)
4611 Geary Blvd.
San Francisco, CA
415-751-6336
Korean

SamWon (billed as Oakland's biggest Korean restaurant) is a fave of *erifc*'s for superior ventilation and less grilling at the table than many other Korean BBQ places—good for those who dislike coming away smelling like a Korean BBQ joint. Excellent variety of panchan (even for single diners). Open until 2 a.m. Word to the wise from *Mark Wallace*: SamWon "seems to be a favorite hangout for cops, so if you're on the lam, don't go." **Lee's Tofu House & Korean BBQ** gets the nod for tofu soups, spicy pork, lots of panchan (you can even ask for seconds), plus free ice cream for dessert. Excellent service. At **Seoul Gam Tong II**, beef bone and oxtail soups with noodles are the specialty; also great pickles and kimchee. **Koryo** is the place to go for smoky, succulent barbecue—at your table over live wood coals. **Pyung Chang**'s good for soon dofu and other fresh tofu dishes. **Chick n' Deli** (aka, Shin Toe Bul Yi) specializes in noodle and rice dishes (bi bim bop, jap chae), sauteed dishes (dokbokki), and soups. **Dong Baek**'s menu is similar to Chick n' Deli's; the food's not quite as good, but the atmosphere is nicer. Hit **Wooden Charcoal** for fresh, delicious, and varied panchan (little freebie appetizer plates), but service may be different for non–Koreans. We've had a couple of reports of really good Korean home cooking at a little hole in the wall at 13th and Harrison in Oakland. Unfortunately, we don't know its name. *Miele Maiale* highly recommends it to anyone with a flexible schedule—meaning that the owner does it all, from cooking to serving to cleaning, so don't go if you're in a hurry. Even $5.95 lunch specials come with plentiful panchan: soybean and mungbean sprout salads, battered sweet potato, potato and scallion pancake, smoked tofu, crisp pickled cucumber in red chili paste, spinach, cellophane nooldes, daikon kimchi, and cabbage kimchi. Also see the cuisine index for more Korean.

KOREAN in South Bay

Gaesung House of Tofu
  (South Bay)
2089 El Camino Real
Santa Clara, CA
408-248-8638
Korean

Korea House (South Bay)
2340 El Camino Real
Santa Clara, CA
408-249-0808
Korean

Myung Dong Tofu Cabin
Restaurant (South Bay)
1484 Halford Ave.
Santa Clara, CA
408-246-1484
Korean

Palace Bar-B-Que Buffet
(South Bay)
1092 E. El Camino Real, #1
Sunnyvale, CA
408-554-9292
Korean

A restaurant in the strip mall
behind Q Lube (South Bay)
El Camino Real, near Bowers
Santa Clara, CA
Korean

Seoul Gom Tang (South Bay)
3028 El Camino Real
Santa Clara, CA
408-615-0370
Korean

Tong Soon (South Bay)
3240 El Camino Real
Santa Clara, CA
408-615-9988
Korean/Chinese

Daveena, on a mission for seafood tofu stew, shares thoughts on tofu houses around El Camino in Santa Clara. **Gaesung House of Tofu** makes the most delicate tofu and most intense, complex broth of the places tried. Attractive interior too. **Myung Dong Tofu Cabin** "has the ambience of a church basement, but you immediately sense that you're getting as close to home cooking as you can in a restaurant." **Korea House** is consistently strong, with the widest selection of panchan, but "can veer towards overly greasy." **Palace Bar-B-Que** is an all-you-can-eat BBQ spot with lackluster panchan but good quality meat and whole, marinated octopi for grilling. **Tong Soon** is a Korean-Chinese spot with excellent spicy seafood soup, and **Seoul Gom Tang** (in the same strip mall as Vesuvio's Restaurant) is exactly what sul long tong should be ("made me crave karaoke"). The **restaurant in the strip mall behind Q Lube** (probably either Corner Place, 2783 El Camino Real; or BCD Tofu House, 2777 El Camino Real) has slightly tough tofu and "less than fresh tasting broth," but deserves high marks for excellent seafood pancake (hae mul pajun).

KOREAN Shopping in Oakland

99 Ranch Market
www.99ranch.com
Chinese store

Pusan Market (East Bay)
2370 Telegraph Ave.
Oakland, CA
510-986-1234
Korean store

Pusan Village Market is smaller than **99 Ranch**, and is strong on Korean foods. Kimchi and radish pickles sold in bulk (as well as more exotic produce) and a large selection of marinated meats, exotic fresh meats, and thinly sliced meats for hot pot, also live seafood and sushi-quality fish. Very inexpensive cookware (portable gas cooktop for $9.99), and the condiment aisle is a cornucopia. This store is worth checking out, says *Bung*; it's clean, well run, and the staff speaks English.

○ **99 Ranch Market:** *see also* **pp. 181, 206.**

Bridging the **KOREAN-CHINESE** Gap

Formosa Chinese Restaurant
  (East Bay)
39119 Cedar Blvd.
Newark, CA
510-745-8688
Chinese (Beijing)/Chinese
  (Cantonese)

San Tung Chinese Restaurant
  (Sunset)
1031 Irving St.
San Francisco CA
415-242-0828
Chinese (Beijing)

Princess Garden (Solano County)
960 Admiral Callaghan La.
Vallejo, CA
707-643-0202
Korean/Chinese

Korean-Chinese is a hybrid cuisine with some dishes of its own, though many such places also offer items strictly from one or the other parent cuisines, or both. Here are some restaurants whose kitchens straddle that border. None, alas, can be recommended unequivocally (you've got to know what to order in each—and of course, we have suggestions), but the cuisine's so interesting and rare that chowhounds gladly take whatever they can get of it.

Princess Garden is a seemingly standard Chinese place (with more upscale atmosphere than you'd expect from its location in a strip mall across the highway from Marine Park) which offers no external indications they serve Korean. In fact, most of the staff can't read their Korean menu! But their chef is of Shandong background from Korea, and makes Korean as well as "Mandarin" dishes. *Melanie Wong* says the kitchen makes liberal use of such ingredients as fresh lily buds and wood ears, and while prices are a little high by San Francisco or San Jose standards, the place is bustling, with a pleasant atmosphere and eager-to-please servers. There are lots of caveats; for example, skip the Mongolian BBQ buffet and chao ma mien (spicy seafood noodle soup with good noodles, but that's about it) and, from the regular menu, egg drop soup (on the house, and worth about that much). And don't expect kimchi. Go for zha jiang mian (a nice version with soft squishy noodles, black bean sauce, delicious irregular shaved pieces of grilled rare beef), la jiao rou (hot chili pepper beef, probably the best dish here, a generous and very spicy stir-fry), and sweet and sour beef (thick sauce but overall good balance of sweet and sour). Noodles are well made here, as is often the case in Korean-Chinese places.

San Tung is a Korean-Chinese place, particularly known for noodles, with menus in English, Chinese, and Korean. Also recommended: Cao rou liang zhang pi, a salad mix with slices of veggies, five-spiced beef, shrimp, calamari, mung bean sheets, and mustard dressing, all mixed at the table—*tanspace* says the literal translation is "stir-fried meat with two pieces of skin," and it's a standard appetizer item in Korean-Chinese restaurants. Gan zha jiang mian, noodles with black bean sauce (dry), is a better-than-average rendition, and dan dan noodles (with minced pork in a spicy sauce) is also a good choice. Kan pong dry sauteed chicken wings, sauteed in dark sweet sauce with garlic, scallions, and chilis, is another standard, and while its quality is a bit variable, it can be killer good. They also make homemade pancakes for mu shu. "Awesome, I'd go back for the mu shu alone," raves *wonki* who also gives a thumbs up for the fresh shrimp and chive dumplings. Entrees can be disappointing, especially sweet and sour beef.

Formosa offers Korean-Chinese dishes on its Chinese menu. *Han Lukito* recommends tsao ma mien (seafood noodle soup, very spicy) and sweet and sour beef (crispy fried beef with sweet-lemon sauce).

KOREAN SNACKS

Kuk Jea Market (Peninsula)
2350 Junipero Serra Blvd.
Daly City CA
650-992-0333
Korean Store

Chowhound *razordog* likes Seoul U & I Snacks, inside **Kuk Jea Market**, for Korean-style bar foods, such as Korean roast chicken, spicy fried chicken, handmade dumplings, green onion seafood pancakes, mung bean pancakes, rice cakes with hot sauce, fish cake with soup. The most expensive item runs a mere $7.99. Korean sweets like candied yams and baked goods are also on the menu. On weekends, look for the stand outside the market selling fried red bean cakes and roasted yams.

Tofu House, also inside the market, has quick, cheap and good typical Korean foods, and a Japanese menu, to boot. Look for the excellent prepackaged spicy chicken (*kam poong gi*) when you order at the counter. After you eat, you can shop for Korean groceries; *vespaloon* says the selection of self-serve panchan and prepackaged fresh seafood noodle soups boggles the mind. And for you drivers, it's easy to get to from 280.

KOREAN TWINKIES

Lee's Sandwiches (South Bay)
2525 S. King Rd.
San Jose, CA
408-274-1596
Vietnamese

Lee's Sandwiches (South Bay)
990 Story Rd.
San Jose, CA
408-295-3402
Vietnamese

Lee's Sandwiches (South Bay)
3276 S. White Rd.
San Jose, CA
408-274-8166
Vietnamese

Washington Bakery & Restaurant
  (Chinatown)
733 Washington St.
San Francisco, CA
415-397-3232
Chinese (Hong Kong) café

Korea's Delimanjoo cream cakes (Delimanjoo.com) can now be found in San Francisco at **Washington Bakery** and in San Jose at **Lee's Sandwiches**—*haochi* describes them as "wafflelike and about the size of a walnut, and come both plain and creme filled. Try to get them hot off the griddle, and in small quantities, because they seem to have a short half-life."

KORYORI (Japanese Small Plates) at Kappa

Kappa Japanese Restaurant (Pacific Heights)
1700 Post St.
San Francisco, CA
415-673-6004
Japanese

"There is no other place like **Kappa** in all of San Francisco. When you walk in it's like you're in Japan," says *chowhoundX*. Kappa serves great koryori, or little dishes (mostly cooked or marinated), like Japanese tapas, meant for sharing. The problem is that their menu and specials are in Japanese, and the English

menu lists only the most basic items. The owners say that they
do welcome non-Japanese speakers, but they may also warn
you they don't serve sushi when you first walk in. Just let them
know that you've heard of koryori and want to try it. The owners seem willing to educate eager customers willing to learn, although it might be best to go early on a weekday when it's less
busy. There's a $75 tasting menu, though you can certainly get
a lot out of Kappa without spending quite so much. The other
obstacle is finding the place. There's no sign; just go up the
stairs in front of Denny's to the second floor, go in the door with
the sign for Club Nishiki, and directly in front will be a sliding
door with a lit sign above (it says Kappa in Japanese). Slide
that door open and you're in. They do take reservations. Prices
are expensive, but not outrageous, considering all the work that
goes into the chef's creations and cooking.

Standout dishes include shiso miso maki (miso wrapped in
shiso leaf and lightly grilled), hitokuchi katsu (bite-size),
tonkatsu (panko-crusted fried pork), aji ichiya boshi (grilled
aji—a small fish—with grated daikon). Merely superb dishes
include Myoga special (thinly sliced myoga, a japanese veggie
like a cross between ginger and onion, topped with bonito
flakes), yamaimo sengiri bainiku ae (julienned yamaimo—
Japanese tuber with an interesting gooey texture when cut—
topped with pickled plum paste), Kinpira gobo (simmered
gobo—burdock root—and carrot), hirame shiokonbu ae (pieces
of raw flounder mixed with strands of salty konbu seaweed),
and shake ochazuke (rice, sesame, and nori flakes in tea and
fish broth, topped with bits of salmon). Just OK: mushi tori as-
apara miso ae (boiled chicken and asparagus in sesame sauce).

LA MOONE: Pan-Asian

La Moone (Castro)
4072 18th St.
San Francisco, CA
415-355-1999
New American/Pan-Asian fusion/Hawaiian

La Moone, a Pan-Asian spot in the Castro, does a fine job with meat dishes in particular. The kalua pork spring roll and chicken karaange is as good as the late night hole-in-the-wall places in Tokyo, reports *bmarea*. Also good: seven-spice spare ribs and Hawaiian-style short rib tacos. Avoid dumplings. Desserts can be hits (caramelized banana split, mango raspberry sorbets) or misses (rum espresso chocolate cake with a "confusing jumble of flavors and much of it had the mealy consistency of warm paste"). The atmosphere's pleasant and relaxed and drinks are good, especially sake sangría.

LATIN AMERICAN Without a Crowd

La Furia Chalaca (East Bay)
310 Broadway
Oakland, CA
510-451-4206
Peruvian

Panchita's #3 (Mission)
3115 22nd St.
San Francisco, CA
415-821-6660
Salvadoran/New American

Both of the following are terrific little-known Latin American restaurants recommended by *nja*:

At **Panchita's #3**, made-to-order Salvadoran pupusas sing with the flavor of fresh masa and corn, and are beautifully presented. Plain cheese offers purity of flavor, but chicken, beef, and pork versions are also good, complemented by refreshing curtido (slaw), salsa roja, and crema. Favorite mains include enchiladas verdes with tasty stewed chicken, and a pork chop with a thick adobo of chiles, garlic, oil, and sauteed onions and peppers. Flan with shaved almonds (the only dessert served) is recommended. Atmosphere and decor are slightly upscale, but the vibe is friendly and relaxed. Despite the lack of other customers, service is nonetheless laggy.

Service at **La Furia Chalaca** is no better, so don't go if you're in a hurry. Anticuchos (skewered beef hearts) are chewy and flavorful. Prawn chowder is a tasty, thick, yellow, shrimpy soup with a poached egg hiding in the center of the bowl; the shrimp themselves are tiny and chewy. Their jalea especial isn't large in total size, but offers a plenitude of tastes, including green mussels, delicious fried white fish, grilled squid, and shrimp. Also memorable, pickled onions with a flavorful vinegar that enhanced the other components. Desserts include mazamorra morada, a Jell-O-like purple pudding with fruit in it, and an exemplary, freshly-made arroz con leche (warm, creamy, spiced rice pudding with raisins).

○ **Panchita's #3:** *see also* p. 288.

LAUREL'S for Friendly Cuban

Laurel's Restaurant (Civic Center)
205 Oak St.
San Francisco, CA
415-934-1575
Cuban

Laurel's Restaurant is a friendly, family-run place offering Cuban classics and more. The very comfortable atmosphere makes for a good presymphony dinner. *Spencer* suggests: tamales de puerco (full of melt-in-your-mouth meat and stone-ground corn flavor), ensalada Cesar con pollo (well sauced and parmed), conejo guisado (half a rabbit pan-seared in a marinade of sweet wine, tomato, onion, and lemon, served with a crown of fried plaintains), and grilled fresh Alaskan salmon with creamy garlic-mushroom-caper sauce. Paella is offered in single portion or for two, but a single could easily have fed two, or even three after appetizers. Perfectly cooked rice is studded with fresh peas and all sorts of tender meats, each retaining its flavor while contributing to the whole. Pollo a la parilla (grilled chicken with black beans and rice, fried plantains, salsa criolla) is another good order, and the cafe Cubano is as good as in Miami, says *Stanley Stephan*. Laurel's menu also includes many interesting vegetarian dishes, including corn tamale with a side of tofu and vegetables marinara; polenta with veggies; okra, tofu, and plantain stew; chickpea and artichoke hearts with tomato sauce, rice, and yucca. Plus, of course, plenty of meaty standards such as ropa viejo, arroz con pollo, masa de puerco, and more.

Tomorrow's LEGENDS

Bix (North Beach)
56 Gold St.
San Francisco, CA
415-433-6300
American

Scala's Bistro (Union Square)
432 Powell St.
San Francisco, CA
415-395-8555
New American/Italian

Moose's (North Beach)
1652 Stockton St.
San Francisco, CA
415-989-7800
New American

Ken Hoffman provides a nice rundown of what are becoming "classic" San Francisco restaurants:

Scala's "has become a veritable institution among the ladies-who-lunch-crowd, but that should not shoo away anyone not of that set." The food is staunchly Italian (not Italian American), like perfect penne with duck ragout. *Rochelle* recommends Scala's for drinks and fried calamari at the bar, especially after a long day of shopping in Union Square.

Moose's serves up "gargantuan" burgers that are flavorful and juicy, hot, crispy fries and "pillow soft" corn cakes. Bix is "the standard for style." Upscale surroundings make it perfect for a celebration. Steak tartar, lobster linguine, great steaks, and martinis are highly recommended. Tuna carpaccio and grilled shrimp appetizer are better elsewhere. Stylish crowd, good martinis, and, everyone agrees, quite the noisy scene. Fish dishes are particularly well done.

- ○ **Bix:** *see also* **p. 271.**
- ○ **Moose's:** *see also* **p. 185.**
- ○ **Scala's Bistro:** *see also* **p. 117.**

Lusting for **LINGUICA** (Sausage)

Cattaneo Brothers
San Luis Obispo, CA
805-243-8537
Mail order source

Fernandes Sao Jorge Linguica
   (Central Valley)
4220 Commercial Dr.
Tracy, CA
209-835-9115
Portuguese wholesaler

Moniz Portuguese Sausage
   (East Bay)
1924 International Blvd.
Oakland, CA
510-261-4940
Portuguese store

9 Islands Bakery Cafe
   (Sonoma County)
1 Padre Pkwy., in Padre Town
   Center
Rohnert Park, CA
707-586-1620
Portuguese café

Sonoma Market (Sonoma County)
500 W. Napa St., #550
Sonoma, CA
707-996-3411
Store

Takahashi Market (Peninsula)
221 S. Claremont St.
San Mateo, CA
650-343-0394
Japanese/Hawaiian/East Asian
   store

Sources for linguica (leen-GWEE-suh), the spicy Portuguese sausage: **Fernandes Sao Jorge Linguica** supplies Grubstake, a Portuguese San Francisco diner, and you can buy both styles of their linguica out of the refrigerator case at **9 Islands** in Rohnert Park, the Portuguese bakery. Sonoma Sausage makes wonderful Hawaiian Portuguese sausage (**Sonoma Market** sells some of the product line). **Takahashi Market** has good Hawaiian-style Portuguese sausage, Hawaiian products (including poke and poi), and friendly staff. And then there's **Moniz Portuguese Sausage**

in Oakland (no reports yet, but it's worth checking out). Finally, you can buy garlicky linguica via mail order from **Cattaneo Brothers**.

○ **9 Islands Bakery Cafe:** *see also* p. 259.
○ **Sonoma Market:** *see also* p. 250.

Buying **LIVE FISH**

Lien Hing Supermarket
   (Richmond)
400 Clement St.
San Francisco, CA
415-386-6333
Chinese store

99 Ranch Market
www.99ranch.com
Chinese store

Sun Fat Seafood Co. (Mission)
2687 Mission St.
San Francisco, CA
415-282-9339
Chinese store

Wing Hing Seafood Market
   (Richmond)
633 Clement St.
San Francisco, CA
415-668-1666
Chinese store

Buying live fish can be challenging for those used to buying precut. **Lien Hing**'s Clement street branch is a good spot to overcome live fish fears. The fish guys are nice, the fish is reasonably priced and fresh, and the tanks are clean, reports *Jupiter*. They'll also fillet your choice and pack up the bones so you can make stock. **Wing Hing**, across from Haig's, is very clean and has a slightly larger selection than Lien Hing. The market **99 Ranch** is always mentioned as a good spot for live fish. Their prices often can't be beat. And **Sun Fat**'s a good choice in the Mission for very fresh fish, precut or live.

○ **99 Ranch Market:** *see also* pp. 172, 206.

Noisy, Exciting, and Delicious at
LUNA PARK

Luna Park (Mission)
694 Valencia St.
San Francisco, CA
415-553-8584
New American

Luna Park is a much loved spot for drinks and reasonably priced great food in a high-energy atmosphere. Best orders include goat cheese fondue, mussels and frites, tuna tartar, tuna poke, lamb shank (tender and tasty), sea bass, fontina ravioli (with spinach and truffle oil), flank steak with salsa, shepherd's pie, and breaded pork cutlet (stuffed with mushrooms and Gruyère cheese). Excellent frites and one of San Francisco's best mojitos.

The main complaint is that the place is loud. As *Dave* put it: "Atmosphere is noisy but kind of exciting in that I'm-too-sexy-for-my-bowling-shoes Mission Street sort of way." *Baker*'s tip is to go for lunch to avoid crowds (and thus noise). Lunch includes very good salads, different daily specials, and great sandwiches (Monte Cristo, hot Reuben, grilled chicken) and "fries that are some of the best in the city." Desserts like bananas Foster and s'mores (with housemade graham crackers and marshmallows) lean toward the big-and-gooey.

○ **Luna Park:** *see also* **pp. 10, 227.**

MALAYSIAN Finds

Banana City Cafe (East Bay)
3241 Walnut Ave.
Fremont, CA
510-790-3988
Singaporean/Malaysian/Thai

Penang Village (South Bay)
1290 Coleman Ave.
Santa Clara, CA
408-980-0668
Malaysian/Singaporean

Chowhound Nametag: nja

∘◯∘

Location:
San Francisco

Occupation:
Marketing and business strategist

Cholesterol Level:
Somewhere between bacon and lard

Farthest Out of the Way Traveled Just for Chow:
- Gas for 90 mile drive to/from taqueria: $6.78
- Panbazo, DF quesadilla, Negra Modelo, tax, and tip: $12.56
- Another Panbazo and DF quesadilla to go: $8.43
- Not hungry during subsequent family dinner at Old Spaghetti Factory: Priceless!

Nabe Most Full of Explorable Unknown Chow: Any of the hundreds of small towns of migrant farm workers in California's central valley

Top Chinatown Pick: Egg custard tart at Golden Gate Bakery—legendary for good reason

Weight Management Tip: Avoid all trans fats entirely, reduce intake of processed food and sugary beverages

Favorite Comfort Chow:
Risotto at Ristorante Bacco

Favorite Gelato Flavor:
Amarena

Penang Village boasts no fewer than nineteen noodle dishes, and noodles are indeed a strength. So is egg roti, a large, flaky pancake filled with a layer of egg and herbs, served with mild curry sauce for dipping. Hokkien char is thick udon noodles stir-fried with chicken, seafood, and veggies in dark soy sauce (seafood and chicken were overcooked, but noodles, bitter greens, and intensely flavored sweet and smoky sauce made the dish). Chendol is shaved ice topped with coconut milk, heavy, dark-brown sweet syrup, and green pea flour strips. Skip Hainan chicken rice and Malay lamb. Large servings of fresh young coconut juice in the shell are only $2.50. Open Monday through Saturday, 11 a.m. to 3 p.m. and 5 p.m. to 10 p.m.

Malaysian-owned **Banana City** serves a large number of Malaysian, Singaporean, and Thai dishes. Chicken sate is better than beef, and prawn mee (shrimp noodle soup) comes in a pleasantly spicy red broth redolent of fish sauce.

MARIPOSA CAFETERIA
Strategies

Mariposa Cafeteria (Potrero Hill)
1599 Tennessee St.
San Francisco, CA
415-285-5105
Chinese (Hong Kong)/Chinese (Cantonese)

Myriad chowhounds have extolled the virtues of **Mariposa Cafeteria's** roast pork. Here *felice* shares her Mariposa strategies. Pay close attention.

Opt for à la carte rather than rice plates. Two à la carte dishes can be shared among five average eaters, whereas one rice plate will only feed two average eaters. Make sure you specify you want à la carte or they'll give you rice plates by default. If eating family style, only send one person to the register to order to minimize confusion. Get one order of rice per every four people. They're only open until 2 p.m., so get there early for the good stuff. Call ahead if you have your heart set on a particular dish. Besides roast pork, order oxtail stew, pork chops, beef with string beans, Singaporean noodles, and pork spare ribs. Skip soy sauce chicken and chow fun.

Old-Fashioned **MARTINIS**

Blondie's Bar & No Grill (Mission)
540 Valencia St.
San Francisco, CA
415-864-2419
Pub

Moose's (North Beach)
1652 Stockton St.
San Francisco, CA
415-989-7800
New American

Orbit Room Cafe (Castro)
1900 Market St.
San Francisco, CA
415-252-9525
Pub

Washington Square Bar and Grill
  (North Beach)
1707 Powell St.
San Francisco, CA
415-982-8123
American/Italian

In the age of brightly colored specialty cocktails, finding bartenders adept at the classics isn't easy. But the following are a few quality spots where the staff mixologists get nods even from picky chowhounds:

The bars at both **Moose's** and **Washington Square Bar and Grill** serve well-made martinis and other classics apropos to their classic American atmospheres. **Blondie's Bar & No Grill** serves martinis high in both quality and quantity—you get a standard glass, plus your own shaker for keeping your drink refreshed and cold. The **Orbit Room** is San Francisco's best-kept bar secret, reports *phat-phil*, a place where the bartenders take their classic cocktails seriously. Standards made with top-shelf liquors for $5 to $7 and a totally unpretentious yet immediately hip art deco atmosphere are the allure.

○ **Moose's:** *see also* p. 179.

MEATBALL SUBS

Goat Hill Pizza (Potrero Hill)
300 Connecticut St.
San Francisco, CA
415-641-1440
Pizza/Italian

King Foot Subs (Haight)
258 Divisadero St.
San Francisco, CA
415-431-5217
Sandwich shop

Mario's Bohemian Cigar Store
  Cafe (North Beach)
566 Columbus Ave.
San Francisco, CA
415-362-0536
Italian café

New York Pizzeria
  (Sonoma County)
65 Brookwood Ave.
Santa Rosa, CA
707-526-9743
Pizza

Pazzo (Potrero Hill)
2 Henry Adams St.
San Francisco, CA
415-487-1509
Italian

Yellow Submarine (Sunset)
503 Irving St.
San Francisco, CA
415-681-5652
American sandwich shop

Who makes a superior meatball sub? **King Foot**'s version satisfies even East Coast expat hounds. Meatballs are made on the premises, are a little small, but firmly packed with balanced flavor. Throw some provolone and tomato sauce on 'em, toast it all on a white grinder roll, and it's something else, raves *phat-phil*. Perennial sub destination **Yellow Submarine** makes a mean meatball sandwich, says *cc*, who also likes the open-faced version at **Goat Hill Pizza**. North Beach institution **Mario's Bohemian** makes a worthy meatball sandwich on Liguria Bakery focaccia, and **Pazzo**'s tasty version (lunch only) comes on untoasted garlic focaccia, with halved veal and sausage meatballs, provolone, and tomato sauce. Raves all around for meatball subs at much adored **New York Pizzeria** in Sonoma.

○ **New York Pizzeria:** *see also* p. 244.

Sit-down **MEXICAN**

Alteña (Mission)
3346 Mission St.
San Francisco, CA
415-647-1980
Mexican

Estrellita Restaurant (Peninsula)
971 N. San Antonio Rd.
Los Altos, CA
650-941-8976
Mexican

Mar Y Tierra (Peninsula)
1475 Broadway St.
Redwood City, CA
650-369-2201
Mexican

Mom Is Cooking (Mission)
1166 Geneva Ave.
San Francisco, CA
415-586-7000
Mexican

Otaez Mexicatessen (East Bay)
3872 International Blvd.
Oakland, CA
510-536-0909
Mexican

Playa Azul Restaurant (Mission)
3318 Mission St.
San Francisco, CA
415-282-4554
Mexican

The Bay Area's known for its taquerias, but good, full-service Mexican restaurants are thin on the ground. Here are some picks:

In San Francisco, **Mom Is Cooking** has unusual dishes not often seen in the US (e.g., tlacoyos), and is perfect for carnivores. The Mexican Potpourri (a sampler of most dishes) is recommended, but *nja* warns about poor rice and beans. **Alteña** is bare bones, and does serve tacos and burritos, but also ceviches, tostadas, enchiladas, etc. Good, freshly made chips, rice and beans, and excellent sopas and al pastor. **Otaez Mexicatessen** reminds *Windy* of the sort of restaurant you'd see in Mexico.

In the Outer Mission, **Playa Azul** makes the usual Salvadoran-Mexican choices, but also lots of seafood and fish dishes—with prices all over the map. Seafood cocktails are definitely the way to go here, *jonnygo* says, served in large glasses with tomato sauce, onions, cilantro. It also does good huevos rancheros for breakfast.

Estrellita in Los Altos is *nja*'s absolute favorite sit-down Mexican place; it's "the only Mexican restaurant my girlfriend's large and food-obsessed Mexican family likes." The menu's not exotic, so expect the usual Mexican standards—enchiladas, burritos, tostadas—but there's love in the details. Red salsa is intoxicating—somewhat sweet, very garlicky and quite hot. If you like it hotter, ask for the good stuff from the back. And *nja*'s favorite dishes: A mole rojo special and Oaxacan chicken tostada (huge tortilla bowl filled with lettuce, tomatoes, cheese, beans, and marinated, grilled red mole chicken), with sides of unfailingly good refried beans and rice. Large selection of Mexican beers and even a few Mexican wines, but margaritas are the slushy machine kind. Very crowded at lunch.

Those craving mariscos (cold Mexican shellfish dishes) on the Peninsula can head to small, unassuming **Mar Y Tierra**, where *RWCFoodie* has enjoyed shrimp cocktail with a generous amount of large, juicy prawns in a spicy tomato juice–type liquid with chopped onion, radish, cucumber, and avocado, served with lots of soda crackers.

○ **Otaez Mexicatessen:** *see also* **pp. 189, 200.**

Fruitvale **MEXICAN** Tour

Cinco De Mayo (East Bay)
3438 International Blvd.
Oakland, CA
510-533-3838
Mexican

El Novillo (East Bay)
Parking lot of Guadalajara
    Restaurant
Oakland, CA
Mexican street cart/Truck

El Ojo de Agua (East Bay)
3851 International Blvd., in the
    parking lot of International
    Produce Market
Oakland, CA
Mexican street cart/Truck

La Torta Loca (East Bay)
3419 International Blvd.
Oakland, CA
510-532-7105
Mexican

Mariscos La Costa Restaurant
    (East Bay)
3625 International Blvd.
Oakland, CA
Mexican

Neza Rosticeria & Taqueria
    (East Bay)
3731 International Blvd.
Oakland, CA
510-534-4795
Mexican

Otaez Mexicatessen (East Bay)
3872 International Blvd.
Oakland, CA
510-536-0909
Mexican

Oakland's Fruitvale is a mecca for authentic Mexican treats. You'll hear tons of Spanish on the streets, and many of the signs are in Spanish, too. International Blvd. is only a couple of blocks from the Fruitvale BART station. Follow this itinerary for a great way to spend a sunny afternoon.

First, don't forget the much loved **La Torta Loca**! Great quesadillas (fried), huaraches de tinga, aguas frescas (Mexico City–like, i.e., less sweet than most US versions, and include tepache—slightly fermented pineapple juice).

Stop at **El Novillo** taco truck for great carnitas tacos (served with pickled carrots and jalapeños and fresh whole radishes). Tripas (or chitlins, as translated on the truck's sign) are good, too—crisp and carmelized yet slightly chewy. Even non-innard eaters will like these, says *Ruth Lafler*.

Try one of the many fruit and corn carts along International selling baggies of fresh-cut fruit and veggies ($2.50). They douse them with lime, salt, and chili for a very refreshing snack. These carts also sell corn on the cob (it's not on display, so just ask for *elotes*, pronoucned ay-LOTE-ays) slathered in mayo and rolled in cheese and chile powder. Also: big bags of chicharrones (fried pork skins that look like those fake onion ring snacks!), also doused with lime and hot sauce. Eat them fast to avoid sogginess!

Seafood's the thing at **Mariscos La Costa** (the restaurant, not the truck, although the truck's good, too). Try tostados with ceviche de camerones (shrimp) and ceviche de pescado (fish), but unless you like fake crab, skip the mixto (shrimp, fake crab, and octopus). And on the nonseafood end, they make a pretty nice (albeit inauthentic) al pastor.

Getting thirsty? Stop at **El Ojo de Agua** taco truck, in the parking lot of International Market. They make great aguas frescas and liquados—strawberry and nut flavors are highly recommended. They also make more-than-decent tortas (sole complaint: the rolls could be crisper).

Then there's **Neza**, a Mexico City–style restaurant whose

specialty is roast chicken with great green salsa. Hit this place at the height of lunch or dinner for the freshest chicken.

Getting full yet? If not, make a stop at **Otaez Mexicatessan**. It's like someone took a classic diner and dolled it up with Mexican murals and artwork. Very good machaca with eggs, chilaquiles verde con pollo, and aguas frescas. Groups are often served complimentary dessert (rice pudding once, another time baked caramelized sweet potato). The attached taqueria (Otaez Taqueria) looks very promising, with its big pile of grilled white onions, griddle for heating tortillas, and al pastor with pineapple on the spit. No firsthand reports yet. Too full by then.

But if you still have room for dessert, check out **Cinco de Mayo** for raspados—chunky shaved ice with fruit or syrup toppings (nuts, pineapple, strawberry, vanilla, etc.).

○ **El Novillo:** *see also* pp. 288, 294.
○ **La Torta Loca:** *see also* p. 288.
○ **Otaez Mexicatessen:** *see also* pp. 187, 200.

Gilroy **MEXICAN**

El 7 Mares (South Bay)
7820 Monterey St.
Gilroy, CA
408-848-5060
Mexican

Many chowhounds agree that El 7 Mares does a fine job with seafood dishes, especially camerones al diablo (succulent, sweet prawns in very spicy roasted chili sauce), campechana (mixed seafood cocktail with perfect-texture prawns and octopus, though the crab's not as good), octopus cocktail, caldo siete mares (full of seafood with well-balanced broth), quesadilla de camarones (full of cheese, shrimp, and savories, deep-fried, served with avocado, sour cream, lettuce, salsa fresca), and camerones ranchero ("a little soupy, not too sweet, and heavy with tomatoes and lots of shrimp").

MEXICANA Auténtica

City Blend Cafe (Mission)
3087 16th St.
San Francisco, CA
415-725-0137
Mexican café

Dos Hermanos truck
    (Solano County)
700 Sereno Dr., in the parking lot
    of Vallejo Furniture
Vallejo, CA
Mexican street cart/Truck

El Charro Restaurant (South Bay)
799 S 1st St.
San Jose, CA
408-292-3710
Mexican

La Costena Custom Burritos
    (Peninsula)
2078 Old Middlefield Way
Mountain View, CA
650-967-0507
Mexican

La Milpa Mexican Restaurant
    (South Bay)
107 N. Milpitas Blvd.
Milpitas, CA
408-945-6540
Mexican

Mi Lindo Yucatan (Mission)
401 Valencia
San Francisco, CA
415-861-4935
Mexican

Savor Mexico (Peninsula)
2595 California St.
Mountain View, CA
650-917-1306
Mexican

Tacos Chavez truck (East Bay)
Somewhere between CompUSA
    (3839 Emery St) and Pak N
    Save (3889 San Pablo Ave)
Emeryville, CA
Mexican street cart/Truck

Tacos Jerezanos truck (East Bay)
40th St. and Horton
Emeryville, CA
Mexican street cart/Truck

Taqueria El Grullense (Peninsula)
1280 El Camino Real
Redwood City, CA
650-368-3737
Mexican

Taqueria/Mercado Marlen
    (Peninsula)
2350 California St.
Mountain View, CA
650-947-1700
Mexican

Tommy's Mexican (Richmond)
5929 Geary Blvd.
San Francisco, CA
415-387-4747
Mexican

Authentic Mexican (as opposed to San Francisco–style burritos and such) can be found around the Bay Area, if you look for it. Best bets (and their best dishes):

Tacqueria El Grullense: carnitas, adobada, and tongue tacos; fiery-hot, chunky salsa

El Charro: seafood, carne asada

La Milpa: enchiladas (stacked, with fried egg on top); mole negro; soups; breakfast dishes; flan

Tommy's Mexican: margaritas and Yucatecan specialties only

Taqueria/Mercado Marlen: barbacoa

Savor Mexico: salsas

La Costena: carne asada burrito (*nja* considers this the best steak burrito in San Francisco)

City Blend Cafe: known for organic coffee, but also serving Yucatecan specialties—panuchos, salbutes, relleños negros, tamales, empanadas, poc chuc, and cochinita pibil—*shocker* praises their panuchos and salbutes

Mi Lindo Yucatan: great chile relleño negro

In Emeryville, the **Tacos Chavez truck** has standard meats (carne asada, pollo, al pastor, lengua) for tacos and tortas, plus tripas and cabeza. Salsa is fruity and aromatic, and tortas are gooey, with lots of cheese and avocado. Recommended: cabeza and al pastor. Open 10 a.m. to 6 p.m., Monday through Saturday.

Tacos Jerezanos adds chile verde, chorizo, and beef birria to the standard lineup, and has better tortillas than Tacos Chavez (here, they get a little crisp from the grill). Tortas are drier, without avocado. Recommended: chile verde, carnitas, al pastor. Open approximately 11 a.m. to 4:30 p.m., Monday through Friday.

Dos Hermanos taco truck in Vallejo has terrific, thin and delicate tortillas; tacos include creamy-textured whole beans and bright orange, freshly made hot sauce. Lengua is buttery soft, and cabeza is tender from long braising. Open late (the truck's been seen at 9 a.m. and 9 p.m.), and food's always fresh.

MIDDLE EAST Tour

Alborz (Russian Hill)
1245 Van Ness Ave.
San Francisco, CA
415-440-4321
Persian

Fattoush Restaurant (Noe Valley)
1361 Church St.
San Francisco, CA
415-641-0678
Jordanian/Palestinian

Garne's Restaurant (South Bay)
4628 Meridian Ave.
San Jose, CA
408-267-1288
Persian

Maykadeh Persian Cuisine
  (North Beach)
470 Green St.
San Francisco, CA
415-362-8286
Persian

Yiasso (South Bay)
2180 S. Bascom Ave.
Campbell, CA
408-559-0312
Greek

Yiasso (South Bay)
10660 S. De Anza Blvd.
Cupertino, CA
408-253-5544
Greek

"**Persian cuisine is** a sultry calling card to an ancient culture, largely mysterious and unknown to the West. **Garne's** delivers the message with a loving hand. The best Persian eating I have experienced, including in private homes," raves *Ken Hoffman*. His favorite dishes here include tahdig ghormeh sarzi ("uniquely crispified, bottom-of-the-crock rice dish that is smothered with a deep green blend of cilantro, parsley, and onion, a robust and satisfying dish"); and koobideh (ground beef kabob); shirin polo (skinless chicken breast "colored and flavored with psychedelic toppings of almond, orange peel, pistachio nut meat, and a mount of marmalade flavored rice. Wonderful, exotic, healthy"). The most savory, fragrant, and rich item is Garne's wonderful, authentic, and uncompromising khoresht gheymeh bodemjan (lentils, braised beef in tomato sauce).

Maykadeh serves up a taste of Persia in North Beach, specializing in meat dishes. Its menu's a bit more adventurous than the one at **Alborz** (a chowhound favorite for Persian; we have no recent reports to relay, however), and includes lamb tongue and brains. Grilled dishes like koobideh (ground lamb and beef skewer), shishlik (marinated lamb chops), sturgeon kabab, barg (filet mignon), and poussin are all favorites. Don't miss lamb's tongue appetizer, perfectly braised and tender with lime juice, sour cream, and saffron sauce, or zeresht polo (steamed rice with saffron and barberries, with marinated chicken thighs). Service is slow and inattentive. *Malik* doesn't believe it shines above other good Persian restaurants in the Bay Area, however.

Fattoush is a smart brunch option, less crowded than other Noe Valley spots. Brunch menu goes beyond traditional Middle Eastern fare with particulary good grilled chicken frittata and salmon platter. For dinner, *nja* says prices are a little high, though the more elaborate dishes are worth it. Opt for the less common, more interesting dishes and get your hummus, baba ganoush, and tabouli fix less expensively at your favorite hole-in-the-wall Middle Eastern joint. Enjoy the Noe Valley sun on Fattoush's little patio.

Yiasso is a small South Bay chain for excellent gyros and Greek salads. We hear best things about the Cupertino and Campbell locations.

MIDDLEFIELD ROAD Taco Crawl

Aguililla Market (Peninsula)
3250 Middlefield Rd.
Menlo Park, CA
650-361-1965
Mexican

Casa Sanchez (Peninsula)
near 3250 Middlefield Rd.
Menlo Park, CA
Mexican

El Grullense II (Peninsula)
2940 Middlefield Rd.
Redwood City, CA
650-364-8449
Mexican

Gonzalez Taqueria (Peninsula)
3194 Middlefield Rd.
Redwood City, CA
650-365-6405
Mexican

La Fuente Agua Purificado
  (Peninsula)
3250 Middlefield Rd.
Menlo Park, CA
Mexican street cart/Truck

La Pachanga (Peninsula)
3102 Middlefield Rd.
Redwood City, CA
650-364-7969
Mexican

Middlefield Road in Redwood City has lots of little restaurants, taquerias, and markets serving pretty authentic Mexican specialties in a neighborhood with a low-key suburban feel. None of that gritty San Francisco Mission vibe here.

Gonzalez Taqueria serves wonderful birria (goat stew) and menudo every day, not just weekends, but they sell out early. Broth in the former is basically a goat stock, meat is wonderfully tender and chewy. "Add a little onion, cilantro, some great peppery hot sauce, fresh lime, and a few bits of the freshly made, fluffy corn tortillas and you're there—big time!" says *ChewToy*. Tostada de pata de puerco en vinagre, pickled pig's part (leg? foot?) with sliced potatoes, cheese, and lettuce is an acquired taste, being gelantinous and crunchy. Chili oils, salsas, and bowls of oregano and epazote with hot peppers are on the tables, and service is friendly and accommodating.

La Fuente Agua Purificado sells purified water (look for the faucet on the street) at 30¢ a gallon. And with this water, they make ice for crushed ice drinks, adding aguas frescas over the ice for $1.50 to $2.50 for refreshing treats in fruit and nut flavors. **La Pachanga's** the hot spot for frozen margaritas in flavors like jamaica (hibiscus), mango, and honeydew. Unfortunately, top-shelf lime margarita was a failure, so maybe stick with other fruit flavors.

Aguililla Market draws mixed opinions, but its carnitas are dry and crispy (you must ask for "doradas con cueritos" for a bit of crisp skin), says *Victoria Libin*, who also recommends Aguililla's chicharron en salsa verde (fried pork rinds stewed in tomatillo sauce), carne asada (grilled beef), guisado de res (stewed beef). Tacos and salsas are just okay, cantaloupe agua is good, but other aguas seem to be from a mix. Cheerful atmosphere with a nice outdoor patio.

A block from Aguililla, **Casa Sanchez** has the "best birria I've sampled outside of Jalisco," says *Victoria Libin*. **El Grullense II** had the best tacos of all, but alas, its famously fiery salsa is not available at this location.

Clean Clothes . . . and
MITCHELL'S ICE CREAM

Joey's Ice Cream, Espresso,
  Sausages, Wash & Dry
  (Tenderloin)
517 O'Farrell St.
San Francisco, CA
Café

Pakwan Restaurant (Tenderloin)
501 O'Farrell St.
San Francisco, CA
415-776-0160
Pakistani

Joey's Ice Cream, Espresso, Sausages, Wash & Dry has it all: thirty flavors of Mitchell's ice cream, sausage sandwiches (though "it's no Rosamunde," according to *Stanley Stephan*) and a self-service laundry, all two doors down from Pakistani-Indian favorite Pakwan.

○ **Pakwan Restaurant:** *see also* p. 50.

Chowhounding MORGAN HILL

Chimichanga Restaurant
  (South Bay)
10980 Monterey Rd.
Morgan Hill, CA
408-779-2928
Mexican

Trail Dust BBQ Joint (South Bay)
16490 Monterey St.
Morgan Hill, CA
408-776-9072
Barbecue

Sicilia In Bocca (South Bay)
25 W. Main St.
Morgan Hill, CA
408-778-0399
Italian

Hound *pugluvr* shares her chow finds in Morgan Hill: **Trail Dust** is her very favorite rib joint of all time, for superb dry-rub spareribs, BBQ chicken, and juicy tri-tip. Sit-down service, dinner only Wednesday through Sunday. No reservations, no credit cards. **Sicilia in Bocca**'s a winner because the owner is such a character and the cooking is simple and down-home Italian. Don't miss the assorted antipasti plate with garlicky artichoke hearts and vividly flavored caponata, or spaghettti with clams and white wine sauce. Look for Silician wines on the wine list. Be nice to the host and he might sneak you an icy limonata for dessert. **Chimichanga** is the best Mexican in the area for chile verde, beef enchiladas, and machaca.

MOROCCAN Feasts

Aziza (Richmond)
5800 Geary Blvd.
San Francisco, CA
415-752-2222
Moroccan

Tanjia (East Bay)
4905 Telegraph Ave.
Oakland, CA
510-653-8691
Moroccan

At Aziza, a $39, five-course tasting menu includes choice of soup, a selection of appetizers, bastilla, and choice of entree or dessert. Soup offerings might include warming and delicious smooth lentil soup with a date on the side, or creamy pumpkin, reports *Millicent*. Assorted appetizers (vegetable salads, skewered lamb meatballs, goat cheese with tomato sauce) are generous, deeply flavorful, and a nice mix of tastes and textures. Bastilla is the classic Moroccan sweet and savory taste sensation of chicken, almonds, and spices in crackly layers of dough (a vegetarian version is also available). Entrees like prawn tagine, couscous with lamb stew, and couscous Aziza (with chicken, merguez, prawn, lamb stew, and vegetables) are enhanced by great, smoky-hot harissa. Desserts are on the lighter side, meant to complement the heavy and rich dishes that come before; apple-rosemary dessert is perfectly balanced.

Tanjia engages your senses as soon as you enter. A traditional Berber tent, wrought iron fixtures, and deep, cushion-filled benches around low tables create an environment that immediately transports you to Morocco, says *Melanie Wong*. A five-course prix fixe dinner is only $21.95 to $23.95. Harira (mildly spicy red lentil soup) is warming. Assorted vegetable salads are distinctive, each seasoned differently. Bastilla can be ordered with chicken or seafood (shrimp and scallops), and both are delicious, made with housemade, hand-stretched brik pastry leaves rather than commercial filo. Lamb with prunes and chicken with lemon and olives are artfully spiced, with well-balanced sweet and savory flavors. And lamb tagine, served in its eponymous terra cotta dish, is intoxicatingly fragrant, the sweet onions still have a little crunch, and the long-cooked lamb is succulent, though sauce can be over salted. Couscous is hand rolled each day in-house, and is very tasty. Clean your hands with warm towels, followed with a bit of delicate, housemade orange flower water, and enjoy an accomplished belly dancer who offers patrons free lessons. Service is smooth and well timed, and servers are happy to explain the cooking methods and cultural context of various dishes.

○ **Aziza:** *see also* **p. 236.**

Chowhounding **NEAR** **UC BERKELEY**

Ann's Kitchen (East Bay)
2498 Telegraph Ave.
Berkeley, CA
510-548-8885
Diner or Coffee shop

Ashby BART flea market taco
   trucks (East Bay)
3100 Adeline St., at Ashby BART
   station
Berkeley, CA
www.berkeleyfleamarket.com
Mexican street cart/Truck

Caffe Strada (East Bay)
2300 College Ave.
Berkeley, CA
510-843-5282
Diner or Coffee shop

Cheese Board (East Bay)
1504 Shattuck Ave.
Berkeley, CA
510-549-3183
Pizza bakery/Cheese shop/Pizzeria

Hummingbird Cafe (East Bay)
1814 Euclid Ave.
Berkeley, CA
510-848-8361
American café

King Pin Doughnuts (East Bay)
2521 Durant Ave., A
Berkeley, CA
510-843-6688
Bakery

Meesha's Berkeley Gyros
   (East Bay)
2519 Durant Ave., C
Berkeley, CA
510-849-4771
Middle Eastern/North African

Mystery Korean/Japanese at
   Durant Food Court (East Bay)
2517 Durant Ave., B
Berkeley, CA
510-848-5968
Japanese/Korean

Ozzie's Fountain in Elmwood
   Pharmacy (East Bay)
2900 College Ave.
Berkeley, CA
510-841-0989
Café

Sufficient Grounds (East Bay)
2431 Durant Ave.
Berkeley, CA
510-841-3049
Café

Yali's Oxford Street Cafe
   (East Bay)
1920 Oxford St.
Berkeley, CA
510-843-2233
Café

Yogurt Park (East Bay)
2433 Durant Ave., A
Berkeley, CA
510-549-0570
Café

UC Berkeley students past and present share favorite nonobvious student hangouts (top obvious choice: Top Dog—see *"Hot Dog!"*). Most of the following are *ctan*'s picks:

Meesha's Berkeley Gyros is a hole-in-the-wall with good grilled meat plates and a personable owner.

Hummingbird Cafe for vegetarian delight sandwich (pesto, avocado, feta, lettuce, tomato, mayo) and good halvah.

Yali's Cafe for "simple but impeccable" soups, pasta salad, baked-in-house focaccia.

The flea market at **Ashby BART** sometimes has booths selling tropical produce and the occasional taco truck (look toward the northeast corner).

Ann's Kitchen has crispy, hearty homefries.

Spoony Bard likes a Korean/Japanese noodle shop in the

Durant Food Court for fresh noodles. It's on the right as you enter, toward the back.

King Pin Donuts, but only if you can get them fresh! A couple of chowhounds report best success between 9 and 10 p.m.—so long as you're willing to buy whatever they're making at that point.

Cheese Board is a bit off campus, but worth the walk.

Caffe Strada is for dessert, outdoor seating, and *Yvonne*'s favorite ham-and-cheese croissants.

Ozzie's Fountain, inside the Elmwood Pharmacy has great milkshakes and that 1940s soda fountain feel. *David Boyk* advises you skip the pancakes.

Sufficient Grounds is a good spot for studying, serving tasty sandwiches on baked-in-house focaccia.

Yogurt Park is perfect for late-night study break snacks.

○ **Cheese Board:** *see also* **pp. 4, 51, 54, 238.**

Chow at the **NET**

Food booths at Network
   Associates Coliseum
   (East Bay)
7000 Coliseum Way
Oakland, CA
510-569-2121
Eclectic

Otaez Mexicatessen (East Bay)
3872 International Blvd.
Oakland, CA
510-536-0909
Mexican

Watching all that physical exertion can make anyone hungry. What are the best in-stadium chow options when the A's or Raiders play a home game? Hit the Black Muslim Bakery stand for fish sandwiches and baked goods (keep an eye out for banana pudding, carrot coconut cupcakes, ginger cookies, and more). Saag's Grill for bratwurst or Polish sausages. Sandwich buffet bar with tables serves up a pretty good roast beef sandwich. Everett & Jones BBQ, the East Bay fave, sells 'cue in the left field stands. When A's regular *Ruth Lafler* isn't enjoying nachos with fluorescent orange "cheese" sauce (ballpark food!) she'd recommend garlic fries—you'll be garlicky for days! (Ask for directions at the info booth on main concourse behind section 119.) The Field, a pseudo-Irish pub, serves decent corned beef sandwiches and Guinness, and is right next to the customer relations desk, where staff has directories and will happily tell you where to get what. The Coliseum's standard hot dogs are chowhound-approved Miller's brand, but alas, come in soggy steamed buns.

Outside the stadium, check out taco trucks (weekends only) on Frontage Road (Coliseum Way) on the 66th Street side of the Coliseum. The one parked closest to the Coliseum often has excellent al pastor. And for more Mexican goodies, the Fruitvale district is nearby. Head a mile north on San Leandro Boulevard (the main street east of the Coliseum), then jog one block east to International. Otaez Mexicatessen, at 40th and International, is a fave.

○ **Otaez Mexicatessen:** *see also* **pp. 187, 189.**

Secrets of **NIEBAUM COPPOLA**

Cafe Niebaum Coppola (Peninsula)
473 University Ave.
Palo Alto, CA
650-752-0350·
Italian

Niebaum Coppola's Palo Alto location has a well-deserved reputation for very slow service and noisy crowds, but here's a very houndish tip courtesy of *Victoria Libin*: "order their margherita made with buffalo mozzarella (which costs extra). It's quite close to real Neopolitan pizza: thin, but not cracker thin, crispy bottom crust with slight charring on edges, small amount of crushed tomatoes, small amount of fior di latte (cow's milk mozzarella) or buffalo mozzarella, olive oil, and some basil. Order anything other than the margherita or marinara pizza at your own risk. And whatever you do, don't attempt this at the San Francisco location where the same pizzas tend to have chewy, dried-out crusts."

NOE VALLEY Chow

Amberjack Sushi (Noe Valley)
1497 Church St.
San Francisco, CA
415-920-1797
Japanese

Cybelle's Pizza (Noe Valley)
3782 24th St.
San Francisco, CA
415-285-3212
Pizza/Italian

Deep Sushi (Noe Valley)
1740 Church St.
San Francisco, CA
415-970-3337
Japanese

Le Zinc French Bistro (Noe Valley)
4063 24th St.
San Francisco, CA
415-647-9410
French bistro

Miss Millie's (Noe Valley)
4123 24th St.
San Francisco, CA
415-285-5598
American

Noe Valley Pizza Restaurant
 (Noe Valley)
3898 24th St.
San Francisco, CA
415-647-1664
Pizza

Ristorante Bacco (Noe Valley)
737 Diamond St.
San Francisco, CA
415-282-4969
Italian

Yianni's (Noe Valley)
1708 Church St.
San Francisco, CA
415-647-3200
Greek

Noe Valley hounds share inside local tips . . .

Ristorante Bacco is one of *nja*'s favorite restaurants in San Francisco. Appetizers, salads, pastas, risottos, veal Milanese, desserts, and service are top notch; wine list focuses on Tuscany; open every day.

Amberjack does a great job with sushi staples. Fish is always fresh and prices are reasonable. Also good cooked items and appetizers.

Deep Sushi has the best cucumber salad (dime-size slices of sweet cucumber in ponzu sauce with fresh toasted sesame seeds), and cool ambience, sexy waiters and waitresses dressed in black, DJ, and yes, great sushi arrangements. Drawback: really uncomfortable wrought iron chairs.

Noe Valley Pizza Restaurant is a fave, run by an Italian family with a real family feel. Big red vinyl booths and very good spinach salad with carmelized onions.

For watching the 'Niners or Giants, you can't beat a pint of Full Sail at Noe's Sports Bar with a pizza from **Cybelle**'s next door. But, *nja* says, Cybelle's, on its own, isn't worth a trip.

Fabrizio's quick suggestions: **Miss Millie's** serves up great brunch (but be prepared for a wait), French-owned **Le Zinc** offers nice French ambience, excellent fries, and good wine list; and at **Yianni**'s, stick with appetizers and moussaka, also their saganaki (flaming cheese) is good and fun.

○ **Ristorante Bacco:** *see also* pp. 152, 217.

Slurp Your **NOODLES**

Slurp Noodle House (East Bay)
2426 Telegraph Ave.
Berkeley, CA
510-644-9292
Korean/Chinese

Slurp, a cash-only noodle shop near UC Berkeley, specializes in housemade wheat noodles and hand-pulled noodles. There are treasures here, but also some duds. Good stuff includes fiery Thai noodles, great home-style fried tofu soup, pork with pickled vegetables soup, dan dan noodles (not authentic, but very nice). Less good: uninteresting beef chow fun and disappointing Thai noodle soup. Recommended by *patrick*: pork and pickled vegetables ("deliriously salty and with lovely contrasting textures of crunchy pickles and chewy noodles") and braised beef with shiitake mushrooms (broth, noodles, and mushrooms are delicious, but the meat's less so). Wok-tossed edamame in chile and ginger is tantalizing and wonderful, with hot spicy slippery little soybeans.

OFFAL in Oakland (and Other Hot Prospects)

La Gran Chiquita (East Bay)
3503 International Blvd.
Oakland, CA
510-533-6484
Mexican

La Gran Chiquita offers offal to please any palate—not just generic cabeza or tripa, but eyeballs, cheeks, glands, brains, reports *Windy*, ever hot on the entrail. And for the less adventurous, there are sincronizadas (flour quesadilla with ham and cheese) and quesadillas with squash blossoms and huitlacoche (corn fungus). They get small details right: excellent salsas, home-made tangy flour and corn tortillas, fresh-squeezed orange juice, made-from-mix horchata and jamaica. Service is friendly and casual.

Only a block or two from Fruitvale BART, there are plenty of other spots to check out in this nabe, including a rotissierie on the west side of International between 37th and 38th for Mexico City–style food (chicken necks three for $1.00, whole chickens for $5.99), a gumbo house and a birrieria (serving birria, stewed goat). Also, many pushcarts scattered up and down the street with snacks, including elote (corn slathered with mayo, rolled in grated parmesean and sprinkled with chile).

ONO HAWAIIAN GRILL

Ono Hawaiian Grill (Peninsula)
3048 Cabrillo Hwy. N.
Half Moon Bay, CA
650-726-8114
Hawaiian

Rick's Restaurant & Bar (Sunset)
1940 Taraval St.
San Francisco, CA
415-731-8900
Hawaiian

A few things to know about **Ono Hawaiian Grill**: call ahead if your heart is set on Kalua pig, which is not always available; blalah-sized plate lunches are enough food for two meals; ask about the fresh catch of the day (but inquire about prices). And be advised that there's very good teriyaki chicken ("not too saucy, not too sweet, incredibly yummy—perfect for kids,") says *Brad Kaplan*, who sums up the restaurant as having built "a winning combination of great island-flavored food, casual family-friendly surfer atmosphere, and convenient coastside location for all the locals and daytrippers down from the city or out from the peninsula."

Ono is closed Mondays, but the first Monday of every month finds **Rick's** transformed into Hawaii night, full of Hawaiian shirts and leis, with "Tiny Bubbles" played on the piano. *Straight Talk* shares his take: "Bar is outstanding, damn tasty piña coladas help set the island tone for the night. Chow-wise, the portions are Mauna Loa–esque, in size. You could bathe a small bird in the bowl of poi. Everything was outstanding." Reservations recommended.

ORGANIC PRODUCE—
Delivered!

Mariquita Farm CSA
   (Santa Cruz County)
PO Box 2065
Watsonville, CA
831-761-3226
Farm or Farm stand

Planet Organics
1-800-956-5855
Mail order source

Mariquita Farms is a CSA (Community Supported Agriculture) farm delivering to San Francisco customers. It has a field in Watsonville for greens and cool-weather crops plus a field in Hollister for warm-weather produce like tomatoes, chilis, eggplants, and melons. Between the two, its baskets should be well rounded. Cost is $18 per week. For more information see its Web site at www.mariquita.com.

Another produce delivery option is **Planet Organics**, a weekly organic produce and grocery delivery service. Since it contracts with many farmers, it customizes baskets for each customer. You can also order Niman Ranch meats and Rosie organic chickens among other items.

More Toothsome **OSTRICH**

Andronico's
www.andronicos.com
Store

Berkeley Bowl (East Bay)
2020 Oregon St.
Berkeley, CA
510-843-6929
Store

Eliza Restaurant (Potrero Hill)
1457 18th St.
San Francisco, CA
415-648-9999
Chinese/New American

Jasmine Tea House (Mission)
3253 Mission St.
San Francisco, CA
415-826-6288
Chinese

99 Ranch Market
www.99ranch.com
Chinese store

Oliver's Market (Sonoma County)
546 E. Cotati Ave.
Cotati, CA
707-795-9501
Store

Polarica (Potrero Hill)
105 Quint St.
San Francisco, CA
415-647-1300
Store

Fresh ostrich meat is hard to find; it's most often frozen. Tastewise, it's more like beef, but leaner than chicken. Read everything you'd ever want to know on the topic at: www.ostriches online.com. Locally, hounds have spotted frozen ostrich meat at **Andronico's, Berkeley Bowl,** and **99 Ranch** markets; **Oliver's Market** (which also carries emu); **Polarica** (always a go-to spot for hard-to-find, more exotic meats); and at various markets in San Francisco's Chinatown. Don't want to cook it at home? *Thea* reports that

Eliza's serves stir-fry mango ostrich and also garlic ostrich. **Jasmine Tea House** also does a nice ostrich stir-fry.

- ○ **Andronico's:** *see also* p. 230.
- ○ **Berkeley Bowl:** *see also* p. 47.
- ○ **99 Ranch Market:** *see also* pp. 172, 181.

OYSTER Season

Alemany Farmers' Market
(Bernal Heights)
100 Alemany Blvd.
San Francisco, CA
415-647-9423
Farmers' market

Hog Island Oysters (Marin County)
20215 State Rt. 1
Marshall, CA
415-663-9218
Farm or Farm stand

To stock up for a home-based oyster bash, head to the source . . . or to the farmers' market. **Hog Island** will sell you an even hundred oysters pulled from adjacent waters for $68—though you don't have to buy that many. If you can't wait to get home, they'll lend you shucking gear and you can slurp 'em right there at a picnic table. Point Reyes Oysters sells its harvest at the **Alemany Farmers' Market** on Saturdays, where small ones are around $5.50 a dozen or $35.00 a hundred, large are around $9.00 a dozen or $65.00 a hundred. Tomales Bay oysters are around $4.50 for 18, and Kumammotos are around $7.00 a dozen. You'll find Manila clams and clustered oysters, too.

- ○ **Alemany Farmer's Market:** *see also* p. 102.

Chowhound Nametag: Felice

○○○

Location:
San Francisco

Occupation:
Graduate student; chemistry

Nabe Most Full of Explorable Unknown Chow:
Mission

Top Chinatown Pick:
Louie's California Chinese

Favorite Comfort Chow:
All good food is a comfort.

Guilty Pleasure:
I have no guilty pleasures.

Favorite Gelato Flavor:
Vanilla

Chowhounding Rules of Thumb:
Get whatever everyone else is getting.

PACIFICA Roundup

Ali Baba (Peninsula)
127 S. Linden Ave.
South San Francisco, CA
650-871-2221
Middle Eastern/North African

Colombo's Deli (Peninsula)
484 Manor Plaza
Pacifica, CA
650-355-5023
Italian deli

La Morena Taqueria (Peninsula)
307 Baden Ave.
South San Francisco, CA
650-553-9707
Mexican

Nick's Seashore Restaurant
   (Peninsula)
100 Rockaway Beach Ave.
Pacifica, CA
650-359-3900
Seafood

Villa Del Sol Argentinian
   Restaurant (Peninsula)
423 Grand Ave.
South San Francisco, CA
650-583-8372
Argentinian

Yokoso Nippon (Peninsula)
2470 Skyline Dr., in Ramallah
   Plaza at Manor Dr.
Pacifica, CA
650-355-1218
Japanese

Hounds agree that Pacifica's not a wonderland of stellar chow, but there are a few standouts tucked away. **Colombo's Deli** is an old school kind of place where large heroes are made from house-baked bread and meat and cheese are cut to order. It takes a while for sandwiches to come out, but the fresh bread and good ingredients make it worth it, says *beanbag*. This is also an Italian grocery where you can stock up on deli and packaged goods.

The owners of "No Name" Sushi (aka **Yokoso Nippon**) on Church in San Francisco moved to a better place in Pacifica with the same name. *Windy* reports cheap but decent sushi, good tempura (especially the vegetable assortment), and cooked fish in double-sized portions (half orders are available). Always ask what's fresh. Chirashi is enormous and quite wonderful for under $7, and two can eat for under $20, including tip. Free green tea, but no beer or wine. Go early for freshest choices. They serve dinner only from 5 p.m., closed Sundays, and cash only (and, for the love of God, don't park in the adjacent mini-mart's designated spaces).

Some feel **Nick's** is tired and overpriced, but *kaplan* reports enjoying an expensive ($16) but huge crab salad sandwich with fries. Prospects are brighter in nearby South San Francisco, where **Ali Baba** serves excellent shwarma, and **Villa del Sol** does Argentine-style meats. **La Morena** is also recommended, but without details. Also see the nabe index for more local choices.

○ **Villa Del Sol Argentinian Restaurant:** *see also* p. 268.

PAELLA

Alegrias Food from Spain (Marina)
2018 Lombard St.
San Francisco, CA
415-929-8888
Spanish

Iberia (Peninsula)
1026 Alma St.
Menlo Park, CA
650-325-8981
Spanish

B44 (Financial District)
44 Belden Pl.
San Francisco, CA
415-986-6287
Spanish

Zarzuela (Russian Hill)
2000 Hyde St.
San Francisco, CA
415-346-0800
Spanish

Cafe de la Paz (East Bay)
1600 Shattuck Ave.
Berkeley, CA
510-843-0662
Latin American

Paella is ideally an evocatively Iberian celebration of saffron-tinged rice, with carefully simmered seafood or meats (and/or vegetables), with the whole amounting to much more than the sum of its parts. But usually restaurant paella is just a lifeless plate of rice-and-stuff. Here are some of the serious places.

Zarzuela's paella boasts a delectable layer of crusty toasted rice at the bottom of the pan. Several paellas are served at **B44**, a Catalan restaurant (paella originated in Valencia, the southern tip of Catalan culture) where *lmswartz* recommends arros a la cacadorais, made with rabbit and chicken. Non-paella dishes here are less reliable. **Alegrias** is recommended for both tapas and paella. **Cafe de la Paz** is inconsistent, but when it's on, its paella is excellent. For paella on the Peninsula, *Heike Bartlett* recommends **Iberia**.

Also see "*Laurel's* for Friendly Cuban" for Cuban paella

○ **Alegrias Food from Spain:** *see also* p. 294.
○ **Zarzuela:** *see also* p. 123.

PANNETONE for the Holidays

Liguria Bakery (North Beach)
1700 Stockton St.
San Francisco, CA
415-421-3786
Italian bakery

Don't miss pannetone season at **Liguria Bakery** around Christmas time. These much praised and fast selling Christmas loaves are baked in limited quantity, so you've got to call and see when they're being made and run right in to snatch one up.

○ **Liguria Bakery:** *see also* p. 238.

PIZZA Tips

Arinell Pizza (East Bay)
2109 Shattuck Ave.
Berkeley, CA
510-841-4035
Pizza

Arinell Pizza (Mission)
509 Valencia St.
San Francisco, CA
415-255-1303
Pizza

Mary's Pizza Shack (East Bay)
2246 Oak Grove Rd.
Walnut Creek, CA
925-938-4800
Pizza/Italian

Mary's Pizza Shack
    (Sonoma County)
1143 S. Cloverdale Blvd.
Cloverdale, CA
707-894-8977
Pizza/Italian

Mary's Pizza Shack
    (Sonoma County)
359 E. Washington St.
Petaluma, CA
707-778-7200
Pizza

Prego Pizzeria (East Bay)
151 Park Pl.
Richmond, CA
510-235-0551
Pizza

Volare Pizza (Haight)
456 Haight St.
San Francisco, CA
415-552-2999
Pizza

XYZ Bar (SOMA)
181 3rd St., in W Hotel San
    Francisco
San Francisco, CA
415-817-7836
New American

Mary's Pizza Shack is a small local chain, mainly in the North Bay. Hounds recommend the Cloverdale, Petaluma, and Walnut Creek branches in particular, but not just for pizza. The Walnut Creek branch makes good pizza and breaksticks, and the Petaluma branch does a good job with comfort foods, well-seasoned meatballs and spaghetti, lasagna, and tripe in spicy tomato sauce (special only). The Cloverdale branch is good for spaghetti and meatball (yes singular—just one big ball!), and its ultra-fresh and amazingly well-stocked iceberg lettuce salad.

For you NY-style pepperoni and sausage pizza lovers, the place to eat is **Arinell**'s, with locations in Berkeley near UC and Valencia in San Francisco. *Shepherd B. Goode* says this is the spot for thin-crust pizza served with attitude, for eating on the street. You're listening to SUV horns, not taxis, but still . . . You'll glow for hours after a garlic slice.

Within shouting distance of 580 and the Richmond–San Rafael Bridge, is **Prego** in Point Richmond. Go for the thin crust Santa Fe Special with veggies and linguica. **Volare** in the Haight consistently has the freshest ingredients, wonderful crust, and super friendly staff, says *Demian*. Delivery is only after 5 p.m. but pick-up is available at lunchtime. In the Yerba Buena/

Moscone/Modern Art Museum nabe, **XYZ Bar** at the W Hotel has great margherita pizza with thin, crispy crust. Good fries too. See the cuisine index for more pizza tips.

○ **Mary's Pizza Shack:** *see also* **pp. 260, 263, 294.**

More than Wine at
PLUMPJACK

PlumpJack Cafe (Marina)
3127 Fillmore St.
San Francisco, CA
415-563-4755
New American/French/Italian

PlumpJack Wines (Marina)
3201 Fillmore St.
San Francisco, CA
415-346-9870
Wine store

PlumpJack Wines Noe Valley
 (Noe Valley)
4011 24th St.
San Francisco, CA
415-282-3841
Wine store

The PlumpJack kitchen does well with seafood (raw ahi appetizer, crab cakes loaded with crab, shrimp risotto) and especially duck. Nice job, too, with rhubarb tart *rick hurley* describes as not too sweet, not too tart, a happy medium—not easy to achieve with rhubarb. *MikeW* thinks PlumpJack has one of the best wine lists in the city, in terms of affordability and selection of hard-to-find West Coast wines. Also, buy any wine at the store and there's no corkage charged at the cafe! Service is very professional.

La Corneta's Particularly Deft Way with **POLLO EN SALSA VERDE**

La Corneta Taqueria (Mission)
2731 Mission St.
San Francisco, CA
415-643-7001
Mexican

La Corneta Taqueria is packed with Mexican families on weekends and, if you're lucky, there may be a couple of live guitar players. Carnitas are porky but moist rather than crunchy, and tostadas de ceviche is served with plenty of fresh, nonmushy white fish, (but could use more spice). But the main reason to go to La Corneta is undoubtedly taco with pollo en salsa verde, made with doubled tortillas and *tons* of meat. The sauce has very deep, lightly smoked, roasted green chili flavor, and the small chunks of meat are permeated with flavor. "After I finished the tacos I scoured my plate for any and all bits of leftover chicken and salsa," reports *nja*.

POTATO CHIPS

Bay Breads (Pacific Heights)
2325 Pine St.
San Francisco, CA
415-440-0356
French bakery

Boulange de Cole (Haight)
1000 Cole St.
San Francisco, CA
415-242-2442
French café

Boulange de Polk (Russian Hill)
2310 Polk St.
San Francisco, CA
415-345-1107
French bakery/Cheese
    shop/Pizzeria

La Palma Mexicatessen (Mission)
2884 24th St.
San Francisco, CA
415-647-1500
Mexican/Salvadoran store

Taqueria San Jose (East Bay)
3433 E. 14th St., at International
Oakland, CA
510-533-5748
Mexican

The superb homemade potato chips (considered best in the continental US by *Jim Leff*, who's tried hundreds of brands) at **La Palma Mexicatessen** are, alas, often unavailable. The proprietors will fry no chips unless they can find exactly the right potatoes.

The **Bay Bread** folks are selling chips with a similar homemade feeling, but these are very anti-Mexicatessen: very thin, but a little greasy, with a mixture of rosemary and other spices, says *chowhoundx* (who adds that Bay Bread's granola is the best he's ever tasted). Their chips have been spotted at the **Boulange de Polk** for $1.50 per bag, and might also be available at the other **Bay Breads** locations and **Boulange de Cole**.

Taqueria San Jose is selling fresh, housemade potato chips from its walk-up window. *Ruth Lafler* got the scoop: they're made late at night and bagged in the a.m.; arrive early before they sell out.

○ **Bay Breads:** *see also* **pp. 48, 76.**
○ **La Palma Mexicatessen:** *see also* **p. 128.**

POTRERO HILL Lunch

Atlas Cafe (Mission)
3049 20th St.
San Francisco, CA
415-648-1047
Café

Cafe Liliane (Potrero Hill)
550 15th St.
San Francisco, CA
415-864-1040
Diner or Coffee shop

Cafe Veloce (Potrero Hill)
200 Kansas St., inside Design
   Center
San Francisco, CA
415-861-1152
American

Henry's Hunan Restaurant
   (Financial District)
924 Sansome St.
San Francisco, CA
415-956-7727
Chinese (Hunan)

Henry's Hunan Restaurant
   (SOMA)
110 Natoma St.
San Francisco, CA
415-546-4999
Chinese (Hunan)

Henry's Hunan Restaurant
   (SOMA)
1016 Bryant St.
San Francisco, CA
415-861-5808
Chinese (Hunan)

Rainbow Grocery Co-Op (SOMA)
1745 Folsom St.
San Francisco, CA
415-863-0620
Store

Slow Club (Potrero Hill)
2501 Mariposa St.
San Francisco, CA
415-241-9390
New American

Looking for lunch around 16th and Potrero? Hounds like these spots best:

Slow Club for solid well-made food—good and good for you, as the cliché goes. Salads are always a solid bet, as are chocolate chip cookies. **Atlas Cafe** for sandwiches, with especially good vegan options. Don't forget **Rainbow Grocery** for premade sandwiches and salads (vegetarian only) and all your grocery needs. At **Cafe Liliane**, everything's made to order (so it can be slow when busy). Soup du jour, muffins, cookies are great, as are its breakfast baguettes with cuke, tomato, sliced hard-boiled egg, and a sprinkle of zatar. **Henry's Hunan** does great lunch specials, especially cold noodles. Get its Hunan pork rice plate, scallion pancakes, hot and sour soup, spicy and hot rock-cod fillets (extra hot!), and smoked ham and green beans. **Cafe Veloce**, a cafeteria in the Design Center, delivers huge portions of all cooked foods (burgers, pastas, etc.).

○ **Rainbow Grocery Co-Op:** *see also* p. 52.

PRIX FIXE Deals

Alamo Square Seafood Grill
   (Pacific Heights)
803 Fillmore St.
San Francisco, CA
415-440-2828
French bistro

Baker Street Bistro (Marina)
2953 Baker St.
San Francisco, CA
415-931-1475
French bistro

Caffe Venezia (East Bay)
1799 University Ave.
Berkeley, CA
510-849-4681
Italian

Chapeau! (Richmond)
1408 Clement St.
San Francisco, CA
415-750-9787
French brasserie

Firefly Restaurant (Mission)
4288 24th St.
San Francisco, CA
415-821-7652
New American/Pan-Asian fusion

Metro Cafe (Haight)
311 Divisadero St.
San Francisco, CA
415-552-0903
French bistro

Ristorante Bacco (Noe Valley)
737 Diamond St.
San Francisco, CA
415-282-4969
Italian

RNM Restaurant (Haight)
598 Haight St.
San Francisco, CA
415-551-7900
New American

South Park Cafe-Restaurant
   (SOMA)
108 S. Park St.
San Francisco, CA
415-495-7275
New American/French bistro

Town's End Restaurant & Bakery
   (SOMA)
2 Townsend St.
San Francisco, CA
415-512-0749
American

Watercress (Mission)
1152 Valencia St.
San Francisco, CA
415-648-6000
New American

Here are some particularly good (and good value) prix fixe deals. Note: call ahead to see if prices have gone up—after all, they're not *permanently* fixed!

South Park Cafe offers a $29.95 three-course meal, and *Mike Lee* thinks this place holds its own against Le Charm and Clementine. **Alamo Square Seafood Grill** offers a $12.95 three-course meal all night from Sunday through Thursday and as an early-bird special on Fridays and Saturdays: soup, main course, and dessert; no choices of main courses or desserts, and mains are mostly French seafood dishes. **Watercress** is a bargain, with three courses for $19.95. Lots of choices for each course and fresh seasonal ingredients.

Firefly also offers three-course menus for $25.00 Sunday through Thursday. Choose any appetizer, entree, or dessert on the menu, plus coffee or tea. **RNM** offers a three-course prix fixe for $25.00 until 7 p.m. This includes two small plates from a list, plus choice of any dessert. The prix fixe at **Chapeau!** offers three courses for $30.00—all your choice. **Metro Cafe** and **Baker Street Bistro** share ownership and both serve three-course prix fixe dinners for under $20.00. Appetizer is usually salad. **Town's End** offers soup or salad, entree (several choices), and dessert for $12.95, with best selection on Tuesdays. Great crab cakes, bread basket, and housemade cheese sticks. **Bacco** has a three-course menu for $25.00 Sunday through Thursday with limited choices. **Caffe Venezia** has always been reasonably priced, but its $16.00 prix fixe dinner (salad, entree, and dessert) is quite a deal. The prix fixe menu changes biweekly (find the current one at www.caffevenezia.com), and may include tasty things like seasonal, lightly dressed salads; green papardelle with asparagus and artichokes; grilled wild salmon; risotto with crab and prawns; or blackberry sorbet.

- **Baker Street Bistro:** *see also* p. 24.
- **Chapeau!:** *see also* pp. 24, 75.
- **Firefly Restaurant:** *see also* pp. 112, 118.
- **Metro Cafe:** *see also* pp. 24, 219.
- **Ristorante Bacco:** *see also* pp. 152, 202.
- **Town's End Restaurant & Bakery:** *see also* p. 30.

Bunny **RABBIT**

China Village (East Bay)
1335 Solano Ave.
Albany, CA
510-525-2285
Chinese (Sichuan)

Delfina Restaurant (Mission)
3621 18th St.
San Francisco, CA
415-552-4055
Italian

Farmhouse Inn (Sonoma County)
7871 River Rd.
Forestville, CA
707-887-3300
New American

Metro Cafe (Haight)
311 Divisadero St.
San Francisco, CA
415-552-0903
French bistro

Oliveto Cafe & Restaurant
  (East Bay)
5655 College Ave.
Oakland, CA
510-547-5356
Italian

Sam Lok Restaurant (Chinatown)
655 Jackson St.
San Francisco, CA
415-981-8988
Chinese (Sichuan)/Chinese

Metro does a good job with rabbit, French-style. And the **Farm-house Inn** serves rabbit cooked three ways, in a wine-friendly mustard sauce, prepped as confit of leg, sliced saddle, and Frenched ribs served as a rack. For Italian flavors, **Delfina** has been known to braise rabbit with green olives and pine nuts.

○○○ Chowhound Tip:

> *Michael* says for the best home-cooked rabbit,
> check out the recipe in Elizabeth David's *French
> Provincial Cooking*, page 385, but leave out the pork
> and beef. And don't forget the square of chocolate.

Chowhound Nametag: Tanspace

○◯○

Location: Fremont/Santa Clara/San Jose

Occupation: Software engineer (coding and chowhounding go hand in hand)

Cholesterol Level: Too high the last time I checked . . . and I know I've been eating more fried calamares lately, so . . . probably still too high.

Number of Visits to McDonald's in Past Decade: Weekly—for the Sausage Egg McMuffin, can't get enough of it!

Farthest Out of the Way Traveled Just for Chow: Moved from Chicago to Bay Area mainly for the food. Really.

Nabe Most Full of Explorable Unknown Chow: Vietnamese mall at Century Mall (Story Road and McLaughlin). Lots of interesting stands selling all sorts of interesting looking small eats. Will definitely take more than an afternoon to try all the different things.

Underrated by Chowhounds:
- Lulai Vegetarian: one of the best *restaurants*—not just vegetarian. The taste of all the dishes is so good it makes you forget you're eating vegetarian.
- King Crab: very good Cantonese with lots of very good entrees, and at good prices
- Tong Soon: one of the better Korean-Chinese places

Favorite Comfort Chow: Any Korean-Chinese place, Tong Soon, China Way, Tsing Tao, etc., and order either cao ma mian (spicy seafood soup noodle) or zha jiang mian (black bean paste noodle)

Guilty Pleasure: Korean-style fried squid at Hancock Market or Popeyes fried chicken. And I'm very often guilty.

Chowhounding Rule of Thumb: Always ask the waiter or hostess what's their specialty, and order the right things at the right place. For example, don't order XLB at a Cantonese restaurant, BBQ pork at a Beijing/Northern restaurant, or lamb at a Shanghai restaurant.

Favorite Snack I Never Get Tired of Eating: Korean-style dried seaweed found at Asian markets

And **Oliveto** does roast stuffed rabbit loin. Try spicy rabbit at Sichuan favorites **Sam Lok** and **China Village**.

- ○ **China Village:** *see also* pp. 59, 77, 267, 294.
- ○ **Delfina Restaurant:** *see also* pp. 123, 294.
- ○ **Metro Cafe:** *see also* pp. 24, 217.

RATTLESNAKE AND ARMADILLO

New Sang Chong Market (East Bay)
377 8th St.
Oakland, CA
510-451-2018
Chinese store

Seafood, armadillo, and rattlesnakes, what more could you want? **Sang Chong**'s fish and vegetables are fresh and it has soft-shell crab for a very good price. And while it doesn't always have armadillo, it regularly stocks snakes, frog, turtle, and more.

REDWOOD CITY MEX

Chavez Meat Market #1
   (Peninsula)
775 Arguello St.
Redwood City, CA
650-367-8819
Mexican store

Michoacan Produce Market
   (Peninsula)
3380 Middlefield Rd.
Menlo Park, CA
650-368-9226
Mexican store

Tacos El Grullo (Peninsula)
2798 Spring St.
Redwood City, CA
650-363-2597
Mexican

Butterflied, marinated chickens are grilled to perfection over charcoal outside **Michoacan Produce Market.** You get a whole, cut-up chicken, seven tortillas, and a pint of salsa for under $9, and several hounds affirm it's killer. Inside the market, pick up and pay for your tortillas and salsa, then give a ticket to the grill men and get your wrapped chicken when it's ready. Chickens are delivered each morning and grilled all day, every day, says *RWCFoodie*, who recommends a squeeze of lime.

Tacos El Grullo, in a bright pink building, serves good carne asada, chorizo, and al pastor tacos. Also tongue, brains, etc. Carnitas and dry chorizo at **Chavez Meat Market** are highly recommended.

A Good **REUBEN,** Already

Follini & Eichenbaum (Sonoma County)
19100 Arnold Dr.
Sonoma, CA
707-996-3287
Eastern European Jewish/Italian

A good Reuben is hard to find, but you'll find just that at **Follini & Eichenbaum**, reports *Jackie Avery*. It's listed as "Gina's Amazing Pastrami" on the menu, and it's rich, Swiss cheesey, meaty, soft, flavorful, and messy.

ROAST SUCKLING PIG

Andrea Foods (Solano County)
1109 Maple Ave., in the strip
   mall behind Kragen, on Spring
   Rd.
Vallejo, CA
707-644-0518
Filipino

Cheung Hing Chinese Restaurant
   (Sunset)
2339 Noriega St.
San Francisco, CA
415-665-3271
Chinese (Hong Kong)/Chinese
   (Cantonese)

Roast suckling pig—be it Filipino or Chinese—is something hounds are always searching for. **Andrea Foods** is one of, if not the, best makers of Filipino whole suckling pig (lechon). It can prepare any size—small, medium, or large. It's golden brown, crispy, and delicious outside, and really flavorful inside, raves *Maryanne Smyth*. Comes with special sauce. For an extra charge, they'll cut it into pieces and reassemble with an apple in its mouth and ribbons on its ears.

The Noriega location of **Cheung Hing** does a great Chinese roast piglet. *Nathan Lee* ordered one and proclaimed it "the best roast piglet outside of Hong Kong and Saigon. Everyone came over to take pieces of the pig. Cheung Hing promised the pig would be special and they delivered." Twenty-pound pigs run about $130.

For other roast suckling pig tips, see also: Koi Palace in *"Dim Sum* in the Peninsula and South Bay," Daimo in *"Cantonese* Favorites" and Legendary Palace in "East Bay *Dim Sum* Picks."

The World's Best **RUGELACH**

Crixa Cakes (East Bay)
2748 Adeline St.
Berkeley, CA
510-548-0421
Bakery

Crixa Cakes isn't just for cake anymore. They make the world's best rugelach, according to *Stanley Stephan*, who's in a positive tizzy over the things, saying they're "exactly the right size, with a puff pastry–like outer shell, poppy seed filling so rich and buttery, words are failing to describe this!" Crixa Cakes, a little bakery around the corner from Berkeley Bowl, also offers cookies, Boston cream pie, and coffeecakes. Don't miss creamy and aromatic coconut tapioca pudding when it's on the specials board; it's the perfect dessert for a hot day. Open Tuesday through Saturday, 10 a.m. to 6 p.m.

○ **Crixa Cakes:** *see also* **p. 37.**

Tokyo Hound **SAKE** Crawl

Ace Wasabi's Rock N Roll Sushi
(Marina)
3339 Steiner St.
San Francisco, CA
415-567-4903
Japanese

Hana Zen (Union Square)
115 Cyril Magnin St.
San Francisco, CA
415-421-2101
Japanese

Juban (Pacific Heights)
1581 Webster St., in Japan
Center, Street Level,
Kinokuniya Building
San Francisco, CA
415-776-5822
Japanese

Kirala (East Bay)
2100 Ward St.
Berkeley, CA
510-549-3486
Japanese

Maki Restaurant (Pacific Heights)
1825 Post St.
San Francisco, CA
415-921-5215
Japanese

Memphis Minnie's BBQ (Haight)
576 Haight St.
San Francisco, CA
415-864-7675
Barbecue

Osome (Pacific Heights)
3145 Fillmore St.
San Francisco, CA
415-931-8898
Japanese

Roy's (SOMA)
575 Mission St.
San Francisco, CA
415-777-0277
Hawaiian/New American

Sushi on North Beach
  (North Beach)
745 Columbus Ave.
San Francisco, CA
415-788-8050
Japanese

Sushi Zone Restaurant (East Bay)
388 9th St.
Oakland, CA
510-893-9663
Japanese

Takara Sake USA (East Bay)
708 Addison St.
Berkeley, CA
510-540-8250
Japanese sake brewery

True Sake (Civic Center)
560 Hayes St.
San Francisco, CA
415-558-6254
Japanese store

Tokyo-based hound *Bryan Harrell* shares his thoughts on where to go for a *hashigo* experience (the Japanese tradition of pub crawling from sake bar to sake bar) in San Francisco. Before heading out, familiarize yourself with what to ask and look for by doing some reading on the subject of craft-brewed sake (www.Sake-world.com is a good place to start). Here's his *hashigo* list:

Hana Zen: a combo sushi bar and yakatori (try a Bishonen or Oyama sake)

Sushi on North Beach: favorite sakes are Katsu-san and Yamagata

Osome: sushi as well as other Japanese foods; favorite sakes are Shirakawa Junmai Ginjo Nigori and Niwa-no-ugisu-daruma

Juban: a Japanese-style Korean barbecue; favorite sakes are Nihonjyo and Karatamba

Ace Wasabi: a place to, as Harrell puts it, *paaaaarty*; funky sushi rolls are their speciality; they have "a formidible" selection of craft-brewed sakes, as well as infused sakes, sake cocktails, and a frat house–reminiscent sake punch—definitely a twenties' hangout which can be checked out live online at www.acewasabis.com

Other chowhound sake know-how: At **Memphis Minnie**, hit up Bob, the owner, for his sake knowledge. Get him talking and you can learn a lot. The place itself offers a limited but excellent selection of sakes—and BBQ to boot! **Kirala** has a big selection but is always jammed, so there's not much personal attention. Try lunch for better service. **Roy's**, a branch of the Hawaiian restaurant, is not usually too busy and has friendly waitstaff. All bartenders may not be up to snuff on sake knowledge, though. Smallish (but high quality) selections. Good sake lists at **Maki** in San Francisco's Japantown and **Sushi Zone** in Oakland's Chinatown (the latter offers 2-for-1 drinks during happy hour). **Takara**, the sake brewery in Berkeley, doesn't offer tours, per se, but there's a tasting room and small museum with a view of the brewery. Its stuff is value priced, and word is it might sell you some sake mash for a small fee—great for marinating fish! For sake to take home, visit **True Sake**, San Francisco's (and America's) first retail shop specializing in fine small-producer sake (look for its lime green sign).

○ **Maki Restaurant:** *see also* p. 157.
○ **Memphis Minnie's BBQ:** *see also* p. 14.

Eat Your **SALAD**

Bow Hon Restaurant (Chinatown)
850 Grant Ave.
San Francisco, CA
415-362-0601
Chinese (Cantonese)

Cafe for All Seasons
   (Westportal/Ingleside)
150 W. Portal Ave.
San Francisco, CA
415-665-0900
New American

Chow (Castro)
15 Church St.
San Francisco, CA
415-552-2469
American

Chow Market (East Bay)
Lafayette Cir.
Lafayette, CA
925-962-2469
American

Desiree (Marina)
39 Mesa, in the San Francisco
    Film Centre building
San Francisco, CA
415-561-2337
New American/French

Firewood Cafe (Mission)
4248 18th St.
San Francisco, CA
415-252-0999
Pizza

La Note (East Bay)
2377 Shattuck Ave.
Berkeley, CA
510-843-1535
French/American

Liaison Bistro (East Bay)
1849 Shattuck Ave.
Berkeley, CA
510-849-2155
French bistro

Luna Park (Mission)
694 Valencia St.
San Francisco, CA
415-553-8584
New American

Nizza La Bella (East Bay)
825-827 San Pablo Ave.
Albany, CA
510-526-2552
French

Park Chow (Sunset)
1238 9th Ave.
San Francisco, CA
415-665-9912
American

Pluto's Fresh Food for a Hungry
    Universe (Marina)
3258 Scott St.
San Francisco, CA
415-775-8867
American

Pluto's Fresh Food for a Hungry
    Universe (Peninsula)
482 University Ave.
Palo Alto, CA
650-853-1556
American

Sunflower Authentic Vietnamese
    (Mission)
3111 16th St.
San Francisco, CA
415-626-5022
Vietnamese

Ti Couz Creperie (Mission)
3108 16th St.
San Francisco, CA
415-252-7373
French

Tu Lan Restaurant (SOMA)
8 6th St.
San Francisco, CA
415-626-0927
Vietnamese

Got that craving for a big bowl of greens and other goodies?
We've got recommendations from all over the globe right here
in the Bay Area. Starting off with the basics, **Desiree** has really

wonderful salads. And **Luna Park** has a "large salads" section on its menu including basic greens, Nicoise with fresh grilled ahi, cobb salad, and more. Romaine-gouda salad at **Cafe for All Seasons** is a much loved favorite (as is its apple cake with caramel sauce). And go for cobb salad at any of the **Chow** restaurants. (*Jupiter* suggests ordering with goat or feta instead of blue cheese.)

An East Bay trio of options for good Nicoise salads is **La Note**, **Nizza la Bella**, and **Liaison Bistro**. Favorites at **Ti Couz** include salade de crudités, seafood salad (full of veggies and tiny scallops and bay shrimp and topped with seared tuna), and special salads of the day (*dutch* notes that the large salad is truly enormous and organic greens are available for a small additional charge). **Pluto's** and **Firewood Cafe** let you mix and match toppings above and beyond the huge bowl of greens.

On the Asian side, *Melanie Wong* recommends a half-order of raw fish salad at **Bow Hon**—low on the greenery, but chock-full of very interesting textures and tastes; *david kaplan* likes Vietnamese **Tu Lan**'s tofu salad, with strips of tofu, cabbage, and other veggies in mildly sweet lime juice and fish sauce dressing. **Sunflower**, another Vietnamese spot, makes good salads as well.

Also see "Downtown San Francisco *Salad Bars*"; "*Chinese Chicken Salad*."

- Chow Market: *see also* p. 30.
- La Note: *see also* pp. 33, 236.
- Luna Park: *see also* pp. 10, 182.
- Ti Couz Creperie: *see also* p. 24.
- Tu Lan Restaurant: *see also* p. 312.

Downtown San Francisco
SALAD BARS

Fountain Cafe (Financial District)
50 Post St., #62B, in Crocker
   Galleria
San Francisco, CA
415-981-3005
Diner or Coffee shop

Lightening Foods (Embarcadero)
3 Embarcadero Ctr., Lobby Level
San Francisco, CA
415-362-8191
American

Lightening Foods
   (Financial District)
1 Market Plaza
San Francisco, CA
415-777-8222
American

Napa Ranch (Financial District)
465 California St.
San Francisco, CA
415-956-2518
American

Sprouts Health Food
   (Embarcadero)
101 California St.
San Francisco, CA
415-434-3343
Vegetarian American

Lunchtime draws downtown workers to salad bars. The best are: **Fountain Cafe** (lots of fresh, high-quality, unadorned vegetables for assembling a green salad; prepared salads can be soggy), **Napa Ranch** (very good grain/legume salads—cracked wheat, vinegary/oniony black bean salad—and cold noodles, soups), **Lightening Foods** (rotating specials—lasagna, jambalaya with mussels, sausage, shrimp, calamari, Chinese chicken salad—and excellent unbreaded fried chicken, sauteed green beans, roasted potatoes, and asparagus with oyster sauce at Market Plaza location); and **Sprouts** (grilled chicken with jalapeño pesto, haricots vertes with olive oil, butter-coated carrots, and fresh fruit).

Also see "Eat Your *Salad*."

Wild SALMON

Andronico's
www.andronicos.com
Store

El Cerrito Plaza Farmers' Market
  (East Bay)
San Pablo Ave. and Fairmount
  Ave.
El Cerrito, CA
510-528-7992
Farmers' Market

Half Moon Bay Harbor (Peninsula)
Pillar Point Harbor, 1 Johnson
  Pier
Half Moon Bay, CA
650-726-4382
Store

Menlo Park Farmers' Market
  (Peninsula)
Crane and Chestnut
Menlo Park, CA
831-688-8316
Farmers' market

Ver Brugge Meat Fish Poultry
  (East Bay)
6321 College Ave.
Oakland, CA
510-658-6854
Store

Whole Foods
www.wholefoods.com/
Store

California wild salmon is on Monterey Bay Aquarium's Seafood Watch "good choices" list (www.mbayaq.org/cr/seafoodwatch.asp), so, besides **Whole Foods** or **Andronico's**, here are options for fresh California salmon: **Ver Brugge**, the popular meat market in Rockridge, runs its own boat and brings in nice salmon at good prices, especially if you buy a whole or half fish. It'll even fillet it for you. Hudson Fishing sells its catch at the North Berkeley Farmers' Market on Thursdays, at the Downtown Oakland Farmers' Market on Fridays, and at the El Cerrito Market on Saturdays—and sometimes from its driveway! Sign up for its e-mail list at yvette@hudsonfish.com or call its hotline for updates: 510-528-8686. It has also had halibut, grenadier fillets, and smoked salmon.

You can pick up wild salmon at the **North Berkeley Farmers' Market** (Thursday), **El Cerrito Plaza Farmers' Market** (Saturday), or Downtown Oakland Farmers' Market (Friday), and Pietro sells it at the **Menlo Park Farmers' Market**. In **Half Moon Bay,** call the Fish Phone at 650-726-8724 to see what's fresh at the Pillar Point Harbor pier.

- Andronico's: *see also* p. 206.
- Menlo Park Farmer's Market: *see also* p. 103.
- Ver Brugge Meat Fish Poultry: *see also* pp. 48, 79.
- Whole Foods: *see also* pp. 52, 73, 280.

SANDWICHES for the (Plane) Ride

Copenhagen Bakery & Cafe
   (Peninsula)
1216 Burlingame Ave.
Burlingame, CA
650-342-1357
Danish café

Darby Dan Sandwich Co.
   (Peninsula)
733 North Airport Blvd.
South San Francisco, CA
650-876-0122
Sandwich shop

For lunch before a flight or while brown-bagging it aloft, **Darby Dan** makes a mean sandwich right near SFO. Order from the open kitchen/grill at the cash register and grab a table, or get big salads and sandwiches to go from the deli counter (where lines can get long). One favorite is crab salad on a Dutch crunch roll, with mustard, garlic mayo, and more (but skip jalapeños, which overpower the crab). Or get the $6.50 half-and-half special—half crab salad, half shrimp salad (Thursday and Friday only)—and grab lots of napkins. Also recommended: Darby Dan (ham, mortadella, Italian salami, cheese), Sleeper (ham, turkey, bacon cheese), and Piccolo (ham, turkey, roast beef cheese), all $6.00.

   Copenhagen Bakery, also close to SFO, has authentic Danish open-face sandwiches and delicacies on its lunch menu, but also a full roster of local standards like Chinese chicken salad and deli sandwiches, including good curried Danish meatballs (like a Japanese curry) and pickled fish appetizers. It serves breakfast and dinner, too, and terrific pastries—check out the chocolate danish!

Road Trip to **SANTA CRUZ**

Cafe Gibraltar (Peninsula)
425 Ave. Alhambra
El Granada, CA
650-560-9039
New American/Middle
  Eastern/North
  African/Greek/French

Creekside Smokehouse
  (Peninsula)
280 Ave. Alhambra
Half Moon Bay, CA
650-712-8862
Store

Cunha Country Grocery
  (Peninsula)
448 Main St.
Half Moon Bay, CA
650-726-4071
Store

Duarte's Tavern (Peninsula)
202 Stage Rd.
Pescadero, CA
650-879-0464
American/Portuguese/Seafood

Garden Deli Cafe (Peninsula)
356 Main St., in San Benito
  House
Half Moon Bay, CA
650-726-3425
Café

Half Moon Bay Fish Market
  (Peninsula)
99 San Mateo Rd.
Half Moon Bay, CA
650-726-2561
Store

It's Italia Pizzeria (Peninsula)
40 Stone Pine Rd., in Stone Pine
  Shopping Center
Half Moon Bay, CA
650-726-4444
Pizza

3 Amigos Taqueria (Peninsula)
200 N. Cabrillo Hwy. (Hwy. 1)
Half Moon Bay, CA
650-726-6080
Mexican

Swanton Berry Farm
  (Santa Cruz County)
25 Swanton Rd.
Davenport, CA
831-469-8804
Farm or Farm stand

There are some good chow spots along the drive between Half
Moon Bay and Santa Cruz. **Creekside Smokehouse** has some of the
best smoked fish *Nancy Berry* has ever eaten, and *tomritza* calls
it "a very chowhoundy kind of place indeed!" **3 Amigos**, a cross between a burrito counter and a lunch plate place, is always busy

serving humongous burritos that will last you all the way to Monterey, promises *Sharuf*. **It's Italia Pizzeria** has more than just pizza. In fact, we've had no reports on its pizza at all, but it makes good seafood and salads and has an interesting wine list (nice little magazine and newspaper shop, too). **Cunha Country Store** is quite chowish, carrying all sorts of interesting picnic items, including Arcangeli Breads. **Swanton's Berry Farm** just before Davenport is worth a stop for heirloom strawberries that often don't even make it to the market. **Garden Deli Cafe** at San Benito House has great sandwiches.

Half Moon Bay Fish Co. is the tiny fish stand you see as you enter Main Street in Half Moon Bay. It carries an impressive selection of fresh fish. *Stanley Stephan* offers two nearby tips: the tiny Mexican market next door is surprisingly good, and the restaurant next door to that does inexpensive fish tacos.

On Pescadero Beach, **Duarte**'s is untouristy and casual, and makes good fried fish and seafood (especially the smelts and crab cakes, sweetly delicious grilled sand dabs, and a half-and-half soup (half cream of artichoke and half cream of chili) that's creamy and fortifying. Very good pies include strawberry and rhubarb a la mode, peach, and pecan. "I've had so many bad versions of pecan pie I'd given up on it, but this one was lacking the sweet gelatinlike filling and was rich in toasted pecans: more like nut tart than the usual American pecan pie. Excellent!" says *Ruth Lafler*. Surprisingly extensive wine list.

oOo Chowhound Tip:

Secret info from *Melanie Wong* on the best spot on Pescadero Beach for mussel gathering: "the set of rocks I prefer are on the spit to the left-hand side of the parking lot (as you face the ocean). The rocks on the right side are much more slippery to walk on and less dense with mussels." Mussel season is fall through early spring, but you've got to buy a fishing license before you arrive.

For dinner, several hounds agree that **Cafe Gibraltar**'s a solid choice in the Half Moon Bay area, is on par with Delfina in terms of value. Excellent moussaka is delicate and complex, with a slight kick of cayenne. Lightly sauteed fish is served with sauce begging to be sopped up with the warm flatbread served with all meals. Servings are huge.

○ **Duarte's Tavern:** *see also* pp. 117, 294.
○ **Swanton Berry Farm:** *see also* pp. 156, 273.

Street Food in **SANTA ROSA**

Santa Rosa Downtown Market (Sonoma County)
4th S. and Santa Rosa Plaza to D St.
Santa Rosa, CA
707-524-2123
Farmers' Market

Wednesday nights on Fourth Street in downtown Santa Rosa is a North Bay calvacade of street food: *ellen roberts* tried and enjoyed items from vendors selling vegetarian dosa (with fresh chutneys and ginger lemonade), tamales (both traditional and nontraditional), chicken kabobs with yogurt sauce, gumbo, barbecued oysters, lots of baked goods, cotton candy, kettle corn, and even hotdogs, also a "Thai Taste" combo plate of spring roll, noodles, slaw-type salad, and pastry shell stuffed with veggies. And myriad Mexican vendors. Here are some of the vendors whose names we caught: Mary's Pizza, Johnny Garlic's, Thai House, Willie Bird (with grilled turkey legs), Pasta King, Cold Stone Creamery, Mom's Apple Pie.

Chowhound Nametag: Melanie Wong

o◯o

Cholesterol Level:
Normal (good genes)!

Top Chinatown Pick:
R&G Lounge

Nabe Most Full of Explorable Unknown Chow: The sleepy town of San Bruno on the Peninsula is not well known except as SFO's flyover zone and the home of Artichoke Joe's card room, but San Mateo Avenue offers a remarkable diversity of restaurants and food stores for chow window-shopping. I've tried every Burmese restaurant in the Bay Area, and Innya Lake is my current favorite. Mings has tasty hand-pulled noodles, and Thai Nakorn can outgun the huge majority of San Francisco's Thai kitchens. Even better is the Sunday luncheon at the local Thai temple for loving, homemade taste. The handful of Japanese restaurants will delight and local taquerias serve up the real deal. There aren't that many places to eat, but standards are high, with a good hit rate. I've just gotta believe that there's more to be found here and chances are they'll be good chow. I've heard about a halal creperie that someone needs to check out . . .

Underrated by Chowhounds:
Little Deli

Favorite Comfort Chow:
Hing Lung, abalone and chicken jook with a yao tieu

Favorite Gelato Flavor:
Gianduja

Spicy **SAUSAGE:** Balkan and Moroccan

Aziza (Richmond)
5800 Geary St.
San Francisco, CA
415-752-2222
Moroccan

Baraka (Potrero Hill)
288 Connecticut St.
San Francisco, CA
415-255-0370
Moroccan/French/Spanish

Chez Maman (Potrero Hill)
1453 18th St.
San Francisco, CA
415-824-7166
French

Del Monte Restaurant (South Bay)
100 S. Murphy Ave., Suite 104
Sunnyvale, CA
408-737-7678
Bosnian or Serbian/Italian/French

Fabrique Delices (East Bay)
1610 Delta Ct., #1
Hayward, CA
510-441-9500
French store

Jeanty at Jack's
(Financial District)
615 Sacramento St.
San Francisco, CA
415-693-0941
French bistro

La Note (East Bay)
2377 Shattuck Ave.
Berkeley, CA
510-843-1535
French/American

Old World German Sausage &
Meat Co. (East Bay)
1367 52nd Ave.
Oakland, CA
510-533-7211
Bosnian or Serbian store

Rosamunde Sausage Grill
(Haight)
545 Haight St.
San Francisco, CA
415-437-6851
American/German

Cevapi (pronounced che-VAP-ee), also spelled cevapcici, are spicy ground meat sausages traditional in the countries of the former Yugoslavia. Following a hot tip at a Serbian food festival, *Joanne Lafler* found that **Old World German Sausage & Meat Co.** makes and sells both cevapi and kobasica ("a smoked sausage, similar to kielbasa but indescribably better"). It is only open to the public Friday to Sunday, and only sells in bulk, so stock your freezer or have a barbecue! Canned and prepared Balkan foods are also available. You can also try cevapi from the menu at **Del Monte Restaurant.**

Merguez are highly spiced Moroccan lamb sausages. Good grilled merguez is served on a roll at **Rosamunde**, in panini with caramelized onions and cheese at **Chez Maman**, and as a sandwich special at **Jeanty at Jack's.** La Note serves merguez in sandwiches and with eggs—though it sells out early on weekends. Or have merguez at **Aziza** or **Baraka.** For home cooking, try merguez made by **Fabriques Delices**, used in many area restaurants under the Made in France label (order from its Web site at www.fabriquedelices.com)

- ○ **Aziza:** *see also* p. 197.
- ○ **Baraka:** *see also* p. 241.
- ○ **Chez Maman:** *see also* p. 24.
- ○ **Jeanty at Jack's:** *see also* p. 272.
- ○ **La Note:** *see also* pp. 33, 227.
- ○ **Rosamunde Sausage Grill:** *see also* pp. 17, 134.

Chowhounding **SAUSALITO**

Pelican Inn (Marin County)
10 Pacific Way
Muir Beach, CA
415-383-6000
British

Sushi Ran (Marin County)
107 Caledonia St.
Sausalito, CA
415-332-3620
Japanese

Sushi Ran serves first-class sushi in a high-end atmosphere, says *Heike Bartlett*. It also has a great sake selection. **Pelican Inn**, a British country pub in Muïr Beach, is casual, with pub fare and darts on one side and a more formal (but rustic) dining room with traditional English food on the other. See the Nabe Index for other nearby choices.

Liguria Focaccia at **SBC PARK**

Liguria Bakery booth at SBC Park
  (SOMA)
24 Willie Mays Plaza, lower level
  booth
San Francisco, CA
415-972-2000
Italian

Liguria Bakery (North Beach)
1700 Stockton St.
San Francisco, CA
415-421-3786
Italian bakery

Hey, Giants fans, Liguria Bakery's focaccia is available at SBC Park, at the same booth on the lower level that sells 40 Cloves of Garlic chicken sandwiches. They also sell arancini (cheesy rice balls).

○ **Liguria Bakery:** *see also* p. 211.

SCONES That Aren't Like Doorstops

Arizmendi (East Bay)
3265 Lakeshore Ave.
Oakland, CA
510-268-8849
Bakery

Arizmendi Bakery and Pizzeria
  (East Bay)
4301 San Pablo at 43rd St.
Emeryville, CA
510-547-0550
Bread/Pizza bakery and sitdown
  café

Arizmendi (Sunset)
1331 9th Ave.
San Francisco, CA
415-566-3117
Bread/Pizza bakery and sitdown
  café

Cakery (Peninsula)
1308 Burlingame Ave.
Burlingame, CA
650-344-1006
Bakery

Cheese Board (East Bay)
1504 Shattuck Ave.
Berkeley, CA
510-549-3183
Pizza bakery/Cheese shop/Pizzeria

Mandarin Lounge
  (Financial District)
222 Sansome St., in Mandarin
  Oriental Hotel
San Francisco, CA
415-276-9888
Pan-Asian fusion

Scone Henge Bakery & Cafe
  (East Bay)
2787 Shattuck·Ave.
Berkeley, CA
510-845-5168
Café

Scone Works (Russian Hill)
814 Eddy St.
San Francisco, CA
415-922-0635
Café

Tired of coffee shop scones that are either big fluffy monsters or inedible heavy pucks? **Scone Henge** scones, carried by many local grocers, are fluffy and small, like scones should be. **Scone Works** bakes many flavors—pumpkin, berries, and ginger are good. They're cakey in texture, like a fruit cookie. **Cakery** offers scones in two sizes. The small ones have more outer crispy goodness, while the larger ones have more soft innards. Raisin and raisin-oatmeal are good choices. **Mandarin Lounge** serves baked-to-order scones with its tea service, but they're pricey. Both **Arizmendi** and **Cheese Board** use the same scone recipe. It's not particularly traditional, but is oh, so good (especially the cherry cornmeal version)!

- ○ **Arizmendi:** *see also* **pp. 3, 102.**
- ○ **Cheese Board:** *see also* **pp. 4, 51, 54, 198.**

SHANGHAI Longing

Mystery Shanghainese restaurant
  at Lion Food Center
  (South Bay)
1838 N. Milpitas Blvd.
Milpitas, CA
Chinese (Shanghai)

Shanghai Restaurant (Sunset)
420 Judah St.
San Francisco, CA
415-661-7755
Chinese (Shanghai)

At Shanghai Restaurant in San Francisco, be sure to ask for the Shanghai specialties menu. If the staff has you pegged for a gringo and demures, just speak the magic words: xiao long bao (soup dumpling). Shanghainese classics are rendered well here. Drunken chicken has a delicious interplay of cold, sweet, sour, and salty, but is best eaten quite cold, as flavors become muted as it approaches room temperature. Rich vegetarian goose is served warm, highlighting textural contrast between crisp tofu "skin" and soft mushroom "meat." Tea smoked duck has charry texture and rich smoky flavor; xiao long bao are substantial and piping hot. Sole disappointment: bland Shanghai pan-fried noodles, garnished with cabbage, beef, and pea shoots.

Lion Food Center in Milpitas boasts three separate **Shanghai restaurants**, and *Han Lukito* is most impressed with the one directly across from Fu Lam Moon (which is at 1678 N. Milpitas Blvd.). Steam table lunch specials are the way to go here for home-style food at very inexpensive prices (about $4 gets you three items plus rice for just pennies more.) You get porridge with items unless you specify rice. English menu is available. Look for these items on the steam table: salt and pepper shrimp, Chinese sausage, tofu strips with pork strips, twice-cooked pork, pork with spicy red sauce, and Napa cabbage with shrimp and mushrooms. Worth ordering off the menu are oyster omelet and steamed fish in soy sauce. Lukito reports that "four of us shared everything, loved everything, total bill was only like $20 and we were stuffed to the gills!"

SHWARMA Heaven

Habibi (East Bay)
3906 Washington Blvd., at Irvington Shopping Plaza
Fremont, CA
510-659-9600
Lebanese

Lebanese Habibi serves fresh, well-made mezze and succulent shwarma totally unlike the mass-produced mediocrity served in so many places around the Bay Area. Tabouleh is refreshing and bright, hummus and baba ganoush are rich and flavorful, and stuffed grape leaves taste fresh and homemade. But it's the shwarma that really wows here: "Large slices of real meat are spiced, skewered, and roasted. The resulting slivers of very tasty beef, rolled in pita with onions and a bit of hummus ensure that I will never voluntarily have any other kind of shwarma," avows *Pia*. A combo plate serving two or three comes with all this, plus falafel and skewers of grilled marinated chicken and beef for around $20. Rich rose-petal ice cream from Shatila in Michigan hits the spot for dessert. So-so Lebanese wines are served by the glass.

SMALL PLATE Places

Baraka (Potrero Hill)
288 Connecticut St.
San Francisco, CA
415-255-0370
Moroccan/French/Spanish

Cesar (East Bay)
1515 Shattuck Ave.
Berkeley, CA
510-883-0222
Spanish/New American

Fonda Solana (East Bay)
1501 Solano Ave.
Albany, CA
510-559-9006
Mexican

Fork (Marin County)
198 Sir Francis Drake Blvd.
San Anselmo, CA
415-453-9898
French/New American

Pesce (Russian Hill)
2227 Polk St.
San Francisco, CA
415-928-8025
Italian

Platanos (Mission)
598 Guerrero St.
San Francisco, CA
415-252-9281
Latin American

Small plates are huge. Tapaslike cooking has become far more popular than real Spanish tapas ever were. The following are choice small plate options, Iberian and way beyond.

Pesce is styled like a Venetian chichetteria (chichetti are the Venetian equivalent of tapas—small plates of seafood to sample and share over a leisurely meal paired with wines by the glass), and gets the feel of these Venetian restaurants just right, probably because Pesce is run by a big, burly Venetian chef. The friendly and hospitable staff appreciates diners who are there for more than the pretty-people Polk Street scene, says *the other zach*. *Paul H* agrees: "I love seafood, but I have never had a meal from the ocean so artfully and creatively prepared. The food at Pesce delights the mind as well as the palate." And the prices are a good value. While virtually all dishes are well received, some really stand out: grilled octopus ("a texture unlike anywhere else," says *nja*, "like fresh roasted turkey breast"), lobster spaghetti in brandy cream sauce ("one bite and we were transported to Rome, where I fell in love with a simliar dish at Settimio all'Arancio," says *the other zach*), grilled fresh sardines, scallop salad, linguini frutti di mare (with clams, mussels, bits of halibut, and shrimp), fresh peas (with caramelized, sweet red onion, and pancetta), and tiramisu. Only a dish of gelato (with peaches, huckleberries, and zinfandel) disappointed, due to below-par peaches. Wine list includes wonderful Italian vintages at bargain prices ($6 to $7 glasses, $20 to $30 bottles) and even passito, a wonderful and rare dessert wine. Validated parking for $6 in Video City parking lot, two blocks south on Polk.

Baraka is a restaurant run by the folks who brought Chez Papa and Chez Maman to Potrero Hill. Hounds rave over the Moroccan and Spanish flavors of their small plates, most in the $6 or $7 range, with the most expensive running $12. Good choices include: bread served with cumin-laden hummus; fresh fava bean falafel with lavash; fabulous warm, pistachio-encrusted goat cheese with sweet onion jam and toasts; and lusty flavored swordfish and lamb brochettes with savory salsa verde. And for dessert, orange blossom beignets with goat yogurt and orange marmalade, and sweet Moroccan mint tea. Extensive wine list (about twenty by the glass), includes a good selection of Spanish wines.

Platanos serves small plates in a warm atmosphere with a great vibe. Recommended items include ceviche (excellent balance of lime, avocado, fish, seasoning), crab salad (large chunks of meat with grilled avocado and mango), and shrimp in mole verde (very rich and creamy green mole sauce) sauce. Four dishes, a few glasses of Spanish wine at $7, tax, and tip, ran $75 and left two hounds with no room for dessert.

Fork holds its own with the best in San Francisco, at more reasonable prices, says *eatingoutagain*, who reports that "from the truffled egg custard with smoked bacon, to the Maine lobster bisque, to the seared scallop on potato puree, everything is perfect." Many small plates and side order–type dishes are offered, and the signature tasting menu runs $49.00 per person. There's also a $19.95 prix fixe menu offered as an early evening special (from 5:30 to 6:15 p.m.). Don't miss awesome butterscotch pudding for dessert. The room is small but tables are well spaced.

Cesar, right next door to Chez Panisse, has a nice selection of sherries by the glass, as well as Eric Bordelet French ciders to go with tapas. And it's open late. As for the tapas themselves, start with complimentary marinated olives and then try any of the following standouts: green garlic and almond soup, fried potatos (garnished with deep-fried herbs and aioli—garlic mayo—on the side), fava bean and Yukon gold potato salad (covered in garlic mayonnaise, per tradition), halibut a la plancha (roasted, served on bed of sauteed mushrooms), cazuela of branade (puree of salt cod and potato), boquerones (white anchovies on toasted baguettes spread with garlic mayo), jamon Serrano (with roasted grapes), pimiento de padron (thumbnail-sized Spanish green peppers lightly fried and salted, with "about every fifth pepper packing a fiery wallop," says *foodfirst*), and bread pudding so good "we'd ordered three servings, and still we were fighting over it" (*Melanie Wong*).

Fonda Solana, much more upscale than your typical "fonda" in Mexico, does small plates with a Latin American flavor. Hibiscus drinks, quesillo, queso fresco, epazote, tequila with sangrita, and very limey margaritas, and a couple of really good dishes: perfectly crispy arepas with spicy and vinegary salsa, fantastic quail with peanut mole, and for dessert: mango sticks served in a glass with lime juice and zest. Service is skillful and dining room has a nice ambience, but it's pricey. Open for dinner only, until 12:30 a.m.

○ **Baraka:** *see also* p. 236.

SONOMA: VARIOUS CHOWING

Borolos Original Pizza
  (Sonoma County)
500 Mission Blvd.
Santa Rosa, CA
707-539-3937
Pizza

George Chung's Chinese & Sushi
  Cuisine-Burgers-Fish 'n' Chips
  (Sonoma County)
18976 Sonoma Hwy., at Verano
  Ave.
Sonoma, CA
707-935-3383
American/Chinese/Japanese/
  Vietnamese

K & L Bistro (Sonoma County)
119 S. Main St.
Sebastopol, CA
707-823-6614
French bistro

La Poste (Sonoma County)
599 Broadway
Sonoma, CA
707-939-3663
French bistro

Moosetta's Russian Piroshki
  (Sonoma County)
18816 Sonoma Hwy., Suites E & F
Sonoma, CA
707-996-4459
Russian/New American

New York Pizzeria
  (Sonoma County)
65 Brookwood Ave.
Santa Rosa, CA
707-526-9743
Pizza

Oakville Grocery
  (Sonoma County)
124 Matheson St.
Healdsburg, CA
707-433-3200
Store

Ravenous Restaurant
  (Sonoma County)
420 Center St.
Healdsburg, CA
707-431-1302
New American

Red Grape (Sonoma County)
529 First St. West
Sonoma, CA
707-996-4103
Pizza

Sake O (Sonoma County)
505 Healdsburg Ave.
Healdsburg, CA
707-433-2669
Japanese

Seaweed Cafe (Sonoma County)
1580 Eastshore Rd.
Bodega Bay, CA
707-875-2700
New American

Western Boot Steak House
    (Sonoma County)
9 Mitchell Ln.
Healdsburg, CA
707-433-6362
Steakhouse

Willow Wood Market Cafe
    (Sonoma County)
9020 Graton Rd.
Graton, CA
707-823-0233
New American

Zin Restaurant (Sonoma County)
344 Center St.
Healdsburg, CA
707-473-0946
New American

Sonoma brims with chowfulness. All tips below are courtesy of Sonoma supersleuth *Melanie Wong* unless otherwise noted.

Willow Wood is an optimal stop for visitors who want to experience the essence of Sonoma's rural life. Graton itself is just a wide spot in the road with wooden sidewalks—quaint without affectation or pretension, nestled among Gravenstein apple orchards and vineyards. From whichever direction you approach, it's a scenic drive and just a slight detour off the main wine-tasting trail. The café (note: no relation to the Willowside, which is out of biz) offers seemingly simple cooking that's beautifully balanced, made from very fresh artisanal ingredients. Especially good: their polenta with local goat cheese, "surely the most wonderful bowl of polenta around, with a plump and creamy grain that satisfies the soul. Several other toppings are available, e.g., pork ragout, but the goat cheese one is the classic version with some squared-off pieces of carmelized sweet onion and a spoonful of fresh pesto to stir in as the bits of goat cheese soften and become even creamier." Willow Wood is uber-Sonoma in its casualness of composition. And it's not expensive (maybe $10 per person with tax and tip, plus beverages, some good value wines by the glass). It's the best bang for the buck in the area and a great value for getting a taste of the Wine Country on a budget.

One chowhound lives twenty miles from **New York Pizzeria** yet went twice the week he first tried it. Believe it or not, this is not an unusual story; from nearly the moment it opened, chowhounds have been obsessed by this place, which indeed makes NY-style, with thin crust and NY attitude otherwise unfindable in the Bay Area. For genuine NY-style, stick with traditional toppings (one or two at most), order extra crispy (blackened crispy crust). Don't miss meatball or Italian sausage subs, either. Shakers of grated cheese, chili flakes, and oregano are offered for custom spice-ups.

La Poste is a tiny place with close-set tables, decorated with bistro paraphernalia. There's an esoteric, intelligent list of mostly local wines served in Riedel stemware. A signature appetizer of salt cod fritters with aioli is incredible—"an explosion of flavor with plenty of garlic leading the charge." Cassoulet and tarte tatin are disappointing, but skate wing with brown butter and capers is excellent, with sweet and delicate flesh under a maximally crunchy crust. A regular recommends seared scallops, steak frites, and chocolate mousse. Great selection of dessert wines.

K & L Bistro is small, but its food made a big impact on *socal boy*, who considers the place a gem. Great appetizers include roast quail with fruit salad sauteed in its juice, and caramelized onion tart with blue cheese. Entrees are large and come with generous sides. Crisp-skinned pan-roasted organic chicken served with its juices comes with mashed potatoes, green salad, and creamy mac and cheese. Huge Niman Ranch ribeye with blue cheese was tender and beefy, and also comes with a salad. Polenta pound cake with poached plums amd whipped cream was great as well.

Manning the kitchen and sushi bar at **Sake O** is Kauru Ishii, recruited from Matsuhisa in Beverly Hills. His menu includes many Nobu Matsuhisa–inspired fusion dishes such as ceviche, miso baked black cod, lobster salad, kobe beef tataki, flamed amaebi, foie gras, warm halibut carpaccio with olive oil, rock shrimp tempura with spicy aioli, and various fish tartars served with Osetra caviar. At Sake O's sushi bar, Spanish mackerel nigiri is perfectly cut and dressed with ponzu. Just as good: tender, fragrant engawa (halibut fluke) nigiri, well-balanced hirame carpaccio with yuzu and warm olive oil, shimaaji (yellowjack) nigiri, and stellar ankimo (topped with finely grated daikon stained orange from chili spice and chopped scallions). We've had a report of undercooked uni tempura (good flavor, though). Fish is of exemplary quality, and sake pours are generous. But you'll pay for it all—as much as $70 with tax and tip for a sushi dinner with a single sake.

Moosetta's offers housemade fried or baked piroshki still warm. The fried beef version (greaseless, with flaky pastry and a filling redolent of dill and onion) is savory, homey, and very satisfying. Many varieties are available for $2 or $3 per, including vegetarian and pepperoni with pepper Jack cheese.

Fresh and seasonal dishes are served at **Zin Restaurant**, like ricotta ravioli with sweet corn and basil in brown butter and halibut on a bed of creamy beans—both excellent. Also recommended: bananas Foster sundae.

Seaweed Cafe is a real gem with an ambitious menu belying its casual name. It serves three meals a day, emphasizing local seafood and seasonal ingredients. Brunch and lunch excels at buttermilk and sourdough pancakes (light and delicious), red flannel hash (perfectly balanced and "did a little dance on my plate," reports *Kim Cooper*), croissants (small, very fresh, house-baked, wonderful), heirloom tomato gazpacho (light and sweet), baked butter beans with sausage and clams (hearty and good) and grape tart, with peeled grapes (excellent). Also good salads and tapas–like dishes. Dinner is prix fixe (three courses for $32, four for $44) and the menu changes weekly.

Andy Jacob shares his top two picks for California-style pizza in Sonoma County. First: **Oakville Grocery** in Healdsburg, which is actually not just about pizza: hit it on Friday or Saturday nights when it showcases a rotating cast of local wineries, vineyards, and tasting rooms with wine tastings. There's also a cheese counter and many prepared foods, including rotisserie ducks ($17.50) on Fridays. Other meats are featured on different days, plus chickens every day. Wonderful patio for (takeout) dining and relaxing. Close runner up: **Borolos**, with friendly staff, fresh, quality ingredients, creative monthly specials, and an extensive vegan menu as well. Only downside: no clam toppings.

Wine-friendly, kid-friendly **Red Grape** specializes in New Haven–style thin-crust pizza (except made in a wood-burning oven, not coal-burning). Plain cheese (red cheese on the menu), margherita, Mediterranean, peppers and gorgonzola, pears and gorgonzola, and mushroom pies are all recommended.

At **George Chung's**, skip bland and greasy Chinese dishes and from-frozen fish-and-chips, and go for a generous bowl of pho at $5.95, replete with correctly cooked tripe, tendon, and brisket (ask for rare beef on the side). Only the broth disappoints, with murky and overaggressive flavors (somewhat tameable by adding fresh lime juice). Dine on the beautiful patio. Fruit shakes (made from soft serve) are not recommended. Not much English spoken or understood. Open daily, 11 a.m. to 8 p.m.

Ravenous exemplifies the casual, fun, and fresh Sonoma style, and has a fairly priced wine list and low $10 corkage. Highlights on the everchanging menu include burgers; cabbage rolls filled with Niman Ranch minced beef, pancetta, spinach and Reggiano; and smoked salmon with black and gold caviar and warm corn cakes. Also good: Vietnamese Dungeness crab cakes and grilled fennel and sage-rubbed pork tenderloin medallions with mustard-onion sauce. If you haven't made reservations and can't stand the wait for a table, hit the bar where you can order the full menu, and chat with the bartender and locals (maybe even a local winemaker).

Western Boot Steak House is a family-oriented restaurant with something for everyone: good, straightforward food, warm and friendly service, and reasonable prices. Its menu is devoted to ranch-style steaks of every size and shape, plus ribs, seafood, chicken, and pasta. Burgers are hand-formed of quality beef and grilled to order. Desserts are housemade. Lots of Western deco, and cowboy memorabilia.

Also see *"Wine Country* Chowing." See the Nabe Index for other Sonoma venues.

○ **K & L Bistro:** *see also* p. 134.
○ **New York Pizzeria:** *see also* p. 186.

SONOMA: PROVISIONING
(Wine, Cheese, and Much, Much More)

Angelo's Wine Country Deli
 (Sonoma County)
23400 Arnold Dr.
Sonoma, CA
707-938-3688
Store

Anstead's Marketplace and Deli
 (Sonoma County)
428 Center St.
Healdsburg, CA
707-431-0530
Store

Big John's Market
(Sonoma County)
1345 Healdsburg Ave.
Healdsburg, CA
707-433-7151
Store

Bodega Goat Cheese
(Sonoma County)
1379 Tannery Creek Rd.
Bodega, CA
707-876-3483
Cheese shop

Bruno's Marketplace
(Sonoma County)
102 Healdsburg Ave.
Healdsburg, CA
707-431-0530
Store

Cheese Course (Sonoma County)
423 Center St.
Healdsburg, CA
707-433-4998
Cheese shop

Dean & DeLuca Market
(Napa County)
607 S. Saint Helena Hwy.
St Helena, CA
707-967-9980
Store

G & G Foods (Sonoma County)
322 Bellevue Ave.
Santa Rosa, CA
707-542-6300
Store

Il Pasticciere Fiorini
(Sonoma County)
248 W. Napa St.
Sonoma, CA
707-996-6119
Italian bakery

Imwalle Gardens
(Sonoma County)
685 W. 3rd St.
Santa Rosa CA
707-546-0279
Store

Janetta's Zuchettas at Sonoma
Plaza Farmers' Market
(Sonoma County)
Sonoma Plaza on the Square
Sonoma, CA
707-538-7023
Farmers' market vendor

Madame de Fromage
(Sonoma County)
P.O. Box 721
Kenwood, CA
707-539-2252
Cheese shop

Martindales's Quality Meats
(Sonoma County)
5280 Aero Dr.
Santa Rosa, CA
707-545-0531
Store

Mekong Market (Sonoma County)
206 Sebastopol Rd.
Santa Rosa, CA
707-544-6201
Vietnamese store

Olive Press (Sonoma County)
14301 Arnold Dr., in Jack
   London Village
Glen Ellen, CA
1-800-965-4839
Store

Oliver's Market (Sonoma County)
560 Montecito Ctr.
Santa Rosa, CA
707-537-7123
Store

Pacific Market (Sonoma County)
1465 Town and Country Dr.
Santa Rosa, CA
707-546-3663
Store

Petaluma Grocery Outlet
   (Sonoma County)
80 E. Washington St.
Petaluma, CA
Store

Powell's Sweet Shoppe
   (Sonoma County)
720 McClelland Ave., in
   Town Green Village
Windsor, CA
707-836-0808
Chocolate/Candy shop

Raymond's Bakery
   (Sonoma County)
5400 Cazadero Hwy., about
   6 miles after turnoff from
   Hwy. 116
Cazadero, CA
707-632-5335
Café

Santa Rosa Grocery Outlet
   (Sonoma County)
1116 4th St.
Santa Rosa, CA
707-566-0530
Store

Sonoma Market (Sonoma County)
500 W. Napa St., #550
Sonoma, CA
707-996-3411
Store

Sonoma Saveurs (Sonoma County)
487 First St. W.
Sonoma, CA
707-996-7007
French store

Spring Hill Cheese
   (Sonoma County)
4235 Spring Hill Rd.
Petaluma, CA
707-762-3446
Cheese shop

Traverso's Gourmet Foods
(Sonoma County)
106 B St.
Santa Rosa, CA
707-542-2530
Italian deli

Vella Cheese Co.
(Sonoma County)
315 2nd St. E.
Sonoma, CA
707-938-3232
Cheese shop

Village Bakery (Sonoma County)
1445 Town and Country Dr.
Santa Rosa, CA
707-527-7654
Bakery

Whole Foods Market
(Sonoma County)
6910 Mckinley Ave.
Sebastopol, CA
707-829-9801
Store

Whole Foods Market
(Sonoma County)
621 E. Washington St.
Petaluma, CA
707-762-9352
Store

Whole Foods Market
(Sonoma County)
1181 Yulupa Ave.
Santa Rosa, CA
707-575-7915
Store

Willowside Meats & Sausage
(Sonoma County)
3421 Guerneville Rd.
Santa Rosa, CA
707-546-8404
Store

Windsor Wine Shop
(Sonoma County)
9058 Windsor Rd.
Windsor, CA 95492
707-838-9378
Wine store

Wine and Cheese Tasting
of Sonoma County
(Sonoma County)
25179 Main St. (Hwy. 116)
Duncans Mills, CA
707-865-0565
Wine store

Continuing with the bounty of Sonoma, here are the best places for do-it-yourself eating. Again, all tips are from Sonoma super-sleuth *Melanie Wong* unless otherwise noted.

At **Sebastopol Fine Wine Company,** a dozen wines are offered by the taste or glass, and there is a small selection of inexpensive daily specials, salads, antipasti, panini, soups, and a cheese plate ranging in price from $5 to $7. **Wine and Cheese Tasting of Sonoma County** is well worth a detour for a one-stop tour of local wines and cheeses. There are up to thirty wines open for tasting, including a selection of dessert wines, many locally made. Proprietors are extrafriendly, make everyone feel at home, and are eager to share wine knowledge with oenophiles and novices alike. Great value for quality (nine wine tastings and a piece of cheese runs $15 with tax and tip). You'll find ample cheese selections at **Cheese Course**, and **Whole Foods** is always a fine cheese option. Both offer tastes before purchase. If you're entertaining, or just willing to purchase large cuts of cheese, call Colette, aka **Madame de Fromage**.

Sonoma County artisanal cheese makers produce prize-winning and nationally recognized cheeses, but they also make fresh cheeses sold only locally, and some offer tastings at their production facilities. Here are some recommendations: **Spring Hill** has a public tasting room and sells its wares on site. Try fresh curd, cheddar, lemon quark, dry Jack. **Vella** has a retail store on site, and sells its cheese through grocers. Try special select dry Jack, half dry Jack. And **Bodega Goat Cheese** is open only by appointment, but sells at area farmers' markets. Try cream cheese, natilla.

Powell's plays *Willy Wonka and the Chocolate Factory* continuously on video and has a "Candy Casino" with roulette wheel and baccarat table marked with sweets. The chocolate case has American classics like turtles, pecan logs, and fudge, and there's a selection of bite-size chocolate bars from international manufacturers for 40 cents each. Twenty or so flavors of Gelato Classico are available, kept at correct tempurature to highlight texture. Servings seem generous.

Raymond's Bakery seems as much community center as bakeshop, with a small lending library, kids' games, and bulletin board, but the homey café and bakery are the draw. Offerings include crusty breads, pizzas, focaccia, quick breads, muffins, brownies, fruit tarts, oatmeal cookies, and lemon bars. Small palmiers are crackly, buttery, and dense; lemon bars have a buttery shortbread crust and a cakey top; and onion rolls filled with fragrant poppy seed and onion are buttery and very good. Indoor and outdoor seating. Cash only; check for seasonal hours.

Il Pasticciere Fiorini in Sonoma boasts about two dozen varieties of cookies, as well as pastries. Both light, meringuelike cookies and butter cookies are very good (*Peter*). **Traverso's**, open since 1922, is one-stop shopping for domestic and imported Italian foods. The house-cured pancetta and guanciale are unique and worth a special trip from the city. Really good imported roasted porchetta and mortadella, too. **Mekong Market** carries live seafood, many South East Asian food products, Asian veggies like galangal, and a wide selection of Vietnamese herbs. **G & G** is a good, big, bustling but slightly scruffy supermarket for Asian veggies. They have seafood tanks stocking live crabs, catfish, etc., at good prices. **Janetta's Zuchettas** offers more than just zucchini squashes. Check out the trombocino, a light-green, curly, tender and sweet variety. You can find them at the **Sonoma Plaza Farmers' Market** or at Dean & Deluca over in St. Helena.

Olive Press presses whole citrus fruits with its olives to make citrus oils in luscious flavors like limonato (organic Meyer lemons) and blood orange. It has a store in Jack London Village.

Sonoma Naturals is another company on the condiment wagon—roasted garlic base is a terrific product to have on hand when you want just a dash of roasted garlic flavor. It also makes great roasted red pepper and tomato pesto. Buy via its Web site (www.sonomanaturals.com) or at select Marin and Sonoma grocers.

Oliver's and **Pacific** are top-notch markets carrying Niman Ranch beef and pork and locally grown produce. Pacific has sushi-grade fish and bakes La Brea bread, and is very open to customer requests. Step next door to **Village Bakery** for fresh baked goods.

In Healdsburg, **Anstead's Marketplace and Deli** has shed its hippy-dippy ambience and taken on a well-lit rural sheen. Specializing in locally grown produce, it's now got an expanded prepared food counter, freezer case packed with organic meats, and fresh organic Rosie chickens are delivered from Petaluma daily. And for those sweet tooth cravings, Studebaker Cheese Cake from Boyes Hot Springs, a smooth, creamy-style cake on a graham cracker crust.

There are a couple of **Grocery Outlets** around the county, for those really cheap specials and special buys. *Jackie Avery* sometimes finds great tamales (chicken, pork, beef, and jalapeño-cheese, with sour cream and tomatillo salsa for $1) outside the Santa Rosa branch.

Martindale's Meats is pricey, but worth it for careful butchers, superb sausagemakers, and excellent beef jerky. **Willowside** caters more to wholesale and restaurant acccounts, but its butchers also serve retail walk-ins. **Angelo's**, with stores in Sonoma and Petaluma, makes great sausages (a bit on the sweet side), a wide assortment of jerkies, ham, bacon, and smoked chicken and duck. **Sonoma Saveurs** is the place for foie gras and other duck products. **Bruno's** carries fresh meats supplied by Martindales Meats in Santa Rosa, including house-cured sausages, hams, bacon, and smoked chickens; imported Italian and conventional American deli meats; and organic produce. Sandwiches are available, including muffaletta, and there are tables on a rose-lined patio. **Big John's** has the best looking meat counter in the North County, including the full range of CK lamb cuts, Niman Ranch pork and beef, and Rosie/Rocky chickens, and butchers on hand. Other features: sushi counter, baked-in-house La Brea breads, Chester fried chicken in the deli. **Sonoma Market** makes what *goingoutagain* calls the best fried chicken in the Bay Area, and they fry up fresh batches all day long.

For year-round produce, check out **Imwalle Gardens**. Open daily, closes at 5:15 p.m. Monday to Saturday, and earlier on Sundays. Also see "*Sonoma: Portuguese*" for info on Joe Matos Cheese Factory, which makes a cheddarlike Portuguese cheese.

○ **Santa Rosa Grocery Outlet:** *see also* p. 255.
○ **Sonoma Market:** *see also* p. 180.

SONOMA: MEXICAN

Delicias Elenitas (Sonoma
    County)
Sebastopol Rd.
Santa Rosa, CA
Mexican street cart/Truck

La Tapatia Taqueria Taco Truck
    (Sonoma County)
16405 River Rd., in parking lot
    of Safeway
Guerneville, CA
Mexican street cart/Truck

La Tejanita (Sonoma County)
Sebastopol Rd.
Santa Rosa, CA
Mexican street cart/Truck

Lola's (Sonoma County)
440 Dutton Ave., Suite 17
Santa Rosa, CA
707-577-8846
Mexican store

Los Mares Market and Taqueria
    (Sonoma County)
434 Center St.
Healdsburg, CA
707-433-4138
Mexican

Mariscos Alex (Sonoma County)
Santa Rosa, CA
Mexican street cart/Truck

Quezada Market (Sonoma County)
700 Sebastopol Rd.
Santa Rosa, CA
707-528-4999
Mexican store

Santa Rosa Grocery Outlet
    (Sonoma County)
1116 4th St.
Santa Rosa, CA
707-566-0530
Store

Tacos La Bamba (Sonoma County)
17400 Sonoma Hwy., behind La
    Morenita Market
Sonoma, CA
Mexican street cart/Truck

Tacos Milagro (Sonoma County)
18140 Sonoma Hwy., across from
    Sonoma Mission Inn
Sonoma, CA
Mexican street cart/Truck

Taqueria Los Primos
    (Sonoma County)
18375 Sonoma Hwy.
Sonoma, CA
707-935-3546
Mexican

Quezada is an all-around Mexican market with butcher, produce, and packaged goods, including some Central American items. There are also housemade beverages (silky horchata made from rice and whole milk, not mix, and seasonal aguas frescas) and an outside cooking setup serving tacos and platos. The prepared meats are impeccable. The carne asada is cooked to order with a different twist. Coarsely cut marinated steak is flash-sauteed on the flat top. (It is much juicier this way.) The grilled version has better flavor but is not as tender and juicy. Carnitas are the moist succulent type that pull apart in nubs. Moist pollo asado, grilled over mesquite, is sold as a half chicken plate with rice and beans. The chickens are cooked in batches throughout the day to ensure freshness. Salsa fresca (pico de gallo) is top-notch and very spicy with a blend of fresh jalapeños and yellow manzano chilis that add a fruity note. The red and green sauces are nothing special. Rice and beans are tasty.

Jackie Avery reports that Santa Rosa's best lunch bargain, the Elusive Tamale Man of Santa Rosa, can be found at a card table outside the west exit door of **Grocery Outlet**—if you're lucky.

Many who've sought him have not been lucky. But if you do connect with the Tamale Man, hot tamales (chicken, pork, beef, and jalapeño-cheese) can be yours for $1, with sour cream and tomatillo salsa. One tamale makes a decent lunch, two is a lot of food.

La Tapatia Taqueria has a taco truck that parks in the Guerneville Safeway's parking lot, with picnic table seating. Tamales contain very smooth and soft masa and are filled with pork cooked with tomatoes and peppers. Tamales and tacos (lengua was tender and buttery) are served with a bright orange, very hot and spicy chili sauce.

Los Mares Market and **Taqueria** offer a number of seafood selections. Nice, bright, limey ceviche (fish) tostada and good tacos de barbacoa de res (shreds of beef stewed in zesty chili sauce). Menudo and birria de chivo are offered on weekends.

Lola's, a large Mexican market, has all the basics and then some for your Mexican cooking needs.

Sam B. offers a brief Sonoma taco truck rundown (they usually arrive at 7 or 8 p.m., and stay till the wee hours); **Tacos La Bamba** (all meats excellent, virtually perfect carnitas; also try enchiladas michoacanas); **Tacos Milagro** (all items excellent, unbelieveable tacos al pastor, and "the best tacos I have ever had." Beware: sister truck "Tacos Milagros 2" isn't as good). **Taqueria Los Primos** (a nearby brick-and-mortar taqueria) is also good. **Mariscos Alex** is a taco truck in Santa Rosa preparing a full range of meats for tacos, burritos, and tortas; eggs for breakfast; and many seafood dishes, like coctel campechana ($7), tender prawns and octopus in citrusy tomato water with sweet red onion, ripe diced tomatoes, avocado, and cilantro. The owner speaks good English and parks weekday mornings and afternoons. We're not sure where he's parking, but he's worth searching down. There are three **Delicias Elenitas** taco trucks and two **La Tejanita** taco trucks that park on Sebastopol Road in Santa Rosa, and all are recommended.

○ **Santa Rosa Grocery Outlet:** *see also* **p. 250.**

Chowhound Nametag: Jim Leff

○◯○

Your Neighborhood: Queens (but I love chowhounding around the Bay Area)

Occupation: Writer, jazz musician, Web guy

Cholesterol Level: That of an eighty-three-year-old deli counterman

Weight Management Tip: Yoga (specifically, shoulder stand followed by fish position)

Farthest Out of the Way Traveled Just for Chow: I traveled to Spain nineteen times, ostensibly to play jazz but really to stock up on an ordinary brand of Italian supermarket cookie I'm in love with (Pannochie, from Mulino Bianco). They're made with corn.

Favorite Comfort Chow: Buko (young coconut) ice cream from Mitchell's, and anything from wonderful wonderful La Palma Mexicatessen (2884 24th Street at Florida), starting with anything fried (especially their potato chips, but all the fried stuff in bags is great), and also cooked stuff like pupusas, etc.

Guilty Pleasure: Like everyone else, Popeyes fried chicken, which serves as firm—vexing, even—evidence to refute the notion that fast-food chains can't be delicious. Important: regular, *not* spicy!

Favorite Gelato Flavor: The best flavor made by the place I'm in (and I'll taste through every single one to make that determination)

Nabe Most Full of Explorable Unknown Chow: The African American areas in East Bay. Everyone makes a beeline to certain vaunted barbecue destinations, but they're missing stuff. I've spotted all sorts of interesting cafés and soul food joints and blues lounges, none of them ever spoken about by anyone. I'm dying to do a thorough investigation.

Top Chinatown Pick: R & G Lounge for baby chicken stuffed with sticky rice—must order the day before. I'm also proud to be the hound who first "outed" Jai Yun Restaurant, the fabulous one man Shanghai joint (that now has become expensive and crowded . . . woops!)

Favorite Comfort Chow: Pizza while driving. Having been raised suburban middle class, this is the only culture I have to cling to. The way a Muslim feels upon hearing the early morning call to prayers, or an Inuit ice fishing, or a Frenchman breaking open a steaming croissant—at one with one's own nature and steeped in long ancestral heritage—this is how I feel eating pizza while driving.

Chowhounding *Negative* Rules of Thumb:

1. Don't look for people of the restaurant's ethnicity eating there. How many Americans have excellent taste in roast beef or apple pie? Why do we assume Chinese, Afghans, or Peruvians are any hipper to their cuisines? Instead, look for people of diverse ethnicity, eating with passion and exuding electric bliss. That is, look for chowhounds.

2. Don't look for crowds. Crowds are attracted by: 1. low prices, 2. advertising, and 3. crowds.

3. Don't ever order what you feel like eating. Only order what you think the place does best. If you crave something specific, find the specific place that best satsifies that specific craving.

4. Immigrant waiters exultant to guide you through their cuisine are a bad sign. It means the place is aiming for gringo clientele, which means they're pandering and diluting their cuisine. Better are sulky, impatient waiters who view your gringo presence as nothing more than potential aggravation. How many overworked barbecue shack counter workers would thrill at the prospect of explaining chopped barbecue to a group of Lithuanian tourists? And would you want to eat in a barbecue shack that offered a Lithuanian menu just in case?

5. Don't solely rely on second hand info . . . even secondhand info as savvy as this book or the Chowhound.com Web site. The search—and thrill of discovery—are half the fun. Do your own chowconnaissance and enjoy the giddy adventure!

SONOMA: PORTUGUESE

Joe Matos Cheese Factory
  (Sonoma County)
3669 Llano Rd.
Santa Rosa, CA
707-584-5283
Portuguese cheese shop

La Salette (Sonoma County)
452 First St. E.
Sonoma, CA
707-938-1927
Portuguese

9 Islands Bakery Cafe
  (Sonoma County)
1 Padre Pkwy., in Padre Town
  Center
Rohnert Park, CA
707-586-1620
Portuguese café

La Salette's carefully selected list of Portuguese and local Sonoma Valley wines includes an impressive variety of ports and Madeiras. Foodwise, choose from an array of fresh seafood on ice; large sardines grilled whole (dressed with Portuguese olive oil, vinegar, and sea salt, served with signature "melted" onions and a confetti of fresh vegetables) are buttery inside, with well-charred skin. Caldo verde, a refined, elegant take on Portugal's potato, greens, and sausage soup, has a creamy, potato-thickened broth, a chiffonade of barely wilted collard greens, and slices of Fernandes Sao Jorge linguica. Note that by the time you read this, they will have moved to a new location closer to the plaza in Sonoma.

Joe Matos Cheese Factory makes a Portuguese raw milk St. George–style cheese, which tastes kind of like cheddar. Stop by the farmhouse, where it's a bargain at $5 a pound (expect to pay around $12 a pound elsewhere).

In Rohnert Park, **9 Islands Bakery Cafe** is a Portuguese bakery. No malasadas, but don't miss the queijadas tarts—almond, orange, and plain custard. "The three are so different from each other and each simply wonderful in its own way. I think it's well worth a detour to try these the next time you're on this stretch of 101" (*Melanie Wong*). Also offered are a soup of the day, sandwiches (including linguica sausage on a roll), and espresso drinks. Tuesdays, you'll find the traditional kale and sausage soup. Imported food items, Sao Jorges cheese, sausages, and bacon are also sold. A small bulletin board displays news from the local Portuguese community, including a schedule of fiestas. Note: Padre Parkway is a poorly marked cul-de-sac off Commerce Boulevard, directly across from Lyon's and Burger King.

○ **9 Islands Bakery Cafe:** *see also* p. 180.

SONOMA: PETALUMA HIGHLIGHTS

Angelo's Meats (Sonoma County)
2700 Old Adobe Rd.
Petaluma, CA
707-763-9586
Store

Hallie's Diner (Sonoma County)
125 Keller St.
Petaluma, CA
707-773-1143
Diner or Coffeeshop

Hiro's Japanese Restaurant
    (Sonoma County)
107 Petaluma Blvd. N.
Petaluma, CA
707-763-2300
Japanese

Le Bistrot (Sonoma County)
312 Petaluma Blvd. S.
Petaluma, CA
707-762-8292
French bistro

Lolita's Market (Sonoma County)
451 Lakeville Circle
Petaluma, CA
707-766-8929
Mexican store

Lombardi's Gourmet Deli/BBQ
    (Sonoma County)
3413 Petaluma Blvd. N.
Petaluma, CA
707-773-1271
Barbecue store

Mary's Pizza Shack
    (Sonoma County)
359 E. Washington St.
Petaluma, CA
707-778-7200
Pizza

Mike's at the Crossroads
    (Sonoma County)
7665 Old Redwood Hwy.
Cotati, CA
707-665-9999
American

Mike's at the Yard
    (Sonoma County)
84 Corona Rd., at the Auction
    Yard
Petaluma, CA
707-769-1082
American

Papa's Taverna (Sonoma County)
5688 Lakeville Hwy.
Petaluma, CA
707-769-8545
Greek

Taco Truck (Sonoma County)
801 E. Washington St., in parking
   lot of Shell Station
Petaluma, CA
Mexican street cart/Truck

Playa Azul Mexican Restaurant
   (Sonoma County)
228 Petaluma Blvd. N.
Petaluma, CA
707-763-8768
Mexican

Thai Issan (Sonoma County)
208 Petaluma Blvd. N.
Petaluma, CA
707-762-5966
Thai

Here are some chowhound-worthy Petaluma stops, courtesy of
Bryan Loofbourrow and *Melanie Wong*.

No wonder **Le Bistrot** is a favorite of Petaluma locals: it serves
affordable and perfectly executed classic dishes cooked with
warmth and grace. Bistro salad made from lettuces more like
gossamer than greens is a mosaic of fresh, crisp flavors. Ex-
ceedingly fresh Dijon-crusted halibut is casually draped over
terrific garlic mashed potatoes and napped with a silky beurre
blanc and capers. Mostly local wines are all under $40.

Lombardi's is worth visiting just to smell the barbecue drums
emitting their fragrant smoke. But its BBQ chicken and ribs
are excellent and full of smoky flavors. Also very good: smoky
barbecued tri-tip on a soft untoasted roll. It makes and carries
Pedroni's famous potato salad in its deli case (*Jennie Sheeks*
calls it the "ambrosia of my Petaluma childhood"). Be sure and
get only the one marked Pedroni's for that loving, small batch,
handmade taste. No eggs, no celery, no paprika, just straightforward cleanness of taste.

Papa's Taverna plays host to a lively party on weekends, and
you're expected to join in. Get in the mood with excellent grilled
octopus and village salad (served only in summer, when perfect
tomatoes are available), but avoid merely okay cold appetizers.
Pork souvlaki is succulent, Greek sausage is nicely seasoned,
and buttery mashed potatoes are addictive. Daily special roast
lamb is disappointing, though. On Saturdays, a live band plays
in the downstairs tavern loudly enough to make you feel you're
in another country but not so loud that you can't talk. There's a
belly dancer with a large snake as an accessory, and servers

offer a quick lesson in Greek dancing so you can join the fun. Great location right on the river.

Quirky **Mike's at the Yard** offers twelve different burgers but not much more, not even fries. Why not? Their stated number one reason: "Mike's too darn lazy to change the grease." But oh what a burger, sighs *Bryan Loofbourrow*, who explains that "the flavor is all about the beef. You could taste this burger loud and clear through all the fixins and it was *good*. I think this is the best burger I've tasted." These burgers are made from a half pound of Harris Ranch beef, cooked to perfection, and come with tomatoes, lettuce, and cheese (no cheese costs five cents *more*). Limited hours: 11 a.m. to 3 p.m. Monday through Saturday. There's another Mike's branch in Cotati.

Hallie's, serving all-day breakfast and lunch downtown, has the feeling of a modern diner without retro pretensions. Very fresh, rich-tasting eggs done over easy are perfection. Fluffy corncakes come with warm maple syrup; and cajun sausage is deftly spiced and very flavorful. Burgers are meaty and flavorful, served on a sourdough roll with impeccably fresh accompaniments. Most ingredients (including eggs) are locally sourced. Open daily 7 a.m. to 3 p.m.

Lolita's for great chicken in mole, very good al pastor (cut to order from the spit—ask for some roasted pineapple, too), fresh made tortillas, tasty, spicy menudo, and intensely flavored birria (goat soup). **Taco Truck** in the Shell station, from about 6 p.m. on, most (but not all) nights, sells terrific $1.50 tacos, including tripa and lengua. Good quesadillas, too. **Playa Azul** specializes in seafood, including delicious ceviche. **Thai Issan** doesn't serve the sour sausage or exotic innards you'd find in traditional Issan cuisine, but does make a bunch of tasty standards. Fried rice balls with dipping sauce and Dungeness crab in yellow curry are winners. Food isn't intensely hot, but maybe if you ask nice? Very friendly service.

Mary's does a good job with gnocchi, spaghetti with meatballs, lasagna, and ravioli, along with special tripe in spicy tomato sauce. For dessert, get lemon ice or hot fudge sundaes. **Hiro's** is a city-quality sushi restaurant, with an engaging (when he's not busy) and creative sushi master. Impressive sake selection (try the Katana). Interesting rolls, including nice fresh uni. If feeling adventurous, try deep fried rolls or the Marilyn Monroll. **Angelo's** (part of the Angelo's empire) sells fab beef jerky and sausages.

○ **Mary's Pizza Shack:** *see also* **pp. 212, 263, 294.**

SONOMA: WHEN IN CLOVERDALE

Cloverdale Coffee & Ice Cream
(Sonoma County)
105 E. 1st St.
Cloverdale, CA
707-894-0846
Café

Cornucopia Natural Food Store
(Sonoma County)
228 S. Cloverdale Blvd.
Cloverdale, CA
707-894-3164
Store

Eagle's Nest Deli
(Sonoma County)
113 N. Cloverdale
Cloverdale, CA
707-894-9290
American

First Mart (Sonoma County)
840 N. Cloverdale Blvd.
Cloverdale, CA
707-894-3633
Mexican store

La Michoacana (Sonoma County)
5 Tarman Dr.
Cloverdale, CA
707-894-5370
Mexican store

Los Pinos Carniceria
(Sonoma County)
3 Tarman Dr.
Cloverdale, CA
707-894-3342
Mexican store

Mary's Pizza Shack
(Sonoma County)
1143 S. Cloverdale Blvd.
Cloverdale, CA
707-894-8977
Pizza/Italian

Pick's Drive In
(Sonoma County)
117 S. Cloverdale Blvd.
Cloverdale, CA
707-894-2962
American

Ruth McGowan's Brewpub
(Sonoma County)
131 E. 1st St.
Cloverdale, CA
707-894-9610
American pub

Starry Net Cafe
(Sonoma County)
512 N. Cloverdale Blvd.
Cloverdale, CA
707-894-0100
American

Sweet Rosebud's Coffee House (Sonoma County)
Broad St., next to the post office
Cloverdale, CA
707-894-9912
Diner or Coffee shop

Here's the best of Cloverdale (eat in, take out, and provision purchase), mostly courtesy of Sonoma sleuth *Melanie Wong*. First of all: be sure to keep an eye out for community breakfasts and barbecues. They'll be publicized on the marquee at the Citrus Fair, on banners over the roadway and along the chain link fence behind the Owl Cafe, and on the bulletin boards at the supermarket. During the summer it seems like there are a couple of civic events per month involving grilling.

Starry Net Cafe has a drive-in menu with good food and attention to quality. Chuck, ground fresh every day for burgers, is full of flavor and stays moist even when cooked medium-well. Garnishes are sliced to order and very fresh. "Big DaddY" a third of a pound burger with pepper Jack cheese is excellent, and a bargain at $3.75, as is a 75¢ order of slender, crisp fries. Milk shakes are made to order with quality ice cream; the spicy chai shake is deliciously exotic. There are some Chinese items on the menu, but the Hokkien-Chinese owner from Rangoon says they're too salty for his taste—that's how his customers like them! This is the only place in town to buy Thai iced tea; coffee is organic from local premium roaster, Taylor Maid. There's seating outdoors on a shaded patio or inside in air-conditioned comfort.

The menu at popular **Sweet Rosebud's Coffee House** includes housemade breakfast pastries and cookies, sandwiches, salads, and a daily quiche. Quality breads, meats, and cheeses are used for sandwiches, but avoid the fake panini. Mayo is used with a heavy hand. Baked goods (like cranberry scone and cookies) are quite good; blueberry-pecan muffins are excellent, with lots of fruit, tender, moist crumb, but surprisingly light, says *Pia*.

The bar at **Eagle's Nest Deli** serves lots of tomato beers to a lunchtime crowd; there are a few tables as well. Smoked pork roast and chicken, and house-barbecued tri-tip (tender, with deep flavor) are among the food choices. Prime rib sandwich has a nice thick slab of roasted medium-rare center cut meat, and is available au jus. Lunch, plus dinner on Fridays (lunch menu plus one entree). Corner Deli is home to **Los Pinos Carniceria,** with Mexican-style meat cuts and a butcher on staff. Cooked selections include carnitas, and chicken and pork tamales. You can get carne seca here. **La Michoacana** carries a selection of pan dulce delivered morning and afternoon from the Healdsburg location (119 Healdsburg Ave, Healdsburg; 707-433-1325), plus Mexican groceries and dry goods. (Note: they also do tax returns.)

Ruth McGowan's Brewpub has an unassuming rural California atmosphere (no yupscale anything) with food that is at once contemporary and comforting, says *Bryan Harrell*. The food's quite good for a brewpub, but stick with the basic sandwiches and salads and don't expect trendy, cutting-edge executions; just honest food. Great service. And what's a brewpub without beer—in this case, stellar beer brewed by Vinnie Cirluzo, of Russian River Brewing Company.

Pick's Drive In makes old-fashioned fast food; burgers are "wet" style with signature red relish, lots of mayo, shredded lettuce, and mushy tomatoes; shakes are made with Clover Stornetta ice cream. Root beer floats are great on a hot day. **Mary's Pizza Shack** is family oriented. **Cloverdale Coffee & Ice Cream** sells pastries from Healdsburg's Costeaux bakery, plus Lappert's ice cream (but be sure to ask which flavors are Lappert's). **First Mart** offers a full range of paletas (Mexican popsicles).

Cornucopia offers a decent selection of fresh, dried, and prepared vegetarian and health foods for when you have a craving for, say, smoked tempeh. The produce section features local, organically grown goods, and Bruce Breads from Boonville. Occasional surprises, like rare fresh turmeric root.

○ **Mary's Pizza Shack:** *see also* **pp. 212, 260, 294.**

SOUL FOOD Tips

Emma's Seafood & Poultry
  (East Bay)
3112 Market St.
Emeryville, CA
510-547-2864
Southern

Ma Pinkie's BBQ & Soul Food
  Restaurant (Peninsula)
207 N. Amphlett Blvd.
San Mateo, CA
650-342-1394
Southern/Barbecue

McNight Family House Fast Food
   (Peninsula)
2118 University Ave.
Palo Alto, CA
650-324-2983
Southern/Barbecue

Miya's Place
   (Westportal/Ingleside)
850 Holloway Ave.
San Francisco, CA
415-239-5741
Southern

Miya's Place ("Soul Food with a Taste of St. Louis") offers three or four revolving daily mains (meatloaf, baked ham, fried or broiled fish, fried shrimp, pork chops, and just about any other kind of meat, often smothered in gravy), plus choice of two sides and cornbread muffins (made with lots of cornmeal and no sugar, not like that cakey stuff you get at corner stores in New England), reports *Justin Cooper*. Oxtails are rich, tender, and even slightly sticky, smothered in a rich gravy that tastes like it's really made from pan scrapings and stock. Yams are sweetened with brown sugar and lightly spiced and are just tender enough without being too mushy; mac and cheese is perfect. But the star of the show at Miya's is fried chicken, cooked with thin, crispy skin that is salty and spicy, while the meat inside is remarkably moist and tender, with no stringiness. Serving breakfast, lunch, and dinner, with dinners under $10.

Emma's offers fried chicken, prawns, oysters, nine kinds of fish, sandwiches, and sides of fries, coleslaw, or potato salad (both of which are offered spicy or regular). Spicy fish is a good way to go. Orders are fairly substantial. Seasoning mix is flour-based (no cornmeal), and chicken can be underseasoned. Coleslaw is of the very wet and mayo-ey camp.

If you've ever been tempted to try turkey tails, **McNight Family House Fast Food** is the spot, selling four of these babies for $5. The tails have a slightly smoky flavor; they're brushed with barbecue sauce and are meatier than expected. The texture is like neck meat, with lots of skin and firm fat (like ham fat). Also good: fried okra, green beans with smoked pork, and catfish. Not so great: potato salad, fries, and ribs.

Ma Pinkie's is known to hounds for good barbecue, but there's also exemplary fried chicken with a crisp, golden, uniformly adherent and nongreasy coating protecting moist breast meat like a well-fitted glove, says *Ken Hoffman*. Service is warm and personal.

Cold-Weather **SOUP**

Cha-Am (East Bay)
1543 Shattuck Ave.
Berkeley, CA
510-848-9664
Thai

China Village (East Bay)
1335 Solano Ave.
Albany, CA
510-525-2285
Chinese (Sichuan)

Los Gatos Brewing Co.
  (South Bay)
130 N. Santa Cruz Ave.
Los Gatos, CA
408-395-9929
Pub

Mario's La Fiesta Mexican
  (East Bay)
2444 Telegraph Ave.
Berkeley, CA
510-540-9123
Mexican

When autumn chill hits the air, chowhounds look to soups for warmth. Albondigas (meatball) soup and its variations at **Mario's La Fiesta** take off the chill for the bargain price of $2, and is perfect for a cold day. At **China Village**, beef stew on noodles, swimming in hot oil, will open up all your pores, as will spicy fish noodle soup, says *Sharuf*. *Kathleen Mikulis* recommends tom kha gai soup (chicken in coconut milk) at **Cha-Am** ("lovely, with a kick of spiciness"). Note: this place may be going downhill, so caveat eater! New England clam chowder at **Los Gatos Brewing Company**, served Friday and Saturday only, is some of the best *Bob* has had; pho (Vietnamese rice noodle soup, seasoned to taste with condiments like chili sauce, cilantro, and garlic) and yuk ke jang (Korean spicy beef noodle soup with shredded beef, mung bean noodles, bean sprouts, green onions, and egg) are dependable options when looking for a bracing hit of spicy soup. Find them at most Vietnamese and Korean restaurants, respectively (see the cuisine index for tips).

○ **China Village:** *see also* **pp. 59, 77, 219, 294.**

Authentic SOUTH AMERICAN

Chola's (East Bay)
4375 Clayton Rd., #6
Concord, CA
925-680-0718
Peruvian

Villa Del Sol Argentinian
  Restaurant (Peninsula)
423 Grand Ave.
South San Francisco, CA
650-583-8372
Argentinian

Villa Del Sol serves good, authentic Argentinian cuisine. The quality-of-food versus price ratio was very high, says *Victoria Libin*, who notes that service is very friendly. Best appetizer: meat empanadas full of ground beef redolent of cumin. Potato and onion tortillas (omelets) and empanadas de humita (grilled corn and custardlike "Alfredo sauce" filling) are pretty good, too. And for you meat lovers: parillada, a platter of grilled meat that includes New York steak, Hawaiian-style short ribs, flank steak, beef sweetbreads, blood sausage, chorizo, pork chop, deboned chicken breast, and grilled chicken drumstick, all well seasoned and of creditable quality. Sweetbreads are amazing, firm yet tender with no strong odor. And, to complement the meat, the house chimichurri (garlicky parsley sauce) is very flavorful with a good balance. And save room for dessert: the Bay Area's best alfajores de maizena (buttery sandwich cookies filled with dulce de leche and dusted with powdered sugar). Wine list features Argentinean and Chilean selections. Corkage is $8 per bottle.

Chola's does authentic Peruvian food. Lunch specials for under $6 include grilled pork cutlet, salad, roasted yellow potatoes, rice, and chibcha morada (sweetened purple corn punch). "These people are pros and know what they are doing," raves *Wylie*.

○ **Villa Del Sol Argentinian Restaurant:** *see also* p. 209.

Alhamra vs. Pakwan:
SOUTH ASIAN Chow-Off

Alhamra (Mission)
3083 16th St.
San Francisco, CA
415-621-3935
North Indian/Pakistani

Pakwan (Financial District)
653 Clay St.
San Francisco, CA
415-834-9904
Pakistani/North Indian

Naan N' Curry (Financial District)
533 Jackson St.
San Francisco, CA
415-693-0499
Pakistani/North Indian

When in the Mission and craving hot and spicy, do you head to Alhamra or Pakwan? Consensus seems to be that **Pakwan** wins for vegetable dishes, naan, lamb chops, and shish kabobs (avoid curries, though!), whereas **Alhamra** does a better job with other meat dishes, especially chicken tikka masala (CTM). *King Masala* deconstructs Alhamra's now legendary CTM thus: "the sauce itself is where the magic happens. Surely passed on from generation to generation, there is a sense of story behind this piece of curry perfection, and just how such a loose and silken sauce can be laced with such complex and exotic flavors I'll never know."

Pakwan's Clay Street location is a welcome addition to financial district lunch options, though dishes seem a little less spicy than at **Naan N' Curry** a few blocks away (and overall quality is below that of the two other Pakwan locations). Meats are especially good, including juicy, spicy seekh kabob and chicken tikka masala with a hint of smokiness. Other recommendations: sabzi (vegetable curry), bengan bhartha, veggie samosas. Two drawbacks: (1) rice pudding portions are very, very tiny, and (2) they tend to forget items on takeout orders, so check before you leave.

Breads and Pastries from the
SOUTH PACIFIC

South Pacific Island Bakery (Peninsula)
110 5th Ave.
Redwood City, CA
650-261-9360
Pacific bakery

South Pacific Island Bakery makes breads (presliced and bagged), sweet yeasted baked goods, turnovers, pastries, and more treats from the South Pacific. Samoan pineapple turnover is like a giant empanada (there's also a Tongan version with different crust) with tasty not-too-sweet filling. Rolls with coconut milk have coconut milk and sweetened condensed milk poured over them. They're all well made with good ingredients, and given the dearth of South Pacific foods in the Bay Area, this is a place worth knowing about says *Ruth Lafler*.

SOUTHERN Quartet

Gecko Grill (South Bay)
855 N. 13th St.
San Jose, CA
408-971-1826
Mexican

Steamer's Grillhouse (South Bay)
31 University Ave.
Los Gatos, CA
408-395-2722
American

Pizza Antica (South Bay)
334 Santana Row #1065
San Jose, CA
408-557-8373
Pizza

Tapestry Bistro (South Bay)
11 College Ave.
Los Gatos, CA
408-395-2808
New American

Ken Hoffman shares tips for four places to the south:
    Gordon Drysdale, of the late Gordon's House of Fine Eats,

runs **Pizza Antica** on the happening Santana Row. Menu offers appetizers, salads, pizza, and pastas. Breadsticks with olives are beautifully authentic—lean and crunchy and pencil thick. Neopolitan-style pizza, with a super-thin, soft, foldable crust is terrific—flavor intense without being filling, the closest thing to what you get in the Campagna. They serve delicious homemade Italian sodas such as limeade and blood orange over crushed ice, and the waitstaff performs with grace and style.

Gecko Grill is an oasis of good food and sly style, serving updated Mexican. House chips are extra thick, chicken avocado salad is full of quality ingredients (grilled zucchini, black beans, queso fresco, grilled chicken, half an avocado, with cilantro dressing), Mexican cheesesteak torta is a generous portion, and there's comfortable outdoor seating.

At **Tapestry**, a charming California-style bistro, every Monday all wine bottles are half price. Other interesting deals, too (info at www.tapestrybistro.com). Good crab cakes and garlic lo mein noodles; outdoor patio; parking in the Soda Works Plaza lot in the rear.

Steamer's is an ode to slickness, but if you find yourself there, get the warm crab-artichoke dip with toasted pita wedges (70 percent crab and 30 percent artichoke with breadcrumbs and no mayo). Add shrimp to margherita pizza for very oceany flavors that meld seamlessly with the tomato and basil.

STEAK TARTARE: Eating It Raw

Andalu (Mission)
3198 16th St.
San Francisco, CA
415-621-2211
Spanish/New
    American/French/Italian

Bix (North Beach)
56 Gold St.
San Francisco, CA
415-433-6300
American

Boulevard (Embarcadero)
1 Mission St.
San Francisco, CA
415-543-6084
New American/French/Italian

Chez Papa (Potrero Hill)
1401 18th St.
San Francisco, CA
415-255-0387
French bistro

Jeanty at Jack's
  (Financial District)
615 Sacramento St.
San Francisco, CA
415-693-0941
French bistro

Syrah Bistro
  (Sonoma County)
205 5th St.
Santa Rosa, CA
707-568-4002
New American

Jeanty at Jack's serves steak tartare as an entrée rather than appetizer. It's a large portion with raw egg on top to mix yourself, plus plenty of toast points. The version at **Chez Papa** isn't as big as Jeanty at Jack's, but is just as tasty. **Bix** preps its steak tartare tableside. It's perfectly seasoned and neither eggy nor slimy. **Andalu** does a nice twist on steak tartare served with a unique sauce. **Syrah** in Santa Rosa offers a unique take on steak tartare that's terrific with a spicy glass of Syrah wine, reports *Melanie Wong*, who adds the tasty version by Nancy Oakes of Boulevard, tasted at the Masters at Highlands Inn, would be worth asking about since it may not be on the regular menu at **Boulevard**: "What I liked about both versions is that the meat was not pulverized into submission and had been coarsely chopped so it retained some texture. The prep at Syrah was actually on the chunky side."

- **Andalu:** *see also* **p. 320.**
- **Bix:** *see also* **p. 179.**
- **Boulevard:** *see also* **p. 28.**
- **Jeanty at Jack's:** *see also* **p. 236.**
- **Syrah Bistro:** *see also* **p. 275.**

STRAWBERRY Delights

Nation's Giant Hamburgers
  (Contra Costa County)
5321 Hopyard Rd.
Pleasanton, CA
925-463-2388
American

Nation's Giant Hamburgers
  (East Bay)
6060 Central Ave.
El Cerrito, CA
510-528-8888
American

Nation's Giant Hamburgers
   (Peninsula)
301 S. Mayfair Ave., in Westlake
   Center
Daly City, CA
650-755-8880
American

Nation's Giant Hamburgers
   (Solano County)
2525 Sonoma Blvd.
Vallejo, CA
707-554-8888
American

Swanton Berry Farm
   (Santa Cruz County)
25 Swanton Rd.
Davenport, CA
831-469-8804
Farm or Farm stand

In season, Nation's sells fresh strawberry tarts (a huge mound of fresh berries with sweet glaze and whipped cream piping) big enough to share. They also have a strawberry cheesecake topped with sliced berries. If you're not a berry fan, *Mike Lee* says banana cream pie's the way to go. Best of all, it's open twenty-four hours for a dessert fix at any time.

Swanton Berry Farm used to make amazing strawberry short-cake during strawberry season, and sold it at their farmstand in Davenport and at the Ferry Plaza Market. Unfortunately, it seems to have stopped making shortcake, but (1) it may change its mind! And (2) if enough of us beg, maybe it'll reconsider! And (3) it's worth checking! So give it a call.

○ **Swanton Berry Farm:** *see also* pp. 156, 232.

Fruhstuck Und Mittagessen at **SUPPENKUCHE**

Suppenkuche (Civic Center)
525 Laguna St.
San Francisco, CA
415-252-9289
German

Breakfast, lunch, or brunch at **Suppenkuche**, it's all good, from herbed quark with potatoes to cured gravlax to very tasty sauteed German ravioli with eggs (*maultaschen*) to big, filling Emperor's pancake. If you want lighter fare, consider salads: simple cucumber salad or butter lettuce salad with mustard vinaigrette. Tables are beer hall style, and you'll share with other patrons. Check out the amazing German beer selection. (Who says you have to drink coffee with brunch?)

SUSHI Trio

Sakae Restaurant (Peninsula)
240 Park Rd.
Burlingame, CA
650-348-4064
Japanese

Sawa Sushi (South Bay)
1042 E. El Camino Real
Sunnyvale, CA
408-241-7292
Japanese

Sushi California (East Bay)
2033 Martin Luther King, Jr.
  Way
Berkeley, CA
510-548-0737
Japanese

Hounds sing the praises of **Sushi California**'s tasty, comforting, reasonably priced fare, which *Derek Glanville* says may be the best sushi for the money in Berkeley. The chef's friendly, and if you sit at the bar and ask for whatever's freshest, you'll be treated well and perhaps be served an extra treat gratis. This restaurant is a bit off the beaten path, but only a few minutes' walk from downtown Berkeley theaters and the BART station.

Sawa's got a reputation as being pricey and kind of exclusive, but the food's terrific. Go *omakase* (chef's choice). Some highlights, courtesy of *suekiyaki*: maguro ("so good that I briefly went blind from pleasure"), unrecognizably huge softball of out-of-season ankimo (a special order—challenging preorders seem to be a special source of joy for this restaurant), fresh wasabi ("you can tell if Steve-san loves you based on which wasabi you get"), amazing hotate (scallop), fresh lobster roll with huge avocado chunks ("a creamy narcotic, I felt despair and loss when the last bite was finished"), and beautifully carved pineapple.

Sakae is pricey, but serves very good sushi. Advice from *xiong xiong*: go before 7 p.m., sit at sushi bar for more attention, and order from the specials board. There's a nice premium sake list, and top orders include uni tempura (fried sea urchin wrapped in shiso), seki saba, whole scallop, and sweet jumbo shrimp. *NipponFan* says ambiance is that of a neighborhood Japanese sushi bar that, over the years, has become popular and, thus, lost some of its homey charm.

Hoorah for **SYRAH**

Petite Syrah (Sonoma County)
205 B 5th St.
Santa Rosa, CA
707-568-3167
Wine store

Syrah Bistro (Sonoma County)
205 5th St.
Santa Rosa, CA
707-568-4002
New American

Syrah Bistro's tasting menu ($55 for five courses) is a bargain. Not every dish is awesome, but on the whole, *Melanie Wong* was very pleased, especially for the price. Others like it more. *Andy Jacob* finds the cooking excellent, especially Syrah's steak tartare ("really tuned in on the musky truffle nuance and right amount of spice to make it sing with the Syrah wines"). The staff goes all out, and takes pride in what they do. This is an especially good spot to enjoy a glass of wine and some appetizers (great cheese plates, too). *Maya* says this is the perfect place for an elegant and relaxed lunch in Santa Rosa. House salad (with pears, walnuts, goat cheese, and cucumbers), chicken pot pie (flavorful, with good crust), seared scallops on angel hair (with red onions, arugula, and tarragon cream), and fresh mascarpone beignets with bittersweet Scharffen Berger chocolate fondue are recommended. This, plus a glass of wine, runs $60 before tip. Service is great. Check out affiliated **Petite Syrah** wine shop next door (open Tuesday to Saturday, 11:00 a.m. to 5:00 p.m.).

○ **Syrah Bistro:** *see also* **p. 272.**

TACO Cravings

El Tonayense Taco Truck (Mission)
Harrison St., between 19th and
  20th St.
San Francisco, CA
Mexican street cart/Truck

El Tonayense Taco Truck
  (Mission)
Shotwell St., just south of
  16th St.
San Francisco, CA
Mexican street cart/Truck

Grocery Clearance Center
  (East Bay)
2079 23rd St.
San Pablo, CA
510-965-1020
Store

Los Cantaros Taqueria (East Bay)
5412 San Pablo Ave.
Oakland, CA
510-601-8545
Mexican

Los Cantaros Taqueria 2
  (East Bay)
3817 Market St.
Emeryville, CA
510-653-4572
Mexican

Mi Casa Mexican Restaurant
  (East Bay)
1408 Webster St.
Oakland, CA
510-835-1813
Mexican

Nick's Crispy Tacos at Rouge
  Night Club (Russian Hill)
1500 Broadway
San Francisco, CA
415-409-TACO
Mexican

Taco truck (Napa County)
Hwy. 128 (formerly Hwy. 29),
  north of Calistoga, north of
  Petrified Forest Rd.
Calistoga, CA
Mexican street cart/Truck

Tacos La Playita (Napa County)
3069 Jefferson St.
Napa, CA
707-258-8443
Mexican

Taqueria El Castillito (Noe Valley)
4001 18th St.
San Francisco, CA
415-621-6940
Mexican

Taqueria Maria (Marin County)
1017 4th St.
San Rafael, CA
415-257-5720
Mexican

Taqueria Mendoza (East Bay)
2031 23rd St.
San Pablo, CA
510-215-9065
Mexican

Taqueria San Jose (Mission)
2830 Mission St.
San Francisco, CA
415-282-0203
Mexican

The taco trucks of El Tonayense are renowned for al pastor that's spicy, savory, juicy, piquant, meaty, charred, and silky. Tripitas "strike just the right balance between chewiness and cracklyness, with some (but not too much) intestinal flavor," reports *chibi*. For chorizo tacos, *chibi* heads to **Taqueria San Jose**, which serves up large mounds of silky moist chorizo piled on substantial tortillas, topped with salsa and lots of finely chopped onions. The chorizo is notably ungreasy (nothing against grease, of course), and the great salsa is "full of torn up pieces of chiles, velvety smooth from pureed tomatillos, smoky tangy, make-your-nose-itch hot."

There's a little market on Highway 128 selling mostly beverages and a few Mexican snack items. It is Napa Valley's northernmost **taco truck**. "Being able to make a taco truck run from slightly snobby, cream and butter clogged St. Helena just puts a little smirk on my face," snorts *Jennie Sheeks*. Chorizo tortas start with large round hamburger type buns, grilled, stuffed with meat, grilled onions, pinto beans, iceberg lettuce, slices of avocado, tomato, and sour cream. Besides tortas, offerings include tacos, burritos, quesadillas, taquitos, tostadas. Pricier than other trucks at $2.00 for a taco, $4.75 for torta, but it's still one of the top cheap lunch options up-valley.

Tacos La Playita's truck is another favorite, last seen on McKinstry (runs parallel to Soscol near the Wine Train depot), due to construction. After 6:30 p.m., it usually parks in the lot of the old Food Fair on Jefferson and Old Sonoma Road. The Tacos La Playita folks opened a small restaurant in a mini-mall (an old Food Fair spot), and it's really busy. Its tacos al pastor are comparable to the truck, while chicken tacos are not quite as good. The menu's more extensive than the truck offerings, though. It's busy, so go at off-peak hours (they open at 10 a.m. daily).

Nick's Crispy Tacos, hidden away inside Rouge nightclub, is, says *Johnny P*, "by far your best option for taqueria-style Mexican food in the area. I consider Nick's to be, at worst, a blessed addition to a neighborhood that is long on pricey meals and short on tasty bites . . . and at best, a sure contender for the best taco outside of the Mission." Best bet: order crispy carnitas tacos. Steak and chicken are worthy too.

Taqueria Maria, across from the big bank building in San Rafael, serves very good food (especially tostadas) at low, low prices. **Taqueria El Castillito** is good to know about if you live nearby or are in the area of Noe and Eighteenth, for unexpectedly good quality and excellent value, says *Jimbo*. It's a branch of the place on Mission, and has particularly choice breakfast offerings. Huge portions, no esoteric Mission meats (tongue, kid, etc.), and pretty creditable gallo pinto. **Taqueria Mendoza,** located in a San Pablo mini-mall, serves working class standards like cabeza tacos (duly gelatinous, reports *Gordon Wing*) and nice portions of chips with flavorful but not-screaming red salsa. Al pastor is just okay. Big bowls of soup and plate lunches are reasonably priced. (To digress, check out nearby **Grocery Clearance** outlet for deals like Cape Cod Kettle Chips Dark Russets at 50¢ a bag, one-and-a-half pint Ben & Jerry's for 99¢, Cabot Farms Sharp Cheddar for $2.99.)

The second branch of **Los Cantaros** (in North Oakland) does excellent tacos, especially fish, and chiles rellenos filled with corn and cheese in a light tomato sauce. The original San Pablo location may not be holding up, though. *Marc Wallace* likes **Mi Casa** in downtown Oakland for lunch. Everything's extremely good, and they're generous with free extras and very glad for customers.

Also see "*Middlefield Road* Taco Crawl," and the cuisine index for many Mexican tips.

TALLULA

Tallula (Castro)
4230 18th St.
San Francisco, CA
415-437-6722
Pan-Asian fusion/Indian/New American

Chez Spencer's Laurent Katgely consulted on the menu at **Tallula,** but don't expect French flavors; it's more Indian fusion.

Special touches make it worth a visit: rose petal garnishes, the location in a groovy three-level house including deck, funky tables in the lounge, arresting pix of India that make for a sumptuous space, and the saucy cocktail menu, says *Courgette*. Tallula is doing creative, nontraditional things with Indian-based cooking, like Tabla or Tamarind in New York City, but not quite as elegant or upmarket $$, says *Jimbo*.

The menu's divided into four sections: puri and chaat (small plates) and tandoori and chulla (entrees), all intended for sharing. Standout small plates include lobster and corn dosa w/curried cream, crowd pleasing spiced pommes frites with mango pickle ketchup, grilled sardines (two) with mango and cucumber relish, and lamb sausauge and kidneys with pink lentils and pickled turnips. Top entrees include fennel-crusted golden trout, crumb-crusted eggplant and portabello mushrooms with tomato chutney, house-cured duck with caramelized pineapple. Rice pudding is highly praised. Note that even entrée portions are small (this isn't obvious from the menu) so be prepared for tiny squab, etc. There's an extensive wine list (but no corkage fee, so BYOB if you like), and lots of cocktail concoctions and gourmet teas.

Ambience-wise, dining here is like eating in a cool house, where larger parties get their own cozy rooms, and the view of the hills from the top level is unique. There's a pleasant lower level bar (no hard liquor) and a dimly lit (romantic or just dark?) mezzanine. Pace is leisurely. Anticlimax alert: as we finished production of this guide, we heard reports that Tallula may have gone a tad downhill. If so, we hope it'll reverse its slide.

The Elusive and Wonderful
TAMALE LADY

Virginia the Tamale Lady (Mission)
San Francisco, CA
415-218-1443
Mexican street cart/Truck

Virginia the Tamale Lady makes the rounds of bars in the Mission, Bernal Heights, Lower Haight, and more on Friday nights. Other times and days, she's harder to track. Give her a call at 415-621-0129 or 415-218-1443.

Serious TEA

Dynastea (Russian Hill)
1390 Pacific Ave.
San Francisco, CA
415-931-8620
Café

Samovar (Castro)
498 Sanchez St.
San Francisco, CA
415-626-4700
Café

Silk Road Teas (Marin County)
P.O. Box 287
Lagunitas, CA
415-488-9017
Mail order source

Teance (East Bay)
1111 Solano Ave.
Albany, CA
510-524-1696
Café

Whole Foods
www.wholefoods.com
Store

Both Teance and Samovar are worthy destinations for tea drinkers or anyone looking to expand their repertoire, reports *Windy*.

Teance is a charming place to enjoy a cup of tea or indulge in an extensive tasting, with low-key expert staff willing to describe and evangelize each tea, encouraging you to examine and smell the leaves, or just allow you to sit back and enjoy the aromas and flavors. Don't miss its superb baochung competition oolong or silver needle. As with so many highly addictive substances, your first tasting is free. Then you pay $2 for each subsequent tasting per person. Teance also carries beautiful tea ware and serves pastries and tea snacks (e.g. great tea-pickled plums and thin biscotti). Open until 10 p.m. Fridays and Saturdays.

Samovar is very unstodgy and inviting (lots of light and pillows). Teas are good, but prices are bit higher than other tea rooms' at $3.00 to $5.00 per pot (someone's got to pay for the dj spinning hip tea music). It offers about thirty quality teas, all (perfectly) brewed by the pot. Presentation is lovely. Outstanding tea snacks include vanilla-flavored roasted pumpkin seeds, Mandarin orange almonds, tea-flavored shortbread cookies, salmon tea toasts, and smoked salmon. For a nice iced tea, check out Samovar's citron oolong, with a strong lemongrass scent. It also offers some rare Korean green teas. And there's special pricing from 7 to 9 a.m. on weekdays and 8 to 10 a.m. weekends, when a pot of tea plus pastry from Sylvie's costs $3.00. Weekend brunch is $10.95 for five small dishes and pot of tea. Plenty of street parking (at least during the week).

David Lee Hoffman imports many great and rare Chinese teas through his company, **Silk Road Teas**. Some of these can be found in bulk at **Whole Foods** markets, while others are available by contacting him directly. *Liz* says his tea tastings are very informative at reasonable prices ("you won't look at tea the same way after a tasting with David").

If you want a place to kick back and relax, **Dynastea** is it, says *Stanley Stephan*. Lovely room with for-sale Asian antiques, comfy couches, tables and chairs, and a back room that feels like a living room ("I asked three times if I was accidently walking into their living quarters"). You may need an appointment, so call ahead. This is a good place for tea beginners, as owner May is very helpful and friendly. She buys directly from the Chinese government, mostly from Fujian province. Free tastings are offered. Most pots run $4 to $6 with the most expensive, Scarlet Robe, at $10. Tea snacks, including vegan tea cookies are avail-

---

○○○ Chowhound Tip:

If you don't like strong tea, ask for a fair pot—a little pot to pour the tea into after it has brewed.

---

able. Open from noon to 10 p.m. Parking's tight in this neighborhood, but the Hyde St. cable car runs right past as do some MUNI lines.

○ **Whole Foods:** *see also* **pp. 52, 73, 230.**

THAI/LAOTIAN Provisions in Santa Rosa

Thailao Market (Sonoma County)
1081 Santa Rosa Ave.
Santa Rosa, CA
707-546-0129
Thai/Laotian store

Thailao Market, owned by a Lao/Issan family, is quite a find for authentic Thai ingredients in the Bay Area. It's bigger than Erawan, the Thai grocery in Berkeley, and offers a wider selection including more fresh produce and frozen foods, plus Thai clothing items, cookbooks, and cookware. There's an extensive selection of packaged Thai goods and condiments (e.g., five brands of canned coconut milk), and some other Southeast Asian products as well.

Fridays are the best days to go; Thailao has extra quantity and selection for the weekend. On her Friday visit, *Melanie Wong* found many fresh herbs (including some she'd not seen before), red and yellowish-green bird's eye chilis sold loose or on their leafy vines, baggies of fresh kaffir lime leaves for $1.25, many types of leafy greens, tiny Thai eggplant, bitter eggplant, Chinese eggplant, and baby loofah okra. Note that the bird's eye chili stalks are boiled in soup and are good for the eyes.

The daughter of the family, Makha, can help choose among packaged goods, and will explain unfamiliar produce. Prices are excellent. Open daily, 9:30 a.m. to 8:30 p.m.

Chowhounding the **THAI AND INDIAN TEMPLES**

Shiva-Vishnu Temple (East Bay)
1232 Arrowhead Ave., in Hindu
    Community and Cultural
    Center
Livermore, CA
925-449-6255
South Indian

Wat Buddhanusorn (East Bay)
380 Bush (look for the stairs
    descending into the depths)
Fremont, CA
510-790-2294
Thai

Wat Buddhapradeep (Peninsula)
310 Poplar Ave.
San Bruno, CA
650-615-9528
Thai

Wat Mongkolratanaram (East Bay)
1911 Russell St.
Berkeley, CA
510-849-3419
Thai

Wat Buddhapradeep (aka San Bruno Thai Temple) serves a wide assortment of home-cooked Thai dishes on Sundays for lunch, and the public's invited. *Melanie Wong* says volunteers at this temple (unlike the bigger and more crowded Berkeley Thai Temple) are thrilled to answer questions and offer encouragement to try their dishes. Since this lunch is smaller than the Berkeley one, you can get closer to the action and watch the cooking (better parking too). Bring a cooler and tupperware to bring leftovers home, as portions can be huge. And the food, you ask? Brilliant! And note that spicy means *spicy*. Be sure to stop by the dessert table first, so you don't miss out on mango sticky rice, coconut coated cassava balls, roti and pork-filled tapioca balls. Also don't miss: fabulous pork larb, green papaya salad (made to order with hand-chopped green papaya), fried bananas, taro and sweet tubers, roti (crispy, sticky, sweet, and made right in front of you), fried pork ribs (a textural cross between carnitas and cecina, with dryish texture and exotic and slightly gingery spicing), fried chicken with sticky rice and sweet chili dipping sauce, and from the steam table, duck curry, anise eggs and pork, and fried fish in spicy garlic sauce. Steamed veggies include: tiny eggplants, blonde zucchini, watercress, green beans, and bitter greens to counteract the heat of other dishes. And if you haven't had enough spicy food, look for the spicy vegetable condiment that looks like ratatouille but is more like caponata on steroids, with a deep and enduring peppery blaze. Buy a tub to take home if you can.

According to *Gordon Wing*, Berkeley's **Mongkolratanaram Temple** serves up a Thai buffet every Sunday, except when fate or other festivals intervene. This Thai brunch takes place in the temple's courtyard every Sunday from 9 a.m. to 2 p.m. (best dishes go fast, so arrive early), with stands offering a wide variety of snacks, curries, and sweets. Of special interest to *Patrick* is som tham, a much sought-after chewy, crunchy salad of shredded green papaya, cabbage, green beans, peanuts, tomatoes, chili/garlic oil, and dried shrimps (customarily served with sticky rice), which is made to order in front of you. *Richard Adams*, a language student at the temple, offers the following tip: when you order the som tham, ask for "som tham bpo," the Isaan (Northeastern) style with salty preserved crab. You will earn a big smile from the woman making the dish plus a great taste treat. By all means, have it with sticky rice (kao nee-o).

At **Wat Buddhanusorn** in Fremont, lunch is served every Sunday from 9 a.m. to 2 or 3 p.m. (arrive early for best selection). It also has special event days that offer a much greater variety of foods. Check its Web site calendar (www.watbuddha.iirt.net) for dates. Flowers and baskets are for sale out front and the food's in the back. *Arlene* says there's a good selection of foods, but not quite as wide as in Berkeley. Recommended: sweet roti (hot off the grill and served with sweetened condensed milk and sugar), steamed fish in banana leaf, chicken satay, chicken

○○○ Chowhound Tip:

The volunteer women who used to cook at Shiva-Vishnu Temple have put out a cookbook of temple foods (it's a Hindu temple so all food is vegetarian), which is available at the temple for a $10 donation.

curry over rice, and BBQ pork. Of the dishes sampled, only two fell flat: seafood noodle soup (a bit too sweet) and fried chicken (kind of dry even though freshly fried).

Word is that the South Indian **Shiva-Vishnu Temple** has hired a professional temple cook (formerly of Ganesh Temple in Flushing, N.Y.) to cook for events. One chowhound reports terrific food and an open atmosphere, but *Jim Leff* warns that this wasn't a particularly highly regarded chef back during his days in Flushing.

THAI TEA ICE CREAM

Chai Yo (and attached sweet
   shop) (Russian Hill)
1331 Polk St.
San Francisco, CA
415-771-2562
Thai

Joe's Ice Cream (Richmond)
5351 Geary Blvd.
San Francisco, CA
415-751-1950
Ice cream or Gelato

Latest Scoop (East Bay)
1017 Ashby Ave.
Berkeley, CA
510-849-0143
Ice cream or Gelato

Mitchell's Ice Cream (Mission)
688 San Jose Ave.
San Francisco, CA
415-648-2300
Ice cream or Gelato

Fans of Thai iced tea, with its reddish cast and sweet, thick consistency (from condensed milk), can now try an even colder version—in the form of ice cream! It's starting to catch on.

The sweet shop attached to **Chai Yo** serves Thai tea gelato from **Latest Scoop** in Berkeley. *Melanie Wong* says it really does taste like a Thai iced tea with a little bit of tannic bite in the finish to balance the sweetness. Thai tea ice cream has also been spotted at **Joe's** and **Mitchell's**.

- ○ **Joe's Ice Cream:** *see also* **pp. 26, 139.**
- ○ **Mitchell's Ice Cream:** *see also* **pp. 20, 26, 139.**

THAI TOUR

Jitlada Thai Cuisine
(Pacific Heights)
1826 Buchanan St.
San Francisco, CA
415-292-9027
Thai

Siam Cuisine (East Bay)
1181 University Ave.
Berkeley, CA
510-548-3278
Thai

Soi 4 Restaurant (East Bay)
5421 College Ave.
Oakland, CA
510-655-0889
Thai

Thai Delight Cuisine (East Bay)
1700 Shattuck Ave., C
Berkeley, CA
510-549-0611
Thai

Thai House Express (Tenderloin)
901 Larkin St
San Francisco, CA
415-441-2248
Thai

Vanni Innovative Cuisine
(East Bay)
1096 Dwight Way
Berkeley, CA
510-843-3646
Thai

Soi 4 is among the more upscale Bay Area Thais. A bit pricier than your basic noodle house, it offers regular entrees and small plates, good cocktails. Thai basics (pad Thai, etc.) aren't necessarily the way to go here. Recommended by *ex culina*: taro and bean curd fries, roti, Shanghai noodle salad, fried catfish salad, braised pork ribs, green curry veggies (grilled, not boiled), and fried banana dessert

Of **Vanni**, *DottieMay* says: "Two words for you: calamari salad. The most beautiful, fresh, slightly smoky, tender calamari I've ever tasted with perfect vegetables and dressing. Go eat it. I'm serious." Special crab curry is good, too. **Thai Delight**'s organic menu costs more, but in Berkeley it's a big draw. Regardless of cultivation methods, hounds like its food. Miang kum appetizer, pumpkin chicken red curry (not on menu), and tofu broccoli are recommended. **Siam Cuisine**'s best dish—and certainly the most popular among hounds—may be fried sweet potatoes. Real good Penang beef, too, we've heard.

Jitlada, in Japantown, offers not-so-traditional Thai with fanciful dish names and bright and unique flavors, accompanied by gracious service, says *Cynthia*. Dishes tried and liked at one recent meal included: deep-fried papaya wedges in a rice flour-coconut batter (served with a sweet and sour sauce); curry puffs (fried pastry triangles of potato, chicken, shrimp, onion, and peanuts) with cucumber salad; paradise pasta (with tofu, vegetables, and spinach noodles mixed with the house dressing); vegetable parade (a platter of crisp seasonal veggies in a garlic bean sauce); and black sticky rice with mango. Price for all above, with Thai iced tea for three, was $46 with tax and tip.

Hounds are divided on **Thai House Express**. Some rave that it's as good as in Thailand, whereas others find it just marginally better than its competitors. Of the one hundred menu items, *ericf* recommends: #7 nuer kem (beef jerky appetizer of unbattered, marinated, deep fried strips of flank steak), #18 bamboo shoot salad (with musty funky flavor, can be an acquired taste), #40 kao ka moo (soy stewed pork Chinese style with garlic sauce and pickled mustard green), #80 gai ga prow (minced chicken with chili and basil), #67 pad kee mow (choice of meat with chili and basil on broad noodles), #51 panang curry beef (in medium spicy red chili), #18 larb (warm ground meat salad in spicy lemon dressing), and #84 moo prig king (pork and green beans in savory chili sauce). One authentic choice, apparently not on the English menu, is fish ball curry served with rice noodles. If you enjoy strong flavors, try fried rice with dried fish and greens. Green papaya salad is crisp and very spicy with lots of dried shrimp. He also recommends braised leg of pork with greens and pickles (which may be the same as #40 kao ka moo—soy stewed pork Chinese style with garlic sauce and pickled mustard green). The restaurant has a reasonably pleasant express atmosphere, and is open late.

Tops Under **THREE DOLLARS**

Cancun (East Bay)
2134 Allston Way
Berkeley, CA
510-549-0964
Mexican

Chipotle
www.chipotle.com
Mexican

El Novillo (East Bay)
Guadalajara Restaurant parking lot
Oakland, CA
Mexican street cart/Truck

Golden Boy Pizza-Sodini's
    (North Beach)
542 Green St.
San Francisco, CA
415-982-9738
Pizza/Italian

Golden Gate Bakery
    (Chinatown)
1029 Grant Ave.
San Francisco, CA
415-781-2627
Chinese (Cantonese)/Chinese
    (Hong Kong) bakery

La Borinquena Mex-icatessen
    (East Bay)
582 7th St.
Oakland, CA
510-444-9954
Mexican

La Torta Loca (East Bay)
3419 International Blvd.
Oakland, CA
510-532-7105
Mexican

Mariscos La Costa Taco Truck
    (East Bay)
East side of International,
    between 29th and 30th
Oakland, CA
Mexican street cart/Truck

Masse's Pastries (East Bay)
1469 Shattuck Ave.
Berkeley, CA
510-649-1004
French/American café

Panchita's #3 (Mission)
3115 22nd St.
San Francisco, CA
415-821-6660
Salvadoran/New American

Picante San Rafael (Marin County)
340 Bellam Blvd.
San Rafael, CA
415-485-6050
Mexican

Saigon Sandwich (Tenderloin)
560 Larkin St.
San Francisco, CA
415-474-5698
Vietnamese

Utopia Cafe (Chinatown)
139 Waverly Pl.
San Francisco, CA
415-956-2902
Chinese (Hong Kong)/Chinese
    (Cantonese)

Wing Sing Dim Sum (Chinatown)
1125 Stockton St.
San Francisco, CA
415-433-5571
Chinese (dim sum) bakery

XOX Truffles (North Beach)
754 Columbus Ave.
San Francisco, CA
415-421-4814
French chocolate/Candy shop

Saving your pennies? Hounds suggest some favorite ultra-frugal treats under $3: *ryan*'s faves are **Panchita's #3**'s pork pupusas, truffle and free coffee at **XOX**, **Saigon's** roast pork banh mi, **Wing Sing**'s shark fin dumpling, **Cancun**'s ceviche tostado, or **Chipotle**'s Niman Ranch pulled pork taco. *Ruth Lafler* covers the East Bay Mexican scene, recommending *huarache de tinga* at **La Torta Loca**, *tostada de camerones* at **Mariscos La Costa**, a couple of carnitas tacos from **El Novillo** taco truck; or tamale and beverage from **La Borinquena**.

Other hounds favor:

- three of any baked goods (egg custard tarts, BBQ pork buns, coconut tarts) at **Golden Gate Bakery**
- flour quesadilla or large soft taco (plus all the salsa you want) at **Picante** in San Rafael
- small berry or lemon tart (or 6 cookies!) from **Masse's**
- focaccia-like thick crust pizza from Golden Boy
- $2 tea-snacks (2:30–5:00 p.m., M–F) at **Utopia**, *jojo* recommends deep-fried soft tofu and fried smelt (nice with a beer, if you're a real spendthrift), and *Yimster* likes small bowls of noodles for $2 (huge ones for $4).

○ El Novillo: *see also* pp. 188, 294.
○ Golden Gate Bakery: *see also* pp. 4, 100.
○ La Torta Loca: *see also* p. 188.
○ Masse's Pastries: *see also* p. 81.
○ Panchita's #3: *see also* p. 177.
○ Utopia Cafe: *see also* p. 168.
○ Wing Sing Dim Sum: *see also* p. 86.

TIM TAMS: Cult Australian Cookies

Australia Fair (Union Square)
700 Sutter St.
San Francisco, CA
415-441-5319
Australian store

British Grocery (Potrero Hill)
726 15th St.
San Francisco, CA
415-863-3300
British store

British Food Center (Peninsula)
1652 El Camino Real
San Carlos, CA
650-595-0630
British store

Roxie's (Sunset)
500 Kirkham St.
San Francisco, CA
415-731-0982
Store

Tim Tams are Australian biscuits (cookies)—*johnnie* fills us in: "They're similar to an English choccy bikkie called a penguin (as in p-p-p-p-p-pick up a penguin, only over-thirties English will get that) . . . here's the trick to Tim Tams: bite off two kitty corners, place one cut corner in your coffee and suck at the other cut corner until you feel the coffee coming thru then quickly stuff it in your mouth . . . it literally explodes in there . . . great party trick." Find them at **Australia Fair** (along with sheepskin slippers, Blunnies, and stuffed koalas). They're available by the case from Arnotts (shops.arnotts.com.au/Store Front.bok); and *Donna* notes that "okay, a case may seem like too many for those of you who've never had Tim Tams, but, really, they are marvelous." Bay Area markets carrying British products (crisps, biscuits, candies, and more) include the **British Grocery** in Potrero Hill, **British Foods** on the Peninsula, and **Roxie's** (formerly Shanahan's).

Lunch Stop Near **TOMALES BAY**

Marshall Store (Marin County)
19225 Hwy. 1
Marshall, CA
415-663-1339
Store

The Marshall Store, near Tomales Bay, is a small grocery store that makes a fine lunch stop. It carries Straus dairy products, Point Reyes blue cheese, Brickmaiden breads, and prepares sandwiches to order. Clam chowder is heavy on clams and dill, light on potatoes, and full of well-balanced flavors. Local oysters are available either fresh or barbecued, seven days a week. Enjoy lunch on their decks overlooking the bay. Cash only.

TOP DRAWER Musings

Fifth Floor (SOMA)
12 4th St.
San Francisco, CA
415-348-1555
French

Gary Danko (Embarcadero)
800 N. Point St.
San Francisco, CA
415-749-2060
New American/French

At Fifth Floor, the chef's choice menu is the way to get the full experience. The cooking of chef Laurent Gras sings, reports *cabrales*: "I see sensuality—as in the undulating folds of the geoduck. I see a willingness to take risks in a measured way—as in the saucing for the scallop or the dipping sauce for the foie gras. I see an openness to certain features of Asian cuisine, with an integration that renders traits of such cuisine subsumed within a larger framework." Fifth Floor's wine list and sommelier team are stronger than those at French Laundry and the maitre d' and his team are on par with those at FL. The restaurant is also luscious looking, in a contemporary and distinctive way. Note: a full dining menu is available in the bar area.

At **Gary Danko,** *cabrales* says to expect professional, earnest, and informed service. If ordering off the menu, look for these outstanding dishes: glazed oysters with leeks, salsify and osetra caviar; warm quail salad with potato cannoli and cherries. GD is generally considered to have the best cheese cart in San Francisco (they have their own aging cave).

Best **TORTAS** Outside Mexico City

La Casita Chilanga #1 (Peninsula)
2928 Middlefield Rd.
Redwood City, CA
650-568-0351
Mexican

La Casita Chilanga #2 (Peninsula)
761 El Camino Real
Redwood City, CA
650-364-2808
Mexican

Tortas are Mexican sandwiches on hard rolls, ideally layered with great precision, and **La Casita Chilanga** has the best tortas outside of D.F. (Distrito Federal, as Mexico City is known in Mexico), according to *Victoria Libin*, who notes that when a torta milanesa is done right, there is nothing better. The secret's in the custom-baked bread (teleras): it's got the proper texture and taste. Condiments include flavorful refritos, avocado slices, lots of jalapeños, marinated carrots, tomatoes, onion slices, mix of crema and mayo, with the same proportion and taste as those Victoria remembers from a great tacqueria in Tlalpan. Milanese (breaded, thinly pounded beef), torta Eva (costilla de res, chuck steak), la tesorito (tender pork), and la Cubana (layers of flavors, including hot dogs) are highly recommended. Huitlacoche quesadillas are stuffed with corn smut and griddled (not fried).

Chowhound Nametag: Cyrus J. Farivar

○○○

Location: Berkeley

Occupation: Senior at UC Berkeley in political economy, and aspiring journalist

Nabe Most Full of Explorable Unknown Chow: Tandoor-loin

Underrated by Chowhounds: Darya in Los Angeles

Weight Management Tip: Light breakfast, skip lunch, focus on dinner; or, fast for Ramadan (It's easier than you think!)

Favorite Comfort Chow: Godmother sandwich at Bay Cities in Santa Monica; hot link from Top Dog in Berkeley

Guilty Pleasure: Double-double at In-N-Out

Favorite Gelato Flavor: Straciatella

Chowhounding Rules of Thumb:
1. Look for the crowd.
2. Look for people of the ethnicity that you're at.
3. Get the daily specials, particularly when they change frequently.
4. Consult chowhound.com.
5. Order your fries well-done, no matter where you go.

Favorite Late-night Food Combo: Top Dog followed by Kingpin Donuts in Berkeley

Favorite Mexican Food Deal: Horchata, taco, burrito for $5.50 at Mariscos La Costa in Fruitvale

Favorite Chow Book: *The Tummy Trilogy* by Calvin Trillin

Favorite Grocery Store: Trader Joe's

Starter **TRIPE**

Alegrias Food from Spain (Marina)
2018 Lombard St.
San Francisco, CA
415-929-8888
Spanish

Balompie Cafe (Mission)
3349 18th St.
San Francisco, CA
415-648-9199
Salvadoran

China Village (East Bay)
1335 Solano Ave.
Albany, CA
510-525-2285
Chinese (Sichuan)

Delfina Restaurant (Mission)
3621 18th St.
San Francisco, CA
415-552-4055
Italian

Duarte's Tavern (Peninsula)
202 Stage Rd.
Pescadero, CA
650-879-0464
American/Portuguese/Seafood

El Novillo (East Bay)
Parking lot of Guadalajara
    Restaurant
Oakland, CA
Mexican street cart/Truck

Gold Medal Restaurant (East Bay)
381 8th St.
Oakland, CA
510-268-8484
Chinese (Cantonese)/Chinese
    (Hong Kong)

Gold Mountain Restaurant
    (Chinatown)
644 Broadway
San Francisco, CA
415-296-7733
Chinese (Cantonese)/Chinese
    (Dim Sum)/Chinese (Hong
    Kong)

Incanto Italian Restaurant & Wine
    Bar (Noe Valley)
1550 Church St.
San Francisco, CA
415-641-4500
Italian

Mary's Pizza Shack
    (Sonoma County)
359 E. Washington St.
Petaluma, CA
707-778-7200
Pizza

Santi (Sonoma County)
21047 Geyserville Ave.
Geyserville, CA
707-857-1790
Italian

Taco window (Mission)
21st and Treat
San Francisco, CA
Mexican

Terra Restaurant (Napa County)
1345 Railroad Ave.
St. Helena, CA
707-963-8931
Japanese/New American/
    Pan-Asian fusion

Some tips for novice-friendly tripe—recommended for those looking to be turned on to tripe, not scared off of it forever. We span the globe for starter tripe, starting south of the border: *Windy* says that the best spot for tripe tacos in the city is the **taco window** on 21st and Treat, just east of Folsom and next door to a restaurant owned by the same people. The tacos are $1 each, come with delicious beans and your choice of great salsas and radishes. It has some very good blood sausage too. We believe that restaurant next door to the window may be El Cahanilla, 2948 21st St. **Balompie** serves mondongo, the ubiquitous Hispanic tripe and tendon soup with veggies. One bowl's enough to feed three. Tasty tripe tacos at **El Novillo** taco truck (one good thing about starting tripe neophytes with a taco is they're small and only cost a dollar or a little more, so if they don't like it you haven't lost much, notes *Ruth Lafler*).

Then, Chinese. **Gold Medal** gets kudos for all sorts of innard dishes (*Michael Rodriguez* is particularly fond of this place, but doctors takeout tripe from there by stir-frying some chopped garlic and black beans, then adding green peppers and onions, and, finally, the tripe. He eats this with steamed rice and finds it delicious). **China Village** actually lists its fried intestines as "tripe"—and it's nicely fried. **Gold Mountain** offers curry tripe on its dim sum carts (the curry mostly obscures the tripe's flavor, so it's a good way to start, but just don't eat the pieces of whatever-else-it-is in there—don't worry, they're easy to distinguish—which seem to involve congealed blood on the inside, warns *Bryan Loofbourrow*).

European versions include honeycomb tripe in spicy tomato sauce, a frequent special at **Mary's** in Petaluma, trippa alla fiorentina at **Santi** (the chef loves this dish so much, he promises it'll always be on the menu), and these three upscale spots with a way with tripe: **Terra** in St. Helena (for tripe and spaghetti), **Delfina**, and **Incanto**. **Duarte's Tavern** sometimes offers Portuguese-style tripe braised in a tomatoey sauce as a special. And **Alegrias** serves authentic Spanish tripas a la Madrilena (stewed tripe in tomato sauce).

- Alegrias Food from Spain: *see also* p. 210.
- China Village: *see also* pp. 59, 77, 219, 267.
- Delfina Restaurant: *see also* pp. 123, 219.
- Duarte's Tavern: *see also* pp. 117, 232.
- El Novillo: *see also* pp. 188, 288.
- Gold Medal Restaurant: *see also* pp. 42, 73, 162, 167.
- Gold Mountain Restaurant: *see also* p. 85.
- Incanto Italian Restaurant & Wine Bar: *see also* p. 141.
- Mary's Pizza Shack: *see also* pp. 212, 260, 263.

Fancy **TUNA** at Outlet Prices

Dave's Albacore Tuna (Santa Cruz County)
310 Coral St., A, across from Costco
Santa Cruz, CA
831-457-2250
Store

While Santa Cruz isn't quite the Bay Area, it's close, and hounds should know there's an outlet store for **Dave's** canned seafood products. Dave's great canned tuna and much more can also can be ordered from his Web site at www.davesalbacore.com.

TURKISH Delights

Bosphorous Anatolian Cuisine
  (East Bay)
1025 University Ave.
Berkeley, CA
510-549-9997
Turkish

Bursa Kebab Mediterranean
  (Westportal/Ingleside)
60 West Portal Ave.
San Francisco, CA
415-564-4006
Turkish

Cafe de Pera (Richmond)
349 Clement St.
San Francisco, CA
415-666-3839
Turkish

Taverna Gyros (South Bay)
133 S. Murphy
Sunnyvale, CA
408-735-9971
Turkish

Gyro King (Civic Center)
25 Grove St.
San Francisco, CA
415-621-8313
Turkish

Good reports have rolled in for **Bursa Kebab**. Mezze (baba ghanouj, hummus, falafel, stuffed grape leaves, yogurt-feta dip) are fresh and tasty, served with fresh-baked flatbread. Kebab plates come with salad, yogurt, and wonderful rice; especially recommended are shrimp, chicken, and ground meat kebabs, and meatball kofta (grilled patties of spiced ground lamb and beef). Turkish coffee made to order with or without sugar. Main courses around $12 to $15.

Taverna Gyros serves housemade doner kebab (called gyros here), in beef-lamb combo or chicken versions, plus a variety of meat and vegetarian plates. It also makes its own basturma—an air-cured beef sometimes called "the original pastrami," which is very rare in these parts.

Cafe de Pera's adana kebab (minced beef with bits of red pepper, parsley, and coarse black pepper) is tasty, but milder than most. Spinach pie (with onions, mushrooms, and cheddar comes with sprightly Greek salad with a zingy herb dressing, and ezme (mashed tomato blend with onion, green and red bell pepper paste, olive oil, toasted walnuts) is an especially good rendition. A selection of Jarritos Mexican fruit sodas is available, apparently popular with the clientele. Go figure!).

Adana kebab at **Gyro King**, aka Taverna Gyros, is a lamb-beef combo, juicy and assertively spiced. If you order it in a sandwich, be sure to have it on house-baked pide bread. Fresh-baked breads and pastries (stuffed pide, lahmacun, boreks, filo pastries) are a specialty.

Bosphorous Anatolian Cuisine, a magnet for Turkish immigrants, is recommended by *Alexandra* for eggplant with ground beef (whole eggplant split open, filled with ground beef and sautéed onions), dana sis (chargrilled cubes of meat, ground beef kebab—very,

very good), and ayran (yogurt drink similar to lassi or doogh—thick and sour). Prices are very reasonable.

Also see *"Kebabs*, Kabobs, Kebaps" for a couple more tips.

TURMERIK

Turmerik (South Bay)
141 S. Murphy Ave.
Sunnyvale, CA
408-617-9100
North Indian

Melanie Wong shares details of a "Chef's Special Spice Flight Dinner" at **Turmerik**. Unfortunately this particular dinner was a one-time thing, but most (if not all) dishes appear on the regular menu. (Which is, itself, ever-changing, so no promises!)

An appetizer of papdi chaat, tomato and chickpea wafers with vegetables and yogurt sauce creates a "brilliant medley of textures—crisp, soft, and chewy, combined with hot and cold temperatures, and flavors that hit high notes, bass tones, acidic, savory, sweet, bitter, salty, and probably some hidden reaches that don't even have names. It certainly woke up my palate and made me pay attention." Soups were vegetarian tomato shorba soup ("light-bodied and almost weightless, the complex and intense flavors made a prickly dance on the palate, then resolved in a sparkling clean wisp of a finish") and coconut-chile shrimp soup ("spicy hot with a mid-palate warmth and herbal tone from fresh chiles. Mouth coating and voluptuous on the palate").

Entrees tried were chicken makhani (chunks of tandoori chicken swathed in rich tomato sauce scented with fenugreek) and paneer makhani (homemade white cheese in similar sauce as chicken). Served alongside: plain and perfunctory lentils, spinach with mushroom, nutmeg, and mace, and perfect saffron rice. Small rosemary naan are tender, pillowy, and well blistered, just perfumed with rosemary.

On weeknights, dinner's served in the bar's lounge area, which is either "cozy" or "dark and closed in," depending on your perspective. Some wine advice: "The well-chosen wine list of unusual offerings seems to have languished. Many vintages were a year or two behind current releases. This means there are some good deals to be had in the interesting wines that have had an extra year or so to develop more fully and are priced below market." One caveat: crab dishes are not the kitchen's forte; crab cakes were too starchy and lacking in crab, and crab in crab masala is overpowered with masala spicing.

UPSCALE Outside San Francisco

Brigitte's (South Bay)
351 Saratoga Ave.
Santa Clara, CA
408-404-7043
French bistro

Chez TJ (Peninsula)
938 Villa St.
Mountain View, CA
650-964-7466
New American/French

Cinq Restaurant (Marin County)
60 Corte Madera Ave.
Corte Madera, CA
415-945-9191
French

El Paseo Restaurant
 (Marin County)
17 Throckmorton Ave.
Mill Valley, CA
415-388-0741
French

La Maison Bistro-Restaurant
 (East Bay)
3774 Castro Valley Blvd.
Castro Valley, CA
510-733-2780
French bistro

Marche Aux Fleurs (Marin County)
23 Ross Common
Ross, CA
415-925-9200
New American/French/Italian

Here are some excellent places where you can feel pampered without coming into town.

In Castro Valley, **La Maison** offers solid bistro fare with high-quality ingredients and careful execution for diner-like prices. A la carte appetizers (e.g., smoked salmon, sauteed mushrooms) supplement a four-course prix fixe menu that starts at $12.50 and maxes out at $20.00. Dinner begins with a small green salad, followed by a generous serving of the day's soup and choice of entree and dessert. Sauces are rich with cream and butter, but still hew to modern tastes and are gratifyingly complex. Recommended: rabbit with mustard sauce (and great side of potato gratin), pork tenderloin, veal medallions. Overall, La Maison serves elegant food that may not be groundbreaking, but is tasty and satisfying. It's located in a charming house with white picket fence and climbing vines, set back from a busy commercial street.

In Santa Clara, **Brigitte's** interior is typical French bistro, with tables a bit too close together. Outside, enjoy patio tables out front facing a park/golf course. Servers are knowledgeable and Brigitte herself visits with customers and even buses tables. Chowhounds hate to invoke the tired cliche by saying a kitchen does simply prepared dishes with the freshest ingredients, but this one really does; all elements, including sauces, are simple, yet taste like you're getting a really fancy meal, says *Alice R*. Nice touch: items come in regular or petite size. Their Cal-Mediterranean menu changes seasonally, but here are some examples: arugula salad with shaved summer truffle, creamy cauliflower soup, vegetarian plate of day, salmon (a new height of bliss for one serious salmon lover), and coffee pot de creme (luciously silky and creamy with right amount of bittersweetness). Sometimes there are wine programs on Saturday nights.

Chez TJ, located in a restored Victorian house in Mountain View, fits the bill when you don't want to drive into San Francisco for a special dinner, says *eel*: "All in all, it's a good dining experience. It lacks the *wow* of Masa's or Elizabeth Daniel, or Farallon, but it is good. Service is professional, but without the elegance of a high-end San Francisco restaurant." Diners have three menu options: (1) Menu gastronimique ($65) offers choice of appetizer, fish and meat courses, salad or cheese course, and choice of dessert. Add a three-wine flight (paired with appetizer, fish, and meat courses) for $24 more. (2) Menu modern ($55) offers fixed soup, meat, fish, and salad courses with choice of dessert. (3) Menu petit ($48) is fixed soup, fish and salad courses, choice of dessert. Highlights from the menu gastronimique: artichoke soup with crab, arctic char on celery root puree with broccoli rabe, lamb loin with spinach and bean ragout, pear brioche bread pudding.

Dana would return to cozy **Cinq** in Marin just for foie gras, but her meal was first-rate from start to finish. That foie gras (seared, with carmelized onions on crispy brioche round, with port sauce) was absolutely amazing, from the texture to the combination of flavors. Sweetwater oysters (with mignonette and tomato sorbet) are perfectly fresh; lamb with French lentils in broth is cooked to perfection; cheese plate has plentiful portions of five selections; and vanilla custard tarte with house-made Valhrona chocolate gelato is a great match for excellent French-press coffee. Service is professional and friendly. Menu and wine list are both short, but have many inviting choices.

El Paseo's the "number 1 recommendation for Frenchiness in Marin. It's not Parisian—the ambience is country inn and terribly charming and relaxing," says *Sharuf*. Check out the wine bar. Your meal will be leisurely; they encourage you to linger. The room facing Throckmorton is more intimate, says *Peter*.

Marche Aux Fleurs—more eclectic than its name indicates—has impeccable charm and service. Food is quite good and wine list offers a small but excellent selection of boutique wines, says *Bill Luby*. Recommended (if on the ever-changing menu): shellfish "escargot," gnocchi, Niman pork chop, chocolate truffle cake. Reasonable prices.

Also consider Old Post Office restaurant, reviewed in the next entry ("Upscale and Downscale in *Vacaville*").

Upscale and Downscale in
VACAVILLE

Downtown Cafe (Solano County)
374 Merchant St.
Vacaville, CA
707-448-0490
Café

Old Post Office Seafood & Grill
  (Solano County)
301 Main St.
Vacaville, CA
707-447-1858
New American

Stanley Stephan reports that little has changed at **Downtown Cafe** since it opened in the fifties and that's a good thing. It still serves serious old-fashioned breakfasts, especially wonderful, flaky, warm biscuits. Coffee always refilled. Waitresses call you hon.

And for dinner—the **Old Post Office**, which holds its own

against any of San Francisco's better upscale restaurants. Seafood's the specialty, served in a relaxed, soothing atmosphere. Nice wine list. Outdoor patio. Small bar. Service isn't up to San Francisco standards (it's pleasant but unpolished). If you're driving, take Merchant Street exit off I-80.

VEGAN Chinese

Bok Choy Garden (Richmond)
1820 Clement St.
San Francisco, CA
415-387-8111
Chinese (Buddhist/Vegetarian)

Lu Lai Garden (South Bay)
210 Barber Ct., in Milptias Sq.
Milpitas, CA
408-526-9888
Chinese (Buddhist/Vegetarian)

Garden Fresh (Peninsula)
1245 W. El Camino Real
Mountain View, CA
650-961-7795
Chinese (Buddhist/Vegetarian)

Totally vegan, the following restaurants specialize in soy and wheat dishes—"fake meat"—plus many other vegetarian preparations.

Bok Choy Garden has the "best Chinese veggie food I've ever had," reports *YinShiNanNu*. There are specials posted on the walls, and friendly and gracious owners happily answer questions. Especially good: vegetarian duck, crispy taro rolls (wrapped in tofu skin and deep fried—crispy outside, meltingly soft inside), deep fried crispy eggplant (silky inside, good with or without tangy red sauce), and seaweed and pine nut fried rice ("screams seaweed," notes *felice*). Also recommended: "meatballs" in black pepper sauce (good texture, taste most like turkey), stuffed shiitake mushrooms (fresh mushrooms stuffed with tofu in brown sauce over broccoli), sauteed green soybeans with tofu and seaweed (great, fresh soybeans, okay tofu and seaweed), and brown rice.

Lu Lai's faux-meat cooking is oftentimes better than some of the meat dishes served at regular restaurants, says *tanspace*, who recommends sizzling vegetarian shredded beef in black bean sauce, braised vegetarian meatballs with cabbage (lion's head meatballs), and vegetarian shredded ham and spiced tofu. There is a chef's specials menu with great dishes, and the regular menu is vast, with appetizers, noodles, fried rice, and congee in addition to entrees.

At **Garden Fresh**, soy products are made in-house, and wheat gluten meat substitues are of superior quality. Recommendations include vegetable bundles with "ham," orange "beef," and sweet-and-sour "pork," says *Reece*.

Luxe and Luscious **VEGETARIAN** in Palo Alto

Stoa (Peninsula)
632 Emerson St.
Palo Alto, CA
650-328-2600
Vegetarian

Pricey vegetarian Stoa comes through with food which chowhounds deem mostly exceptional. The chef has a sure hand with sauces and an eye for beautiful presentation (e.g. wheat bread comes to the table with addictive pea and walnut pâté). Avoid Asian-inflected dishes, and stick with Mediterranean, the forte here, suggests *Windy*. Top choices include caramelized baby eggplant with roasted peppers and garlic balsamic pan juices; polenta lasagna with layers of cheese, tomatoes, and pesto (incredible mingling of flavors and textures); vegetable tempura with coconut dipping sauce; truffled spinach ravioli with out of this world creamy tomato sauce; and spinach souffle with mixed mushroom stew.

Salads are $8 to $9.50; appetizers $9 to $12; entrees $17 to $21, and portions vary dramatically from skimpy to copious. Beer and wine lists are extensive and reasoble, but nonalcoholic choices (fruit juice spritzers, tea from tea bags, Illy espresso) are overpriced. Service is attentive and friendly, and warm interior and a gorgeous bar area make this a good choice for celebrations.

We Want Meat, They Want
VEGGIES

Alma (Mission)
1101 Valencia St.
San Francisco, CA
415-401-8959
Latin American/New
    American/French

Minako Organic Japanese
    Restaurant (Mission)
2154 Mission St.
San Francisco, CA
415-864-1888
Japanese

Helmand Restaurant
    (North Beach)
430 Broadway
San Francisco, CA
415-362-0641
Afghan

Nonvegetarian restaurants which offer truly great vegetable options:

The vegetables platters at **Alma** blow away the other entrees, says *Maya*.

Minako does home-style Japanese with all organic ingredients, and half its menu is vegetarian. Food's made with care and cooked to order (so it helps to arrive early), and there's a deluxe vegetarian meal for around $30. Specials and gyoza are particularly recommended.

Helmand puts together an impressive plate of vegetarian Afghan dishes, including delicious pumpkin with herb-yogurt sauce.

Chowhound Nametag: Celery

∘◯∘

Location:
Berkeley

Cholesterol Level:
163

Nabe Most Full of Explorable Unknown Chow:
Fruitvale—if only I spoke Spanish!

Weight Management Tip:
Lots of walking and never keep ice cream in the house

Guilty Pleasure:
Potato chips and cottage cheese for dinner

Favorite Gelato Flavor:
Pistachio

Favorite Mail Order Chow:
Duke's Mayo from Lee Bros, leebros.com.

San Jose and Environs:
A Hotbed of **VIETNAMESE**

Anh Hong Restaurant (South Bay)
1818 Tully Rd. #150
San Jose, CA
408-270-1096
Vietnamese

Anh Hong Saigon (South Bay)
233 W. Calaveras Blvd.
Milpitas, CA
408-946-9046
Vietnamese

Asian Garden Restaurant
   (South Bay)
304 E. Santa Clara St.
San Jose, CA
408-279-8764
Vietnamese

Bun Bo Hue #1 (South Bay)
Senter Rd.
San Jose, CA
Vietnamese

Da Lat Restaurant (South Bay)
408 E. William St.
San Jose, CA
408-294-6989
Vietnamese

Minh's Vietnamese Restaurant
   (South Bay)
1422 Dempsey Rd.
Milpitas, CA
408-956-1000
Vietnamese

Pho Ga An Nam (South Bay)
740 Story Rd.
San Jose, CA
408-993-1211
Vietnamese

Pho Ga Hung (South Bay)
1818 Tully Rd. #120
San Jose, CA
408-238-2543
Vietnamese

Pho 909 (South Bay)
72 S. Park Victoria Dr.
Milpitas, CA
408-946-1937
Vietnamese

Pho Thien Long Restaurant
   (South Bay)
1111 Story Rd., in Grand Century
   Shopping Mall
San Jose, CA
408-282-1666
Vietnamese

Pho Xe Lua Noodle House
   (South Bay)
1460 Halford Ave.
Santa Clara, CA
408-244-9721
Vietnamese

Pho Y1 Noodle House
(South Bay)
1660 E. Capitol Expy.
San Jose, CA
408-274-1769
Vietnamese

Quang Da (South Bay)
348 E. Santa Clara
San Jose, CA
408-297-3402
Vietnamese

Saigon City Restaurant
(South Bay)
4725 Lafayette St.
Santa Clara, CA
408-986-8383
Vietnamese

Thanh Da Restaurant (South Bay)
1111 Story Rd., in Grand Century
Shopping Mall
San Jose, CA
408-993-9229
Vietnamese

Thanh Duoc Restaurant
(South Bay)
1228 S. Abel St.
Milpitas, CA
408-945-8580
Vietnamese

Thanh Hien Restaurant
(South Bay)
2345 Mckee Rd.
San Jose, CA
408-926-1056
Vietnamese

San Jose is home to one of the country's largest Vietnamese populations, and boasts a corresponding wealth of great Vietnamese chow, quite a bit of which spills into nearby areas in the South Bay, making the region a rich hunting ground for Vietnamese cooking from all regions of Vietnam.

Pho Thien Long in Grand Century Mall makes cha ca, a Northern-Vietnamese specialty of sauteed fish filets with turmeric and dill. Pho Thien Long's version is made with catfish, and is served over a gas burner. The fish rests on top of a pile of herbs and greens, and as it sits, the greens wilt and their bottom layer browns with the heat of the pot. One order is huge. *Alice* says this is as good as cha ca she's eaten in Hanoi. Also worthy: che hat sen nhan tuoi (longan and lotus seed) with shaved ice.

Minh's offers an interesting assortment of dishes not commonly found in Bay Area Vietnamese restaurants, including some Northern specialties like cha ca thanh long—skewered cubes of catfish marinated in slightly sweet tumeric-based marinade. One order is two skewers served on a sizzling platter, with a separate plate of various greens: romaine lettuce, cilantro, basil, dill, and other herbs, plus a good amount of soft rice noodles and a small bowl of sauce heavy in shrimp flavor, vinegar, fish sauce, and sugar. To eat, mix it all together. Portion's large enough for two. *Banh xeo,* a Vietnamese crepe filled with bean sprouts, shell-on shrimp (to be eaten shell and all), and small pieces of meat, also comes with plenty of greens and herbs. Claypot and nonsoup dishes are also consistently good, while pho's below par. Minh's is busy at lunch, when service is minimal.

Thi N says that "after searching throughout LA and the Bay Area, the best pho I've yet found is **Pho Y1**, in San Jose." *Melanie Wong* agrees: "highly recommended—the light and intense broth really is all that. Pure and cleansing, not sucked up by sugar, MSG, or too much herbal influence."

Pho Ga An Nam's specialties are pho ga (chicken pho) and free-range chicken dishes. The house specialty, pho ga dac biet (#7), comes with your choice of chicken cuts (including gizzard and unborn young eggs!). Broth is rich, fragrant, and sweet with chicken flavor; don't add too many condiments, or you'll obscure those nuances. *Mien ga thit* (#30) is cellophane noodles with shredded chicken breast and chicken livers, and tastes strongly of black pepper, per tradition. Com ga (#11), boiled chicken and rice cooked in chicken broth, is served with a dipping sauce of nuoc cham and minced ginger, and sweetish pickled cabbage that looks like kimchi. Sauce is flavorful, chicken is tender and tasty, and rice is perfectly cooked.

South Bay Vietnamese aficionado *pierre 1* calls it overall the most consistently executed pho ga place in the SB, and suggests asking for your favorite chicken parts (dark meat, on-bone, shredded). Cash only.

Bun Bo Hue #1 is a small café specializing in central-Vietnamese foods, and is one of the few places around serving banh (appetizers or small cakes, akin to dim sum) made from scratch and steamed to order. The list of banh is in Vietnamese only, but the following descriptions will help non-Vietnamese speakers: banh beo (steamed rice flour disk topped with ground shrimp and green onion, with crispy pork bits on the side and nuoc cham to pour over the top), banh ram it (sticky rice flour ball filled with small cubes of pork meat, on top of fried shrimp fritter; eat a bit of each in each bite), and mi quang (yellow rice noodles topped with shrimp, pork, onion, thin shredded green and red cabbage, bean sprouts, chopped mint, peanuts, and fried shallots, moistened with a bit of broth and served with puffed black sesame crackers). Nuoc cham (fish sauce, water, sugar, hot pepper, and lemon-lime vinegar) here is too weak, but the rice and tapioca flour preparations have just the right consistency.

Salted crab is the dish to get at **Thanh Hien**. It has the cooking process down to soften the shells and let you get at the meat fairly painlessly, and the flavor of the crabmeat together with the condiments is rich and deep (saltiness is not overpowering but adds a gentle kick to the somewhat delicate native flavor of the crab), says *Ken Hoffman*. Grilled beef and onion bun is delicious, with vermicelli noodles carefully folded into the bottom of the bowl and adorned with colorful carrots and greens. The meat is grilled to a perfect tenderness—no knife necessary!

Quang Da is a homey, inexpensive place serving authentic Vietnamese. Its menu lists forty dishes, half each from Hue and central Vietnam, plus eight vegetarian options and some sides. Pleasant staff speaks minimal English, but provides a very helpful annotated photo album of all dishes. *Nathan P* found the cooking boldly seasoned with no holding back on fish sauce and dried shrimp. Highlights include: steamed rice cakes with minced dried shrimp and pork "Quang Da" style; BBQ pork and shredded pork (with steamed broken scented rice, lettuce, cucumber, papaya, and carrot) and country noodle soup (with prawn, crab claw, BBQ pork, bean sprouts, lemon, and celery leaves). *Nathan* found its quang da good, though not stellar, but says its interesting menu deserves further exploration. Prices are low. Closed Wednesdays.

Chao Vit #2 is a "purple duck" dish at **Thanh Da** in the Vietnamese food court at Grand Century Shopping Mall recommended by *Melanie Wong*. Chao Goi Vit #1 adds cabbage. This is a rice porridge that's more brothy than Chinese jook—a dark stock full of intense and concentrated porcine and duck flavors, nutty, toasty rice, chopped scallions, and silky-textured cooked blood. Add to that a quarter duck hacked on bone, shredded cabbage, basil, rau ram, cilantro, and, most important, the brilliant sweet-sour-spicy-salty green dipping sauce. Word is Thanh Da is expanding into a full restaurant with full English menu. Also in that food court is a stand serving killer banh xeo (Vietnamese crepe). *Josh Fredericks* claims it's the best banh xeo he's had outside of Saigon; much less greasy and wet than most places here, almost the consistency of Indian dosa. Also good:

ground crab soup (either bun rieu or bahn canh on dac beit—specials list). There's also good ground crab soup (in a clearer broth) at the stand to the far right.

But the very best Vietnamese seafood soup might be the baby clam soup at **Pho Ga Hung** (in Call Me Dragon food court at San Jose's Lion Plaza). It's not on the English menu, but just ask for clam soup—a tomatoey broth with tons of tiny shelled clams. Surprisingly, the same soup with snails *is* on the English menu!

Anh Hong Saigon's San Francisco and SJ locations have been known as the places to go for the famous Vietnamese seven courses of beef (bo 7 mon). The Milpitas location's bo 7 mon offers excellent value for the amount and quality of food, says *Ruth Lafler* who suggests ordering the seven courses of beef served with rice paper wrappers, veggies, herbs and greens, and, of course, lots of beef: (1) goi bo (special beef salad); (2) bo nhung dam (fondue with special vinegar sauce); (3 through 6), served on single platter: bo cha dum (steamed beef pate), bo nuong mo chai (grilled beef sausage), bo nuong la lot (beef wrapped in Hawaiian lot leaf), bo nuong sa (grilled beef in lemongrass), and (7) chao bo (beef rice soup). Grilled beef dishes can all be ordered à la carte from the house special (mon an dac biet) section of the menu if you don't want all seven courses. House special Vietnamese crepe (banh xeo) was a standout dish. Servers offer help with assembly and condiments. Wine service is handled well (correctly poured half-full glasses topped up several times). Corkage $7.50, and there's a wine list.

Saigon City is pretty good if you stick with Vietnamese dishes (they also do Chinese). Mi quang (yellow egg noodles topped with seafood and pork, herbs and fried shallots, with complex, flavorful broth on the side) is the best bet, and hu tieu (or banh canh—seafood soup) is tasty, too, says *Alice R*.

Pho Xe Lua has the best pho, if you can get past the dingy atmosphere and nonexistent service; but even so, it's just very good, not great, pho, says *Alice R* (who, you must bear in mind, is a tough customer after growing up on her mom's amazing Northern-style pho).

Thanh Duoc is an okay restaurant with a few really great dishes. One standout: pineapple salad (shredded pork, pineapple, daikon, carrots, herbs, and lettuce served in a pineapple shell with sliced shrimp on top). It's not cheap, but it's an incredible combination of flavors, says *Josh Fredericks*.

Da Lat is family-run, serving up a great variety of dishes with flair and attention to flavor, according to *Ken Hoffman*, whose standard for bun (rice noodle salad bowl) is **Asian Garden**. **Pho 909** gets the nod for banh xeo (Vietnamese crepes). One pho to avoid: Kim Su, on the corner of El Camino and San Tomas.

VIETNAMESE Chow Tour in San Francisco (and East Bay)

Ba Le (East Bay)
10175 San Pablo Ave.
El Cerrito, CA
Vietnamese sandwich shop

Da Nang Vietnam Restaurant
   (East Bay)
905 San Pablo Ave.
Albany, CA
510-524-6837
Vietnamese

Golden Flower (Sunset)
Clement St. between 25th and
   26th Ave.
San Francisco, CA
Vietnamese

Golden King Vietnamese
   Restaurant (Chinatown)
757 Clay St.
San Francisco, CA
415-217-6888
Vietnamese

Lotus Garden Vietnamese
   (Mission)
3452 Mission St.
San Francisco, CA
415-642-1987
Vietnamese

Mai's Vietnamese (Richmond)
316 Clement St.
San Francisco, CA
415-221-3046
Vietnamese

New Loi's Vietnamese Restaurant
   (Sunset)
890 Taraval St.
San Francisco, CA
415-664-7898
Vietnamese

Nha Trang Restaurant (East Bay)
1611 2nd Ave.
Oakland, CA
510-663-0818
Vietnamese

Pho Hoa Hiep (Richmond)
239 Clement St.
San Francisco, CA
415-379-9008
Vietnamese

PPQ Vietnamese Cuisine
   (Richmond)
2332 Clement St.
San Francisco, CA
415-386-8266
Vietnamese

PPQ Vietnamese Cuisine (Sunset)
1816 Irving St.
San Francisco, CA
415-661-8869
Vietnamese

Tu Lan Restaurant (SOMA)
8 6th St.
San Francisco, CA
415-626-0927
Vietnamese

Turtle Tower (Tenderloin)
631 Larkin St.
San Francisco, CA
415-409-3333
Vietnamese

Vietnamese Stand in the
   International Food Center
   (Financial District)
380 Bush (look for the stairs
   descending into the depths)
San Francisco, CA
Vietnamese

Wrap Delights (Tenderloin)
426 Larkin St.
San Francisco, CA
415-771-3388
Vietnamese sandwich shop

Yummy Yummy (Sunset)
1015 Irving St.
San Francisco, CA
415-566-4722
Vietnamese

New Loi's cha ca vong (grilled turmeric fish served with dill on sizzling platters—a North Vietnamese dish) is made with fresh striped bass (it's usually done with catfish), has less turmeric than others and some more exotic spicing, and dill is served raw on the side as a garnish rather than being cooked with the fish. Unlike other local places, New Loi serves this dish as components (fish, herbs, fish sauce, shrimp paste, shrimp chips) to be wrapped in lettuce leaves and eaten out of hand. Other wrap-and-eat dishes include sugarcane shrimp served with beef, pork, or chicken (grilled beef was tender and flavorful, but didn't blend well with shrimp); ban xeo (Vietnamese crepe with shrimp and pork); and bun cha ha noi (juicy marinated grilled pork with rice noodles and vegetables, not usually served this way). Pho at New Loi is made with complex, well-flavored broths. The broth in BBQ shrimp and chicken pho (served with grilled five-spice chicken leg and skewered shrimp) is a revelation, tasting of the sweet brininess of fresh shrimp, with none of the tinny or overly salted, fishy flavors of other versions, says *Melanie Wong*. Sauteed beef and vegetable pho is slightly thickened and so polished and subtle versus the aggressive anise and herbal character of other pho soups. BBQ shrimp pho with roast pork or grilled pork chop is good, too. For dessert, fried bananas come with a choice of jasmine, black sesame, or litchi ice cream. All three have interesting and distinctive flavors, but are marred by off-textures. New Loi's is open every day but Tuesday, 11 a.m. to 9:30 p.m. Beer is served, but no BYO wine is permitted.

Turtle Tower specializes in North Vietnamese (Hanoi) food. One typical Hanoi dish, cha ca va bun (grilled fish with vermicelli) consists of a fillet cut into small pieces coated with turmeric, tossed with sauteed scallion tops and fronds of fresh dill, and served in a small sautee pan, along with a small bowl of white onions in vinegar and a dish of roasted peanuts. Dill, surprisingly, seems to be a common ingredient in northern Vietnamese and Lao dishes, though we don't see it used often in Bay Area Vietnamese restaurants. Pho ga, chicken soup with fresh wide rice noodles (#9 on the menu, $4.95), is the house specialty. It's served in the northern style, with fewer condiments than in other regions—just lime and sliced jalapeños. Its broth is both delicate and rich with chicken flavor, says *Ruth Lafler*. Also enjoyable: pho bo ap chao nuoc, stir-fried beef with stir-fried rice noodle soup (#6, $5.95) that's a haimish affair with wok-charred flavors, black carbon flecks and oil slicks on the surface of the broth. Turtle Tower is open 9 a.m. to 5 p.m. daily except Tuesdays.

Wrap Delights (aka Discount Deli) is a favorite for banh mi (Vietnamese sandwiches), including the not-so-easy-to-find vegetarian banh mi. **PPQ** is best for pho, garlic noodles, crab, egg rolls, BBQ pork plate, chicken curry, vermicelli soup. Fabulous at **Pho Hoa Hiep**: pho, seafood fun (noodles), fresh spring rolls. Memorable at **Mai's**: Hue-style pho, lemongrass chicken, and catfish in claypot (a one way ticket to nirvana, promises *wedge-headjunkie*). Yummy at **Yummy Yummy**: raw beef salad, Hanoi-style bun, tomato-based pho, Vietnamese potstickers, crab in tamarind sauce. Tops at **Tu Lan**: pork and imperial roll bun, tofu salad, goi cuon (spring rolls). Loved at **Lotus Garden**: raw beef salad, Vietnamese potstickers, crab, ban xeo (crepe). Great at **Golden King**: pho bo (beef), pho ga (chicken); superior broths. Be sure to add the steamed lemongrass chicken leg for $1 to your pho ga order. Good bets at **Golden Flower**: pho, and super cheap fried spring rolls. At the branch on Clement in the Sunset, catfish claypot and crepe are outstanding, says *TomG*.

Vietnamese stand in International Food Center (aka "The Food Dungeon" downstairs food court: look for the stairs descending into the depths at 380 Bush). Best bets: imperial rolls, BBQ meats over rice or noodles (when fresh off the grill); other nearby stands not recommended.

Over in the East Bay, at **Ba Le** in El Cerrito, *Brian Stack* recommends tasty banh mi on fresh baguettes, generously stuffed with grilled pork and chicken, shredded carrot, and daikon. Three sandwiches plus an order of shrimp salad rolls (average but fresh) came to just under $9. Delicious Vietnamese beef jerky, too. **Nha Trang** has the best imperial rolls *Missy P*'s ever tasted. The menu includes goat and frogs legs as well as standards, and a special seven courses of fish. (A California play on the famous Vietnamese seven courses of beef?) Another plus: the beautiful open air patio with views of Lake Merritt, very lovely at dusk. **Da Nang** is a lunchtime fave for noodle bowls with cha gio and pork, goi cuon and bo la lot.

○ **PPQ Vietnamese Cuisine:** *see also* p. 77.
○ **Tu Lan Restaurant:** *see also* p. 227.

Celebrity VIETNAMESE

Ana Mandara (Embarcadero)
891 Beach St.
San Francisco, CA
415-771-6800
Vietnamese/French

Ana Mandara, actor Don Johnson's upscale Vietnamese place near Ghirardelli Square, sounds like a good place for a date, with jazz in the lounge and beautifully romantic pagodalike enclosures in the dining room. Presentation of the food is very beautiful, staff is attentive, and it's an altogether wonderful experience, reports *mirch-masala*. Dishes to enjoy: seared Mekong bass; grilled tofu with fried yucca cake; crispy spring rolls with crab and shrimp; organic baby greens with ginger vinaigrette; spicy garlic prawns with housemade rice wine sauce on Asian noodle galette; wokked garlic noodles; spicy chicken in claypot; and chocolate and walnut mousse.

Great Food and Great **VIEW** . . . Really!

Eagle Cafe (Embarcadero)
Pier 39 #201
San Francisco, CA
415-433-3689
American

It's a miracle, says *Stanley Stephan*: a restaurant in San Francisco with a spectacular view, great food, and reasonable prices. The view from the **Eagle Cafe** at Pier 39 is one of the Bay's best, taking in the Golden Gate bridge, the ships of Fisherman's Wharf, Sausalito, Mt. Tam, Angel Island, and Alcatraz. Seagulls circle round drifting along on the breezes. There are picnic benches outside where you can view the sea lions at the end of the pier. And it has updated the lunch menu, adding some healthier choices. Breakfasts under $10, lunch for not much more. Don't miss excellent corned beef hash, a revelation of chopped corned beef with hint of potato, and beautiful golden crust. And home fries are everything home fries should be. Not too crispy, golden cubes of potatoes with grilled onions and green peppers, and just the right amount of grease. At dinnertime, the Eagle dresses up slightly and the view just gets better at sunset. Twelve dollars and ninety-five cents buys your choice of entree with salad or clam chowder. On the appetizer list, spring roll with ginger dipping sauce (with a nice hot ginger bite) is real good. Small wine list, beer, and full bar.

Place your order at counter and pick up, no table service. Full bar. Gilding the lily, you get an hour of free parking in garage with validation during the day (you get two hours' free parking after 6 p.m.). If you eat dinner here, for an awesome view the next morning over breakfast, see Mountain Home Inn, the first item in our "Bay Area Monster *Breakfast* Survey."

Looking for Lunch on
WINCHESTER BOULEVARD

Russian Cafe & Deli (South Bay)
1712 Winchester Blvd.
Campbell, CA
408-379-6680
Russian

There are all sorts of Russian and Eastern European foods at family owned and operated **Russian Cafe & Deli**. Some of the goodies are found on the deli shelves: boxes of cherry juice and black currant juice, small but interesting selection of Eastern European wines, vodkas, and liqueurs, Russian pickles, Georgian red pepper sauce, pomegranate sauce, sour cherry preserves. Desserts made by Russians in LA and flown in. Handmade frozen pelmeni. The selection of smoked fish is mind boggling, says *Jennie Sheeks*, who says the café serves real Russian food. The colder, more windy and darker it gets, the better this food tastes. This is the kind of food your grandmother would cook for you if she lived in St. Petersburg (not Florida), which is where the gracious owner, Rimma Brisker, and her husband lived before moving to San Jose.

Blintzes (think: Russian burrito), piroski (pastry made with flour, cream cheese, butter, stuffed with savory meat filling), solyanka sbornaya soup (sausages, olives, pickles, and barley), buckwheat kasha, beef stroganoff, pelmeni (boiled stuffed pastry), vareniki (semicircular stuffed dumplings), borscht, golubtsy (cabbage rolls stuffed with beef and rice), sazivi (boneless chicken with lots of garlic, walnuts, cilantro—like Russian pesto). Lunch and dinner.

WINE COUNTRY Chowing

Cafe Citti (Sonoma County)
9049 Sonoma Hwy.
Kenwood, CA
707-833-2690
Italian

Celadon (Napa County)
500 Main St, in Napa River Inn
Napa, CA
707-254-9690
New American/Pan-Asian fusion

Foothill Cafe (Napa County)
2766 Old Sonoma Rd.
Napa, CA
707-252-6178
New American

Langley's on the Green
(Sonoma County).
610 McClelland Dr.
Windsor, CA
707-837-7984
New American

Restaurant Mirepoix
(Sonoma County)
275 Windsor River Rd.
Windsor, CA
707-838-0162
French

Zinsvalley Restaurant
(Napa County)
3253 Browns Valley Rd.
Napa, CA
707-224-0695
New American

Three Napa tips from *Melanie Wong*: **Zinsvalley** serves CaliCuisine with very nice outdoor patio dining and reasonable prices (for Napa!), also full bar and no corkage. **Foothill Cafe** is fresh, reliable, unfancy, and value-priced. Food is fresh, competent, and homey. And, unlike some of Napa's better-known spots, it's not hard to get in. Appetizers are particularly good, service is friendly, and corkage is $10. And **Celadon** makes a heckuva American Kobe burger served with rémoulade sauce, arugula, ripe tomato slices, and sweet red onion. Fries are skinny, extra crispy, and tossed with fresh chopped tarragon. Lunch is a bit pricey, but is so pleasant and perfect on the patio that you won't begrudge the cost.

When on the wine trail in Sonoma: **Mirepoix** is in a small converted house in Windsor (just south of Healdsburg). The limited California-French menu changes daily (about five choices each of appetizers and entrees). Two wine lists available: one with thirty locally produced wines at $20 to $40 (about half available by the glass), and another with thirty rare local wines, including some half bottles, in the $50 range. No corkage for Sonoma wines, $10 for others. Can be noisy when crowded. All in all, it's a very nice experience, the food's very good, and the service is unobtrusive and competent, says *svL*.

Cafe Citti makes for a fine casual, relatively inexpensive stop in the Sonoma area. Really good rotisserie chicken, garlic noodles, and very garlicky caesar salads, plus a patio for outdoor dining.

Langley's on the Green is one of few upscale-ish restaurants in Windsor. Impressive bar, corkage $15, good bets include baby back ribs, salads, and sandwiches.

Also see "Sonoma: Various *Chowing*" and see the Nabe Index for many more Napa and Sonoma tips.

○ **Zinsvalley Restaurant:** *see also* p. 126.

WINE COUNTRY Picnics

Bartholomew Park Winery
  (Sonoma County)
1000 Vineyard Ln.
Sonoma, CA
707-935-9511
Winery

Basque Boulangerie
  (Sonoma County)
460 1st St. E.
Sonoma, CA
707-935-7687
Basque/French/Pizza bakery

Bothe Napa Valley State Park
  (Napa County)
3801 St. Helena Hwy.
Calistoga, CA
707-942-4575

Buena Vista Winery
  (Sonoma County)
18000 Old Winery Rd.
Sonoma, CA
800-926-1266
Winery

Dean & DeLuca Market
  (Napa County)
607 S. St. Helena Hwy.
St. Helena, CA
707-967-9980
Store

Genova Delicatessen
  (Napa County)
1550 Trancas St.
Napa, CA
707-253-8686
Italian deli

La Luna Market (Napa County)
1153 Rutherford Rd.
Rutherford, CA
707-963-3211
Mexican store

Rutherford Grove Winery
  (Napa County)
1673 Hwy. 29
Rutherford, CA
707-963-0544
Winery

Rutherford Hill Winery
  (Napa County)
200 Rutherford Hill Rd.
Rutherford, CA
707-963-1871
Winery

Sebastiani Vineyards
  (Sonoma County)
389 4th St. E.
Sonoma, CA
707-933-3230
Winery

Sunshine Foods
  (Napa County)
1115 Main St.
St. Helena, CA
707-963-7070
Store

V Sattui Winery
  (Napa County)
1111 White Ln.
St. Helena, CA
707-963-7774
Winery

W F Giugni & Son Grocery Co
  (Napa County)
1227 Main St.
St Helena, CA
707-963-3421
Italian deli

For old-fashioned sandwiches and Italian foodstuffs, check out **Genova Delicatessen** in Napa or Guigni's in St. Helena. **Dean & DeLuca's** St. Helena outpost carries tons of picnic goodies. **Sunshine Foods** has remodeled its deli and meat counters and offers beautiful selections of cheeses, salads, and sushi. For Mexican, head to the back counter at **La Luna Market** in Rutherford for burritos, tacos, and more to go. **Basque Boulangerie**, in the main plaza of Sonoma, serves Basque-infused sandwiches, salads, soups, quiches.

As for where to actually eat your picnic, hounds have many favorite spots. **V Sattui** is just across Highway 29 from Dean & DeLuca. It also sells picnic fixings and premade foods. You can picnic on their grounds, but it's not particularly tranquil, what with Highway 29 right there and the wine train running by every once in a while. **Rutherford Hill Winery** has a picnic area on top of a hill in an olive grove with a great valley view. **Bartholomew Park Winery** is about two miles from the Sonoma plaza, as is **Buena Vista Winery. Sebastiani Vineyards** (an old historic winery that's fun to tour) has picnic tables in its vineyards, just skip their wines. *Jennie Sheeks* shares some of her favorite secret picnic spots: under the eucalyptus trees at **Rutherford Grove Winery,** on the knoll at La Famiglia, the park in St. Helena across from the post office, and the north end of Bothe State Park.

WINERY TOURS and Tastings

Andalu (Mission)
3198 16th St.
San Francisco, CA
415-621-2211
Spanish/New
    American/French/Italian

Bottle Barn (Sonoma County)
3331 Industrial Dr.
Santa Rosa, CA
707-528-1161
Wine store

Domaine Chandon (Napa County)
1 California Dr.
Yountville, CA
707-944-2280
Winery

Gary Farrell Wines
    (Sonoma County)
10701 Westside Rd.
Healdsburg, CA
707-473-2900
Wine store

Hartwell Vineyards (Napa County)
5795 Silverado Trail
Napa, CA
707-255-4269
Winery

Iron Horse Vineyards
    (Sonoma County)
9786 Ross Station Rd.
Sebastopol, CA
707-887-1507
Winery

J Rochioli Vineyards & Winery
    (Sonoma County)
6192 Westside Rd.
Healdsburg, CA
707-433-2305
Winery

Kendall-Jackson Wine Center
    (Sonoma County)
5007 Fulton Rd.
Fulton, CA
707-571-8100
Winery

Pride Mountain Vineyards
  (Napa County)
4026 Spring Mountain Rd.
St. Helena, CA
707-963-4949
Winery

Wine Counsel (Marina)
350 Bay St.,#328
San Francisco, CA
415-203-9602
Mail order source

Vine Cliff Winery (Napa County)
7400 Silverado Trail
Napa, CA
707-944-1364
Winery

The following just skims the surface of the many wineries in Sonoma and Napa to visit, tour, and taste.

Hounds recommend **Iron Horse** for its outdoor tasting room and particularly good sparkling wines. **Domaine Chandon** offers what *nja* calls a fantastic and informative tour of sparkling wine production. **Kendall-Jackson**, which owns Edmeades, La Crema, Robert Pepi, Calina, Hawley, Hartfort, Mantanzas Creek, and more, does a good tour through its extensive gardens. You'll taste wines with different foods and see how the tastes change—very educational and fun. **Gary Farrell** is a smaller producer with gorgeous vineyards. Call ahead for tour and tasting information. *Philosopher* recommends **Hartwell Vineyards** in the Stags Leap District for a really good, high-end, small winery (tasting and tours by appointment only). **Rochioli** is a favorite stop, but the best wines sell out quickly and are rarely available for tasting. Call ahead to see what they've opened for pouring that day before making a special trip, and you might just hit the jackpot. *Hannah* recommends **Vine Cliff** for tours and tastings by appointment only. There is a tasting fee, but it's waived with purchase. **Pride Mountain Vineyards** is worth a visit not only for the wines, but to see how it can switch its crush equipment from county to county. That's right, it's perched right on the border between Napa and Sonoma so it can process Sonoma fruit in Sonoma and Napa grapes in Napa!

Two independent organizations to check out: The **Wine Counsel** puts on great tastings with exceptional wines at a reasonable prices—check their Web site (www.winecounsel.net) for current events. And Bay Area Wine Project pours top-flight wines at its events. If you don't want to have your wine sitting in the car all day, the **Bottle Barn** in Santa Rosa is the spot to shop where the locals do. You won't find everything from the tasting rooms, but you will leave happy and with money in your pocket, says *Andy Jacobs*.

For restaurant wine tastings, **Andalu** sometimes hosts wine dinners: *laurie* has attended two and reports great wine thoughtfully paired with great food for a very solid value. Check its Web site at www.andalusf.com for upcoming events.

○ **Andalu:** *see also* **p. 271.**

eXtremely IMPORTANT

It's extremely important that we never settle for anything undelicious when there are so many geniuses, hold-outs, and proud craftsmen investing hearts and souls into cooking edible treasure which can sate our deepest hankerings. Just venture a bit further and care a bit more, and all occasions can be special— and the good guys will win.

ZONG ZI (Sticky Rice Dumplings)

Unnamed Deli (East Bay)
near 46881 Warm Springs Blvd.
Fremont, CA
Chinese store

Yu-Tai Chinese Market (Peninsula)
next door to 360 Castro St.
Mountain View, CA
Chinese store

Zong zi, or sticky rice dumplings, are traditionally eaten during the Chinese Dragon Boat Festival on the fifth of the fifth Lunar Month in the Chinese Calender. *Dyno* shares a couple of fresh zong zi finds: **Yu-Tai Chinese Market** sells a very good imported version from Jiaxing (Hou Chow), that has pork cooked with the rice, no egg, and sticky rice, that's a bit softer than other versions. And the **unnamed deli** next to Lion Market (which is at 46881 Warm Springs Boulevard in Fremont) sells six or seven different zong zi, including Cantonese, Taiwanese, white rice with red bean paste, soda rice with red bean paste.

ZUNI'S Best Bites

Zuni Cafe (Civic Center)
1658 Market St.
San Francisco, CA
415-552-2522
New American/American

Zuni Cafe is a San Francisco classic—love it or hate it. Hounds share their "can't miss" favorites: oysters, roast chicken with bread salad (for two, expect a forty-five-minute wait); Caesar salad; burgers (served on focaccia instead of a bun); gnocchi appetizer; pasta carbonara; frito misto (especially when it includes fennel or Meyer lemon); sauteed chicken livers with onion marmalade; house-cured anchovy appetizer. For desserts: trifle, granita, pots de creme (especially caramel or ginger), or cheese (they pair fine nuts and fruits with their impeccable cheeses, says *Mrs. Smith*). The kitchen's especially good with produce. And *shocker* suggests that adventurous diners opt for less mainstream choices.

○ **Zuni Cafe:** *see also* p. 10.

Alphabetical Index

Restaurant/Store	Neighborhood	Cuisine	Page

Alphabetical Index

INDEX
NABE

○○○ East Bay ○○○

ALAMEDA

ALBANY

BERKELEY

○○○ Marin County ○○○

CORTE MADERA

Cinq Restaurant	French	299
Marin Joe's Restaurant	Italian, American	161

GREENBRAE

Victoria Pastry Co.	Italian, Bakery	97

KENTFIELD

Half Day Cafe	Diner/Coffee shop	30
Taqueria Mexican Grill	Mexican	58
Willie's Cafe	Diner/Coffee shop	30
Woodlands Market	Store	52

LAGUNITAS

Silk Road Teas	Mail Order	280

LARKSPUR

Emporio Rulli	Italian, Café	4

MARSHALL

Hog Island Oysters	Farm/Farm stand	207
Marshall Store	Store	291
Straus Family Creamery	Farm/Farm stand	140

MILL VALLEY

El Paseo Restaurant	French	299
Mountain Home Inn	New American	30

MUIR BEACH

Pelican Inn	British	237

Restaurant/Store	Cuisine	Page

POINT REYES STATION

ROSS

SAN ANSELMO

SAN RAFAEL

SAUSALITO

○○○ Mendocino County ○○○

BOONVILLE

YORKVILLE

○○○ Monterey County ○○○

CASTROVILLE

○○○ Napa County ○○○

CALISTOGA

NAPA

RUTHERFORD

ST. HELENA

Restaurant/Store	Cuisine	Page

PESCADERO

Duarte's Tavern	American, Portuguese, Seafood	117, 232, 294

PORTOLA VALLEY

New Bamboo	East Asian	62

PRINCETON-BY-THE-SEA

Half Moon Bay Brewing Co.	New American, Pub	17
Mezza Luna	Italian	152

REDWOOD CITY

Chavez Meat Market #1	Mexican, Store	221
El Grullense II	Mexican	194
Gonzalez Taqueria	Mexican	194
Indian Grocery & Spice	Indian, Store	57
La Casita Chilanga #1	Mexican	292
La Casita Chilanga #2	Mexican	292
La Pachanga	Mexican	194
Mar Y Tierra	Mexican	187
South Pacific Island Bakery	Pacific, Bakery	270
Tacos El Grullo	Mexican	222
Taqueria El Grullense	Mexican	191

SAN BRUNO

Hon Lin Restaurant	Taiwanese, Chinese	66
India Foods	Indian, Store	57, 142
Innya Lake Restaurant	Chinese, Burmese	35
Mings Restaurant	Chinese, Korean	66
South Seas Market	Eclectic Store	115
Wat Buddhapradeep	Thai	283

SAN CARLOS

British Food Ctr	British, Store	290
Laurel Street Cafe	French	79
Rihab's	Iraqi	166

CASTRO

CHINATOWN

CIVIC CENTER

RICHMOND

RUSSIAN HILL

TENDERLOIN

UNION SQUARE

WESTPORTAL/INGLESIDE

○○○ South Bay ○○○

○○○ Bakery ○○○

○◯○ Café ○◯○

○○○ Cheese Shop ○○○

○○○ Chocolate or Candy Shop ○○○

○○○ Farm or Farm Stand ○○○

○○○ Italian Deli ○○○

○○○ Mail Order Source ○○○

○○○ Pub ○○○

○○○ Sandwich Shop ○○○

○○○ Store ○○○

(Grocer, Supermarket, Meat, Fish, Produce, etc.)

Cuisine Index: Store

○○○ Street Cart or Truck ○○○

○○○ Wine Store ○○○

○○○ Winery ○○○

○◉○ Miscellaneous ○◉○

○◉○ African ○◉○

ETHIOPIAN OR ERITREAN

○◉○ American ○◉○

AMERICAN

Cuisine Index: American

BARBECUE

CAJUN OR CREOLE

DINER OR COFFEE SHOP

NEW AMERICAN

Cuisine Index: American

○◯○ Caribbean ○◯○

○◯○ East Asian ○◯○

CHINESE (BEIJING)

CHINESE (BUDDHIST/VEGETARIAN)

CHINESE (CANTONESE)

CHINESE (DIM SUM)

CHINESE (HAKKA)

CHINESE (HONG KONG)

CHINESE (HUNAN)

CHINESE (MUSLIM)

CHINESE (SHANGHAI)

KOREAN

Cuisine Index: European

FRENCH BISTRO

Cuisine Index: European

Cuisine Index: European

POLISH

PORTUGUESE

RUSSIAN

SPANISH

SWISS

○○○ Latin American ○○○

ARGENTINIAN

BRAZILIAN

LATIN AMERICAN

MEXICAN

○○○ Middle Eastern/North African ○○○

LEBANESE

Habibi	Fremont	240
Sinbad Mediterranean Cuisine	San Mateo	166

MIDDLE EASTERN/NORTH AFRICAN

Ali Baba	South San Francisco	209
Bongo Burger	Berkeley	133
Cafe Gibraltar	El Granada	232
Kabob House	San Jose	165
Leila	Financial District	166
Mediterranean	Concord	121
Meesha's Berkeley Gyros	Berkeley	199

MOROCCAN

Aziza	Richmond	197, 236
Baraka	Potrero Hill	236, 241
Tanjia	Oakland	197

PERSIAN

Alborz	Russian Hill	193
Garne's Restaurant	San Jose	193
Maykadeh Persian Cuisine	North Beach	193
Shalizaar Restaurant	San Mateo	166
Shoma Deli	Healdsburg	166

TURKISH

Bosphorous Anatolian Cuisine	Berkeley	296
Bursa Kebab Mediterranean	Westportal/Ingleside	296
Cafe de Pera	Richmond	297
Gyro King	Civic Center	297
Taverna Gyros	Sunnyvale	297

○○○ Pacific ○○○

AUSTRALIAN

Australia Fair	Union Square	290

Cuisine Index: South Asian

○○○ Southeast Asian ○○○

BURMESE

CAMBODIAN

FILIPINO

LAOTIAN

MALAYSIAN

SINGAPOREAN

THAI

VIETNAMESE

○○○ Vegetarian ○○○

FOR THE BEST IN PAPERBACKS, LOOK FOR THE

In every corner of the world, on every subject under the sun, Penguin represents quality and variety—the very best in publishing today.

For complete information about books available from Penguin—including Penguin Classics, Penguin Compass, and Puffins—and how to order them, write to us at the appropriate address below. Please note that for copyright reasons the selection of books varies from country to country.

In the United States: Please write to *Penguin Group (USA), P.O. Box 12289 Dept. B, Newark, New Jersey 07101-5289* or call 1-800-788-6262.

In the United Kingdom: Please write to *Dept. EP, Penguin Books Ltd, Bath Road, Harmondsworth, West Drayton, Middlesex UB7 0DA.*

In Canada: Please write to *Penguin Books Canada Ltd, 10 Alcorn Avenue, Suite 300, Toronto, Ontario M4V 3B2.*

In Australia: Please write to *Penguin Books Australia Ltd, P.O. Box 257, Ringwood, Victoria 3134.*

In New Zealand: Please write to *Penguin Books (NZ) Ltd, Private Bag 102902, North Shore Mail Centre, Auckland 10.*

In India: Please write to *Penguin Books India Pvt Ltd, 11 Panchsheel Shopping Centre, Panchsheel Park, New Delhi 110 017.*

In the Netherlands: Please write to *Penguin Books Netherlands bv, Postbus 3507, NL-1001 AH Amsterdam.*

In Germany: Please write to *Penguin Books Deutschland GmbH, Metzlerstrasse 26, 60594 Frankfurt am Main.*

In Spain: Please write to *Penguin Books S. A., Bravo Murillo 19, 1° B, 28015 Madrid.*

In Italy: Please write to *Penguin Italia s.r.l., Via Benedetto Croce 2, 20094 Corsico, Milano.*

In France: Please write to *Penguin France, Le Carré Wilson, 62 rue Benjamin Baillaud, 31500 Toulouse.*

In Japan: Please write to *Penguin Books Japan Ltd, Kaneko Building, 2-3-25 Koraku, Bunkyo-Ku, Tokyo 112.*

In South Africa: Please write to *Penguin Books South Africa (Pty) Ltd, Private Bag X14, Parkview, 2122 Johannesburg.*